To Clive Rosten:

With Best Wishes

Michael Gambon

★★★★★★★★★★★★★★

Name
Dropping

★★★★★★★★★★★★★★

To
Maya, who has heard it all
And to
Carolyn, Timothy and Tara, who haven't

★★★★★★★★★★★★★★★★★★★★★★★★★★★★★★★★

NAME DROPPING

★★★★★★★★★★★★★★★★★★★★★★★★★★★★★★★★

The Autobiography of
MICHAEL PERTWEE

Leslie Frewin of London

© Valery Productions Limited and Michael Pertwee, 1974

World Rights Reserved, including the right of reproduction in whole or in part in any form whatsoever.

First published 1974 by

Leslie Frewin Publishers Limited,
Five Goodwin's Court,
Saint Martin's Lane,
London WC2N 4LL, England.

This book is set in 11 on 13 pt Century

Photoset and printed in Malta by St Paul's Press Ltd

ISBN 0 85632 071 4

★★★★★★★★★★★★★★★★★★★★★★★

Contents

★★★★★★★★★★★★★★★★★★★★★★★

A Selection of Alphabetically Dropped Names

French, Hugh (Agent)   180.
French, Valerie (Actress/wife)
   137, 139, 145, 147, 151, 159–160.

GABLE, CLARK (Actor)   140.
Gabor, Zsa, Zsa (Actress)   121.
de Gaulle, General   81.
Gelbart, Laurence (Screenwriter)
   196–197, 201.
Gershwin, Ira (Lyricist)   181.
Grant, Cary (Actor)   185–187.
Grigg, Sir James (Politician)   79.
Guest, Val (Screenwriter)   36, 157.
Guha, Maya (Model/wife)   171,
   173, 176–177, 183, 189, 191,
   198, 207.
Gunn, Albert (Newspaper editor)
   161.

HAMER, ROBERT (Film director)
   105–106, 127.
Hancock, Tony (Actor)   168.
Harding, Gilbert (TV personality)
   141, 150–153, 157, 163.
Harrison, Rex (Actor)   179.
Harvey, Laurence (Actor)   132–
   133.
Hastings, Sir Patrick (Barrister)
   12, 125.
Havelock-Allen, Anthony (Film
   producer)   127, 140.
Hay, Will (Actor)   36, 74.
Hemmings, David (Actor)   190,
   194.
Hepburn, Audrey (Actress)   126–
   127, 168.
Herbert, Sir A P (Author)   46.
Hicks, Seymour (Actor)   116.

Hitchcock, Alfred (Film producer/
   director)   35, 134, 180, 183.
Hobson, Harold (Drama critic)
   111, 208.
Howells, Ursula (Actress)   171.
Howes, Sally Ann (Actress)   46,
   130.
Humphrey, Hubert (U.S. politician)
   184.
Hunnicutt, Gayle (Actress)   190,
   194.
Hunter, Hayes (Agent)   33, 35,
   108.
Hylton, Jack (Impresario)   37.

IRONSIDE, FIELD-MARSHAL LORD
   (C.I.G.S)   71.

JUSTICE, JAMES ROBERTSON (Actor)
   141, 150.

KAYE, DANNY (Actor)   131–132.
Kempson, Rachel (Actress)   110.
Kenny, Sean (Theatrical designer)
   202.
Kersh, Gerald (Author)   142.
Khan, The Aga   122.
Khruschev, Nikita   183.
King George V   5.
King George VI   21, 80–81, 97, 152.
Korda, Sir Alexander (Film
   producer)   104–105.

LANDI, MARLA (Actress)   159.
Larner, Elizabeth (Actress)   204.
Laughton, Charles (Actor)   8.
Launder, Frank (Screenwriter)
   35, 37–38.

PREFACE

In its issue dated 15th November 1957, The *TV Times* wrote:

> "No three plays could be more dissimilar than those presented this week. This is not difficult to believe when one considers the authors—Shaw, Michael Pertwee and Balzac."

How is that for name dropping? I like it. I also like the billing. I had no objection to taking second place to George Bernard Shaw but would have certainly resented being billed below Balzac who was, after all, a foreigner.

Name Dropping is my autobiography. It is awe-inspiring to think of the millions of people who will not want to read it. Only a handful of relatives and friends may feel tempted—and, no doubt, they will expect a free copy.*

Why, then, did I bother to write it? Primarily, it was for my own enjoyment, and secondly, because, in the course of an unimportant life, I have come into contact with a number of well-known people about whom I have something to tell—hence my title.

Herein will be found an alphabetical list of about two hundred names I have dropped, with some of the page numbers on which they are mentioned. This will assist the reader to skip details of my life and instantly to refer to people of real interest.

Many other famous names, which I drop in passing, do *not* appear on the list, simply because I found nothing particularly interesting to recount about them. Others, including close friends and relatives, are not mentioned in the book at all, through lack of space.

Such people are my cousin, Ethel Strachan, who made delicious fairy cakes; William Rees-Davies, MP, with whom I play poker; the Duke and Duchess of Abercorn, who invited me to lunch at Government House, Northern Ireland, (twice); and a girl called Cynthia Bennett-Evans, whom I met at a dinner party, (once).

This is not to say that I did not thoroughly enjoy the fairy cakes, the four aces, two excellent luncheons, and above all, the lovely Cynthia Bennett-Evans, (twice).

Michael Pertwee

*They are in for a disappointment.

Part 1

★★★★★★★★★★★★★★★★★★★★★★★★★★★★★★★★★★★

Parent Dropping

★★★★★★★★★★★★★★★★★★★★★★★★★★★★★★★★★★★

I WAS BORN on 24th April 1916.

To start as I mean to go on, and drop a name, my Godfather was Henry Ainley, a most famous actor. He was late for the christening, so it began without him. It was a cold day and the water in the font gave off steam as I was held above it; then a magnificent voice reverberated down the aisle: 'Good God! What are they going to do? Boil the little bugger?'

Henry Ainley had arrived. He gave me a silver tankard, then departed from my life for twenty-five years, until, on the birth of my daughter, Carolyn, in 1941, he wrote me a letter of congratulation, a poem to *Pretty Polly Pertwee*, and added some scurrilous remarks about the morals of certain of his own children.

I was lucky to be born at all. Shortly before my arrival my mother was the target of a bomb dropped from a Zeppelin. It missed her narrowly, and damaged Swan and Edgars.

Perhaps this prenatal experience had some psychological effect on me, for my earliest memory is of a German daylight air-raid on London. I was only eighteen months old, but I clearly remember my pram's-eye-view of the airplanes glinting in the sun over Kensington Gardens. My nanny must have panicked. There follows an impression of travelling at great speed, then, later, of nanny, a cup of tea in hand, talking to a policeman. I assume that, while rushing back to Pembroke Villas, Earl's Court, some Good Samaritan must have thought she looked like a panicky nanny who needed a nice cup of tea.

In his own autobiography, written in 1940, my father, Roland, described

1

himself as a jack of all trades and master of none. It is true that as an actor he was only moderate, as a painter he failed to make an adequate living, despite being hung in The Academy; but he was a successful and prolific writer of novels, short stories, films and plays. In his own genre of short story alone, he was a master.

I am the elder of his two sons. At sixteen, I decided I would be a writer, too. My father took this with admirable calm. How dare a schoolboy simply announce he is going to be a writer?

My brother, Jon, three years younger, simultaneously decided to be an actor. In view of the uncertainties of that profession, this must have been depressing, too.

As it turned out, Roland was lucky. I was making a fair living by the age of twenty-two, and Jon was self-supporting at eighteen.

Soon after the Second World War, Jon became a household name on radio. My father was at the height of his own career when a fellow member of the Garrick Club asked him: 'Are you Jon Pertwee's father?'

'No,' said Roland. 'He is my son.'

With a family so steeped in show business one is inevitably asked from where it originated.

My paternal great-grandfather, Edward Moore, was a chemist and public analyst in Hove, Sussex. He was an uncouth bully, who suffered from wind, and left drawers open ready to be slammed to drown the noise of his rousing farts. If anyone complained, he would look at them coldly, and say: 'Would you have me suffer pain?'

His other hobby was fishing. He would leave the shop and set off in a boat to hunt dabs. If a customer arrived, my great-grandmother blew a whistle, and Edward rowed ashore, protesting angrily at the interruption.

They produced a family of nine daughters and one son. Two daughters died in infancy. Their son built up a successful motor business in the early days of cars, and died a rich man.

The seven surviving daughters, raised on a shoestring, in the restricted atmosphere of a Victorian household, were all artistic.

Eva Moore was a renowned actress on both sides of the Atlantic. She married H V Esmond. Their daughter, Jill Esmond, became a star, and acted with the young Laurence Olivier in the first production of Noël Coward's *Private Lives*.

Decima was one of the original D'Oyly Carte *Three Little Maids from School*.

Bertha was a singer and well-known accompanist. Her son, Harold Huth, became a star in the early days of talking pictures, and went on to be a film producer.

Emily, my grandmother, was a good singer. She also wrote one immensely long novel, which she gave to my father to read. He left it on a bus, and it was never heard of again.

So this show business family originated from a union between a mild little woman, who would not say boo to a goose, and a bully who said boo to everything.

All I remember of my mother when I was a child, is lying in bed beside her while she sang *Over the Sea to Skye*. She fell in love with my father's best friend while he was away fighting in France. She was banished from our lives as if she had never existed. I remember photographs of myself apparently suspended in mid-air, because pictures of mother had been carefully cut out of them.

In those days divorce cases were fully reported in the most intimate detail and, since Roland was a celebrity, he made the headlines in a big way. Good friends of his, Monty and Alice Chapman, decided to give him a sympathetic dinner during this trying time. Unfortunately, Monty fortified himself heavily before Roland arrived. He met him at the door in a confused state, stuck out his hand and said: 'Congratulations, my dear fellow! I read the notices and they are wonderful!'

I was only three, and Jon was eighteen months old, when all this happened; but in 1919 there was no question of the parties in a divorce sensibly discussing what might be best for the children. Whoever broke the rules automatically forfeited all parental rights. Thus I lost my mother, who I was not to see again for fifteen years. In a way I also lost my father. He had been quite unprepared for the disaster which suddenly destroyed a happy marriage. When he surveyed the wreckage, he was understandably appalled at the prospect of coping with two small children.

At this time my grandmother stepped into the breach and we were sent to live with her. From this point on my father became a shadowy and remote figure. I do not think he resented us, but we were a constant reminder of acute unhappiness and, without being aware of it, he kept himself aloof and emotionally uninvolved. I did not really get close to him until I was an adult.

When she took over, Granny was sixty-three, a small woman with an aggressive bosom. She was a wonderful friend, and a formidable foe, who conducted a running battle with maids, nannies, taxi drivers, and the London

3

General Omnibus Company. She never tipped taxi drivers more than three-pence. Come rain or shine she always insisted that the rear section of the roof be opened to the fresh air. This caused the highly polished leatherwork to crack but any driver who refused was reported to the police, because legally she was within her rights.

In those days you could hail a bus between stops and, with luck, the driver stopped to pick you up. Granny made it a point *never* to use a bus stop. She stood grimly between them, with a threatening umbrella raised, and any driver who ignored her would have his number taken and a letter went off by the next post.

With maids she was a martinet. Discipline was strict, and wages minimal. No conversation was allowed unless they were properly dressed in cap and apron.

To nannies she was a dragon. She did not subscribe to the then current belief that childrens' place was in the nursery, with nanny in charge. Nannies did what they were told and were expected to hold no opinions.

But to us she gave out a wonderful, all embracing love and devotion. We were her world. I have never loved anyone so much, and never will. She died in 1938, and I still miss her.

Granny's relationship with her two sons was interesting. Guy lived with her, and remained a bachelor until he died. He was an excellent teacher of elocution, but earned very little. By 1920, Roland was already successful and kept her generously supplied with money; yet, to Granny, the writing profession was not respectable, and it was Guy who had made good. She lived to see my first play produced, but still begged me to give up writing and take up a decent, steady job, like Uncle Guy.

Uncle Guy and Granny had a house in London during the winter. In the spring they made a fifteen mile move to Torcross, a mock Tudor house on the hills above Caterham in Surrey. This was called: 'Moving to the country.'

It was a very conservative and reactionary household. Granny and Uncle Guy read *The Morning Post*. Socialists were 'Swine'. Mister Baldwin was 'Magnificent'. Winston Churchill was 'A Cad'. Unhelpful shop assistants were 'Little counter jumpers'. Children who did not wash properly had 'Ploughboy's hands'. I was once sent to bed for daring to suggest the Suffragettes had been crazy to blow up a lot of innocent ducks in Regent's Park.

Granny and her sisters had been active supporters of Mrs Pankhurst. Aunt Decima had chained herself to the railings of Buckingham Palace.

Decima, who lived to be ninety, was a wonderfully jingoistic lady. She ran an Officers' Leave Club in Paris during the First World War, and returned to do the same in the Second World War, when she was all of seventy years of age. She narrowly escaped being captured when the Germans took Paris, and was evacuated from Saint Nazaire.

She must also have been the only person in Britain to threaten to give a white feather during the Second World War. This she threatened to give to her own son who had served with great distinction throughout the First World War, and was considered unfit for the Second World War by everyone except his mother.

There was nothing Aunt Decima liked better than to invite me to her flat—three floors up and no lift—for a chat about my experiences in the Second World War. She always referred to Field-Marshal Montgomery, with whom I served in a lowly capacity, as 'Your Monty'. After one of my visits she sent me a postcard, which read:

> 'So enjoyed seeing you yesterday, dear boy. It must be magnificent to look at yourself in the mirror each morning and say: Thank God I did my bit!'

Her second marriage was to a Governor of The Gold Coast, Sir Gordon Guggisberg. After his death she called herself Lady Moore-Guggisberg. She was proud of her title. At my grandmother's funeral she approached the local newspaper correspondent to make sure he got the spelling right. He failed; and among the mourners was reported to be a Lady Mona Buggerleg.

Granny herself gained some rather obscure Belgian decoration for her work during the First World War. There is a story, how apocryphal I do not know, that she wore this when she and her fellow workers were paraded before King George V, who walked straight down the line of rigid ladies but paused as he reached Granny, stared at her magnificent bosom, leaned closer, then pointed a finger and said: 'And what have we here?'

I used to lie awake in the early mornings at Torcross listening for the clink of crockery as Granny awoke to make a cup of tea on a methylated spirits burner. I would get up, crawl in beside her, lay my head on that huge, welcoming bosom, and receive my first lessons in geography.

She told an endless serial story of Jasper, Jim, Bill and Rupert, four brave lads, who travelled the world in their own craft. In retrospect, I realise they were a horribly bigoted bunch, who called a spade a nigger, and were fanatical supporters of the British Empire.

After the lesson, Granny would rise and march round the house, tearing the sheets and blankets off the beds and hurling them in all directions, thus forcing the servant to make the beds properly.

Uncle Guy was a simple man with simple tastes, who smoked a pipe, drank an occasional glass of sherry and was normally in bed by ten o'clock. He had little interest in anything outside his own activities, but had total recall for trivia. He could remember exactly what he had said, done and eaten precisely a year before, or, for that matter, five years before. He was never ill, and had no patience with anyone who was. He despised medicines and one of his proudest boasts was that he had last taken an aperient on 21st June 1912. It seems unfair that a man who lived such a moderate and well-ordered life should have died at seventy.

The memories of the seven years we spent with Granny are all happy ones; sunny days (*was* the weather better then?); a sandpit; sweet-peas; a doll called Gladys Cooper; ladies in big hats, and men in white flannels playing croquet; a mongrel called Tyko, who was killed in the tube chasing a bitch up the Piccadilly Line; first pedal car; first fairy cycle. Once I cut off all my hair with the garden shears because a passing errand boy said I needed a bleeding haircut. Granny cried for hours. She believed in long hair, and favoured putting us in Little Lord Fauntleroy suits.

I had a recurring nightmare. It was of a fire, an enormous, terrifying blaze and the flames made music. They kept telling me it was only a dream, but it came true twenty years later.

Uncle Guy's first car was an ancient, open Citroen, which he drove very slowly. He never conquered any other cars but his own. Put him at the wheel of an exactly similar car to his and he was lost. After much crashing of gears, he would throw up his hands and jump out, saying that the beastly thing did not work.

One phrase was dinned into me from an early age.

'Never,' said Granny, '*Never* speak to the man at the wheel.'

The London house was in Camden Grove. When I was six I went to a nursery school from which I was one day sent home in disgrace for making a close examination of my penis, instead of listening to a Bible tale.

I also discovered God at about the same time and became deeply religious. (Perhaps some of the Bible tale sunk in after all.) I do not know how or why this occurred, because Granny was a militant agnostic.

One Christmas I went alone to an early morning service. I noticed that many of the congregation were walking down the aisle, kneeling, and being given something to eat and drink. Thinking this was connected with the Christmas festivities, I joined the queue, and eventually knelt at the altar. I was given a sip of wine, and something which appeared to be a rather meagre ice-cream wafer. The first time round the clergyman did not turn a hair. Perhaps he thought I was a midget, since at six, I could not have been confirmed. It was so enjoyable that I decided on a second helping. He came round again. I took a larger swig and a couple of wafers for good measure. This time he gave me a glassy stare. I was quite prepared to try for a third helping, but a lady sitting in one of the front pews, rose and gently led me away.

I was an avid reader and by the age of seven knew the adventures of Bulldog Drummond by heart. One day, I was in a corridor train with Roland when the door slid open and a slight man in a baggy tweed jacket and plus-fours looked in at Roland and said: 'Tiny! My dear old fruit! Come along down and put your nose inside a wet.'

I asked who the funny man was? It was Bulldog Drummond's creator, 'Sapper', (H C McNeile.) I was disappointed. He did not resemble Bulldog Drummond, and to make it worse, he spoke like Algy Longworth.

The first straight play I saw, aged about nine, was *The Spider*, which Roland had adapted from an American play.

The first woman I saw stark naked was Tallulah Bankhead.

There is a connexion between these events, because Miss Bankhead starred in *The Spider*. I was taken backstage afterwards to meet her. Roland knocked on her dressing-room door, and a voice said: 'Come in,' and there was Miss Bankhead, smiling and nude. She was not put out, but we moved out fast.

I enjoyed Miss Bankhead in the nude more than I did the play.

The second straight play I saw was *Interference*, which was Roland's first big hit in London, New York, and eighteen other countries throughout the world. He collaborated with Doctor Harold Dearden, then a fashionable psychiatrist. The stars were Gerald du Maurier and Herbert Marshall. A young man named Frank Lawton, from the Actor's Orphanage, had his first stage part in it.

I was terribly impressed by Herbert Marshall, who had an artificial leg as a result of a war wound. He moved beautifully, with the slightest swaying movement, as if aboard ship in a mild swell. He had enormous charm, but apparently made enemies as well. I heard a typically bitchy show business story about him. Two people were discussing him, one who liked him and the other who did not. The first said: 'Isn't Bart marvellous about the loss of his leg?'

'Yes,' said the other. 'Serve him right if he grew another.'

7

One night, on arriving at the theatre, Herbert Marshall had a blinding headache. He walked into what he took to be the nearest chemist and demanded an aspirin. In fact, the shop sold only surgical appliances and contraceptives.

'I'm extremely sorry, Mr Marshall,' said the assistant, 'but we only deal in the *lighter* side of pharmacy.'

The third straight play I saw was *SOS*. This was memorable for two reasons. First, Roland took over the joint starring role opposite Gerald du Maurier when Herbert Marshall left the cast. Secondly, the woman star was Gracie Fields. It was, I think, her first and only appearance on the legitimate stage. It was certainly Roland's last.

Du Maurier was an inveterate practical joker, and made Roland's life a hell. Matches exploded in his hand when he lit a cigarette. Loud thunderstorms broke out to drown his dialogue. Water would drip from above when he sat on a settee. It was useless to move further up the settee because extra jets had been carefully planted to cope with all three places.

Du Maurier was not afraid to speak his mind if the occasion warranted it. He had been very much impressed by a performance of Charles Laughton's, some time before Laughton became a major star. Du Maurier wrote him a glowing letter and sent him a present, a first edition of some book. Neither the letter nor the present was acknowledged. Later, someone brought Laughton to the Garrick Club and introduced him to du Maurier.

'Oh, yes!' said du Maurier. 'Charles Laughton, a gentleman who can read but not write.'

It was inevitable that Roland should fall in love and marry again. She was the widow of one of his great friends, Geoffrey Colbourne, who died, while still in his thirties, of cancer. They had one son, also Michael, but always known as Coby, who became our stepbrother, eventually a doctor, and is now a world authority on tropical diseases.

Dorothy was petite, extremely pretty—and Granny hated her. One is inevitably biased about personal relationships, but in all fairness I must say that Dorothy also had every reason to dislike Granny, who fought ruthlessly to prevent the marriage. Whether she had some instinctive maternal feeling that it would not work, or whether she just dreaded the thought of losing Jon and me, I do not know. To do her justice, we children were quite unaware of all this. She said nothing to prejudice our feelings. I still remember the day Dorothy took me for a walk to tell me she and Roland were getting married, and that we should in future be living with them.

I already knew her well and liked her enormously, for she and Coby had spent two summer holidays with Roland, Jon and myself at an old rectory in Horsted Keynes, Sussex.

I have only one unhappy recollection of those holidays, although with hindsight it can be seen as a pointer to what lay ahead.

In the garden of the rectory stood a dead tree with a long branch pointing horizontally like a deformed arm. Roland, who had already shown signs of thinking that Jon and I were a little 'soft', urged me to climb the tree and work myself along the branch. I was nine at the time. I studied the branch, and then refused, on the grounds that it would break and I might hurt myself. Coby, eighteen months younger, was then invited to try it. Without hesitation he did so. The branch broke. Coby crashed to the ground and was led back to the house in tears, bleeding profusely from a cut nose. I felt a great wave of relief. My caution had been justified. Surely I was vindicated? Not at all. Coby remained the hero and I was still stamped as a coward.

I must be an oddity because even now, forty-seven years later, I still think I was right.

Roland and Dorothy were married in 1927, and life turned sour from the outset. Dorothy was no fool, but she was, without doubt, the worst child psychologist in the history of step-motherhood. She immediately made it clear that she considered everything Granny had done in the way of our up-bringing was wrong. She failed to realise that Granny was our one, solid, indestructible prop. No criticism, even tactfully put, would do anything but create resentment. Unfortunately, Dorothy despised tact as a sign of a lack of moral courage. Children should be told the truth——her truth——even if it hurt. It did not occur to her that children long to be appreciated, crave praise for their dreadful little paintings, poems or stories. For us there was always the bloody truth game——castration before the testicles had even dropped.

Roland found himself in a painful dilemma. He could not undermine Dorothy's authority by defending us in public. Thus he would hurt Jon and me during the day, and ruin their own evenings by endless arguments at night. Their marriage never really got off the ground.

Coby sailed through unscathed, partly because, having been brought up by Dorothy, he was assumed to have had a perfect start in life; but, largely, because he was naturally well-behaved and a hard worker. Neither Jon nor I shone at school. The day I left my public school my form master (another great psychologist) said: 'You have been a failure here and you will be a failure all your life.'

9

I wish I could remember his name for I would gladly give him some publicity, but he was a very forgettable man.

Some years later Jon was politely asked to leave the Royal Academy of Dramatic Art as being unlikely to achieve anything in any branch of the theatrical profession.

We had two homes—a big, dark house in Drayton Gardens, Kensington, and Highleigh, a country place near Dulverton in Devon, which was perched high on a hill overlooking the River Exe. There were a hundred acres of woods and farm land and two miles of trout and salmon fishing.

We hunted with the Devon and Somerset Stag Hounds, which was the fashionable hunt of the area, and with the Tiverton Stag Hounds, which was more of a farmers' affair, run by a family called Yandle.

The Master of the Devon and Somerset was a wonderful, retired Colonel who, I think, had one eye, one arm and one good leg. He had to be strapped on to his horse. He rode magnificently. His only difficulty was when caught short during a hunt. To deal with this he had an ADC who rode beside him, and when nature called, undid the Colonel's flies and directed the stream away from the horse. The story goes that the Colonel needed to relieve himself during a particularly exciting chase. The ADC undid the flies and started to fumble, but had no luck in finding the Colonel's part.

'Hurry up, man! Hurry up!'

'I'm terribly sorry, Sir, but I can't find it.'

'What do you mean, you can't find it? *You had it last*!'*

There was one post a day at Highleigh. It was delivered by an old postman, who trudged some twenty miles over fields and rough cart-tracks delivering the mail to outlying houses. He wore gum-boots, and was reputed to have walked the equivalent of three times round the world before he retired. He was addicted to 'scrumpy' (the harsh Devon cider). Sometimes he was unable to negotiate our steep hill, and would chuck the letters in a heap in the farmyard at the foot of the hill.

Years later Jon made himself famous in the radio programme *Waterlogged Spa*, with the character of the West Country postman whose invariable cry was: 'What's it matter what you do so long as you tear 'em up?'

---

*I have just read this same anecdote in a book entitled *Out Of My Mind* by my good friend Monja Danischewsky. He attributes it to General Carton De Wiart VC, who also had one eye and one arm, and who also appears later in this book. From this the reader can draw one of two conclusions. (i) That one of us is a liar, (ii) That both of us are liars.

In London we did not have many friends of our own age. I can remember Christopher Robin (A A Milne's son, who said his celebrated prayers) coming to tea. We hated him, not that he was unpleasant, but because he arrived in a full suit of armour which his father had given him, and we were very jealous.

We rarely received exciting presents. Roland was a generous man, too generous in many ways, but he was not one of those parents who spent a day in Hamleys searching out something nice for the kids. He once returned from Hollywood, and we waited with bated breath to see what he had brought us, only to receive three pairs of braces, bought at the last moment on the ship coming home.

One Christmas party my cousin, Jill Esmond, shyly produced her new beau to be vetted. She was then a successful actress. Some doubts were expressed about the beau, especially by Granny. He was an up-and-coming actor, but actors were not considered very reliable breadwinners. He was even shyer than she, and hardly spoke the whole evening.

Eventually, she married him. His name was Laurence Olivier.

Every Christmas I wrote, starred in and directed a play. Coby took second lead and Jon invariably played a character called 'Stinker—The Butler'. We were ahead of the Royal Academy of Dramatic Art in thinking that Jon showed little aptitude for acting.

Jon always chose Christmas Day for emotional outbursts. Every year, after he had been sent upstairs in disgrace, heads would be shaken and people wondered when he would improve.

The Christmas parties were quite fun. We played charades. Roland would recite Kipling and Dorothy would cry at *The Ballad of the Bolivar*. The strangest things made her cry.

One Christmas, Granny gave me a pair of ice skates. The first day I went skating I left them behind on the tube. I told Uncle Guy about it, and we both agreed it would break Granny's heart. He gave me £3 to replace the skates. This was done entirely to spare Granny's feelings. I rushed home to tell Roland and Dorothy the happy ending to the tragedy. Roland was furious, and accused me of being a moral coward. He insisted that I should go straight to Granny and tell her the truth. I vainly explained I was not scared of Granny's reaction, but that we had merely been thinking of her. Neither he nor Dorothy could see it in any other light than as a further example of my lack of moral fibre. Neither of them seemed to appreciate that I was displaying considerable courage in standing up to them, which I continued stubbornly to do.

It was a repetition of the tree incident, and another example of an odd facet to my character. I am not particularly courageous or stubborn, but there have been a few occasions in my life when I have made up my mind to say 'No', and a whole army would not have been able to shift me. Years later the British Army did try—and failed.

Many famous names passed through our lives. The du Mauriers; Leslie Howard smiling but rather quiet; Patrick Hastings the brilliant KC, bushy-browed and aggressive, with an impish love for insulting people in a joking way, and sometimes a poor choice of victim. At a dinner celebrating one of Roland's first nights, Patrick Hastings found himself seated next to Granny, and said: 'Oh, no! Look what I've got!'

She never forgave him.

He was even more unfortunate at another first night party, many years later. Roland and Dorothy had finally separated and Roland was with his third wife, Kitty. Patrick Hastings made a speech to toast the play's success. For once he decided to be serious and a little sentimental, for he liked Kitty very much.

'I want to be serious for a moment,' he said. 'And to say, with all my heart, how happy it makes me to see my old friend, Roland, sitting here, with his beloved Dorothy at his side.'

When he realised what he had said, for perhaps the only time in his life, he was struck totally dumb.

The nearest we moved to high society was through Sir Archibald and Lady Weigall. She was an amusing, bright lady who was condemned to a wheel-chair which she drove at immense speed and with consummate skill.

At a party given by the Weigalls in London we met our first Royalty— Princess Helena Victoria, Princess Marie Louise and Prince Arthur of Connaught. The Prince sat on a pin and made a fearful fuss. While everyone was rushing around as if he had been mortally stabbed, Coby carried out a minute search of the area and ultimately located the pin. We kept it, for years, in a matchbox labelled:

THE PIN WHICH PRICKED A PRINCE.

On a couple of occasions shortly after Roland and Dorothy were married we went to Dieppe for a summer holiday.

Roland took Coby and me on a tour of the old battlefields, where he had fought in the war. It was an exciting day. The countryside still looked like a battlefield. New young trees were springing up, but the stunted trunks of the old ones still stood like stark monuments. There were overgrown pill-boxes by

12

the roadside. We found a German helmet and a British helmet, both with shrapnel holes in them.

He took us into the barn near a tiny hamlet called Gondecourt where he had been billeted for some months. As he told us of his experiences, we could almost hear the boom of guns and rattle of machine-gun fire.

I have to digress here and go forward seventeen years to the next war, at the time of the breakout from the allied beachhead, when the British Army was streaming west in the direction of Brussels. I had been sitting comfortably at Montgomery's Headquarters when I received sudden orders to head west and catch up with the Guards Armoured Division. I chased them for two days and, on the second night, still not having found them, I moved off the main road and decided to stay the night in the nearest barn. As I removed my equipment, I felt: 'I have been here before.' I had. I was in the same barn where Roland had been thirty odd years before, where I had stood as a child seventeen years before. It was a strange moment. I felt sure some fate had led me, that I was probably destined to die there. I sat down and wrote Roland a long letter, sitting where he had sat. I still get a little shiver down my spine when I think of it.

Part 2

Testicle Dropping

MY SCHOOLING PROPER started in 1925, two years before Roland and Dorothy were married. It was planned along traditional lines, boarding at preparatory and public schools.

I went to Aldro School, Eastbourne, when I was eight. The day of my first term started badly, when Roland announced the time had come when I must stop kissing him. I was already feeling a little empty inside. This made me feel emptier. I asked why. He said it was not manly. That I still vividly remember this incident reinforces my determination never to say the same thing to my son, who is at liberty to go on kissing me for so long as he wishes.

Roland and Granny saw me off at Victoria Station. I forgot his instructions, and kissed him; but that was the last time.

My first impressions of the school were of piercing wind, rattling windows, and a dormitory which had a linoleum floor, high beds with individual pots under them. We said our prayers, and one boy cried all night.

The Headmaster was Mr F E Hill—and Granny hated him. She disapproved of boarding schools, and Mr Hill was the first nail in the coffin of her influence on our lives. She found it unbearably frustrating not to be able to treat Mr Hill like one of the nannies.

Mr Hill was a sincere, well-meaning, if rather humourless man. He was deeply religious, possibly a clergyman *manqué*. He took the daily services in the school chapel, wearing a surplice. He had a delightful wife, who was everybody's temporary mother. They had a beautiful baby boy, who is now Headmaster of the school.

My 'best friend' for a while was Geoffrey Hallowes, who eventually married the famous French Resistance heroine, Odette.

14

My 'worst friend' for a while was Ivor Sainsbury, who was the best boxer in the school at his weight. Fighting was strictly prohibited and there was a rule that any boys seen fighting would box three rounds in front of the assembled school.

I should add here that I was a wretched boxer, younger and lighter than Sainsbury, small for my age, and a dedicated physical coward.

We were out for a walk on the Downs one day. I had been given the coveted honour of walking Mr Hill's dog. Ivor Sainsbury approached, twisted my finger and hi-jacked the dog. The enormity of this crime so enraged me that I forgot the difference in our ages and weights, and clocked him a beauty on the nose, which made him retreat in tears.

I had a brief hour of glory, and became a hero, but it was short-lived. Pursuing a blind adherence to his rules, Mr Hill announced that, since I had struck Sainsbury, I must box three rounds with him in public.

Anyone who has seen Cassius Clay demolish second-rate opposition will have some idea of the massacre which followed this decision. An American boy called Lee shouted: 'Stop it!' midway through the first round, and was promptly sent to bed. The slaughter continued to the end of the three rounds.

I never felt any ill-will towards Sainsbury, and not long afterwards we became 'best friends' but I have always considered this the grossest injustice ever inflicted on me.

Other than that I have few complaints about Aldro. The food was good and the staff pleasant.

I underwent a bad case of hero-worship for a Mr Heath, a tired, cynical man who had been a pilot in the '14—'18 War, and displayed a plane's propeller on the wall of his digs. He was part of my first Walter Mitty dreams. A new war had broken out. England was desperate for volunteers and, at the age of eight, I had got myself into the trenches. I saved Mr Heath's life. (He had abandoned the air for the infantry.) For this I gained the vc and Mr Heath wept on my shoulder.

The senior master was a Mr H B Craft. He had thick, pebble glasses, thick lips and walked on thick, rubber soles, which enabled him to creep up behind you without a sound. I was terrified of him at first—and he could be terrifying; but he was devoted to the school. Every Christmas he sent out scores of Christmas cards to old boys. Later, he rarely missed one of my plays or films, but never asked me for a free seat. Periodically, until shortly before he died, he would give luncheon parties at the Comedy Restaurant in London. He would have liked to have been a professional singer. He had a wavering tenor voice and performed at the drop of a hat.

It is to his eternal credit that he eventually counted me among his friends, since he had good reason to dislike me.

For a start, when the school was out walking, Mr Craft used to entertain by recounting thriller stories. These were told in the first person, with himself as the hero, fearless, ruthless and strong. I was bored by his adventures. I could not visualise him as a hero. He looked even less of a hero than Sapper. So I set up a splinter group and told stories of my own. Before long I built up quite an audience, which considerably reduced his. He did not care for this at all but there was nothing he could legitimately do about it except occasionally to turn round and interrupt my flow by telling me I was lagging.

Mr Craft chose me to sing with him at a Christmas concert. I was the smallest boy in the school and my role was *The Boy* to his *Good King Wenceslas*. We rehearsed long hours together. In case I should be nervous I was allowed to sit next to him in chapel during the service which preceded the concert.

What I had not bargained for was that he would dress up as Good King Wenceslas. I had expected my Mr Craft to walk on to the stage on thick rubber soles, wearing his sports coat and baggy trousers. Instead, he had really gone to town. He wore a crown and his entire face was hidden beneath an enormous beard. As we started to sing, 'snow' was thrown from above and landed on the beard. This was too much and I began to giggle. Mr Craft hissed at me to control myself, but I was unable to. The audience joined in and in moments the whole building rocked with joyous laughter. We did not get beyond the first line. When it became clear that neither I nor the audience was going to stop laughing, poor Good King Wenceslas turned on his heel and, with considerable dignity, left the stage, to increased laughter and a storm of applause.

Sports Day was a big occasion. Granny and Uncle Guy came one year. Granny wore black, with an enormous hat. She was standing in a prominent position when her bloomers fell down about her ankles. She was most put out, forgot which century she was in, and bellowed: 'Guy! I must go back to the coach!'

I was mercilessly teased and for the first and only time in my life felt ashamed of her.

Jon duly joined me at Aldro and was an instant failure. He was bullied. He was miserable. He was intractable. He was coddled, cajoled and punished. Nothing made any difference. Mr Hill was completely defeated by him and talked ominously about him 'having to go'. Granny, meanwhile, had to be restrained from invading Eastbourne, with umbrella poised, to give Mr Hill a piece of her mind——if not of the umbrella. Finally, Roland made a sudden decision to remove him, which evidently shocked Mr Hill for he then pleaded that Jon be given another chance; but he was taken away and went to a school in Westgate-on-Sea where he was very happy, with a headmaster called Mr Underhill. I have always thought he should have been called Mr Overhill.

I had an undistinguished career at Aldro. Mathematics completely defeated me. Classes bored me, and I just drifted off into a little dream world of my own.

The only prizes I ever won were, every year, without fail, the Elocution Prize. Sometimes Uncle Guy would be the judge. He always awarded me the prize. He was, of course, accused of favouritism.

Coby, meanwhile, was winning prizes every term at a school in Brighton.

I failed my Common Entrance to Marlborough. Roland pulled some strings and, surprisingly, had the choice of sending me either to Eton or to Sherborne, in Dorset. He chose Sherborne, perhaps because we lived so much of the time in the West Country.

I had an undistinguished career at Sherborne. Mathematics completely defeated me. Classes bored me, and I just drifted off into a little dream world of my own. The only prizes I ever won were, every year without fail, the Elocution Prize. I know I am repeating myself, but there was a distressing similarity in my career at both schools. I should, perhaps, note that Uncle Guy did *not* come to Sherborne to do the judging.

Coby joined me in School House and won prizes every term.

Jon came on later and was an instant failure. He was bullied, he was miserable. He was intractable. He was coddled, cajoled and punished. So he was taken away and sent to a co-educational school at Frensham Heights, where he was very happy.

In my first term I wrote my one and only poem. It was so bad I have never written another. I had been deeply distressed by the death of Sir Henry Segrave in his speed boat on Lake Windermere.

AN ODE TO SIR HENRY SEGRAVE.

'Oh, you who cut the waters calm and clear,
and raced your boat across The Windermere,
making it rough and terrible to see,
Oh, Sir Henry Segrave, we take off our hat to thee.'

I also received my first caning by my form master. He was in his first term, too, and he had not beaten anyone before. The punishment was to take place in his digs. He lived in one small room, crowded with large

17

furniture. When I reported for the caning it was immediately apparent that there was too much furniture to make the caning possible. Paler, and, I think, more nervous than I, he asked if I would help him move the furniture. We worked together to create enough space for him to swing the cane. I was not unduly worried. I knew he was inexperienced, and had padded my behind with two layers of blotting paper. When he had finally moved the furniture to one end of the room, he told me to bend over and I waited calmly for the beating. Unfortunately, I had miscalculated on one important factor—his nerves. His aim was deplorable. The first stroke hit me somewhere just above the ankles. The second hit the central hanging light, was deflected and struck me on the back of the neck. He muttered an apology for that one, then took a wild, low swipe, which nicked my thighs and knocked something off the mantelpiece as he followed through. The fourth stroke, a chopping movement, broke the cane; at which point he gave up. Looking extremely embarrassed, he said I could go; but I couldn't. We had stacked the furniture in front of the door, so we had to team up again to remove it.

People sometimes ask why I write so much farce, and do not try something more true to life. In answer, I can only point to this episode, and say that I have never used it because I have always believed the public would think it too far-fetched.

I was useless at sports, and was excused from the OTC after two terms owing to flat feet, which made marching an agony. Before I gained this welcome release I joined the band, became a drummer, but was swiftly retired after I had put the drumsticks through two drums. That was the end of my musical career.

The headmaster was a Mr Boughey. He had a round, grim face, a tooth-brush moustache, and was reputed to have a metal plate in his head, following a war wound. Granny hated him.

He started every term with a personal medical inspection of every boy in the house. We had to drop our trousers, while he closely examined our crutches. The ceremony was known as 'Spots or marks on face or legs'. He was looking for a disease called *Tinea Cruris*. Whether this examination took place in other houses and in other schools I do not know. I think not, and believe he must have a thing about *Tinea Cruris*.

One of the worst crimes in the book was to be caught chatting up a member of the Sherborne Girls' School. One boy, caught walking with a girl in the woods, was beaten publicly.

18

Me—at Sweet Seventeen—note the lack of lines of the face: you should see me now . . .

(*Left*) The Pertwee brothers—
Jon and me (Jon's on the left).
We really *did* want to be engine
drivers.

(*Below*) Jon and me—a *few*
years later! While collaborating
on his TV series in which I
appeared. Jon didn't speak one
of the lines I had written for
him which, in turn, 'dried' me
and swiftly put an end to my
career as a bright new
comic . . .

There was no sex instruction whatsoever and, since the only talk Roland ever gave me on the subject was: 'Don't do anything I wouldn't do,' it was not surprising that at fifteen I still thought that sleeping with a woman was a more heinous crime than playing around with a boy.

My first sex instruction came from my great school friend, Bob Rainey, who was a doctor's son, and seemed qualified to talk. He is now a doctor in Loughborough, and I am Godfather to one of his two very lovely twin daughters. Had his description of the sex act been true his family would never have been born. Men and women, it seemed, were built the same. When you wanted to have a baby you joined your private parts together with a piece of tubing rather like a thin garden hose.

I continued with my Walter Mitty dreams. They were a little more realistic now. I had written a West End play. At the end the audience rose to their feet with shouts of: 'Bravo!' and 'Author!' I came on to the stage to make a modest little speech, which had them cheering again.

In those days playwrights were always crouched in the wings just before the final curtain, and would leap smartly onto the stage to make a speech, even if it was only their mother shouting for them.

There is only one thing I did at Sherborne of which I am quite proud; this was the creation and publication of the first school magazine ever to make money. There already existed a semi-official magazine run by senior prefects which was dull, pompous, pseudo-witty and a financial disaster. This was called *The Magenta Clarion*.

Bob Rainey and I decided to produce a rival publication, *PEP*. It was a brave decision and a great deal of Mafia-type pressure was brought to bear on us as soon as word got out, since junior boys just did not do this kind of thing.

We capitalised by issuing 3d shares, and made money by conning a number of local shops to insert advertisements in the magazine. By the second edition they were fighting to get space.

At sixteen, life started to open up and become exciting.

Uncle Guy provided me with my first date at a dinner party in the London flat he shared with Granny. She was his favourite pupil at the Guildhall School, Betty Fergusson. She was blonde, blue-eyed, one day older than me, and I fell in love within half an hour. In my diary of that day I wrote:

> '*She is most awfully nice, very pretty, too.*
> *I am to meet her at the skating rink on Tuesday,*
> *I wish it was tomorrow.*'

19

We met on Tuesday, skated, had lunch, went to The Plaza Cinema to see *If I had a Million,* and followed this with tea and dancing at the Kit Kat. She danced 'awfully well', and I went to bed that night 'at the end of a perfect day'.

It seems almost incredible to imagine a time when a boy of sixteen could become a celebrity at school because he had found himself a girlfriend: but this was the case in 1933, when I confided the news to my circle of friends.

A boy called 'Cave Man' Young accused me of lying. He was a tough, hairy chap who spoke his mind. I was angry and swore that I would prove it to him the following holidays.

The simplest method would have been to invite 'Cave Man' to join Betty and me for tea at the Kit Kat; but the arrangement was made with the secrecy of a spy thriller. Betty knew nothing about it. I was to make an appointment to meet her outside Swan and Edgars in Piccadilly Circus at a certain hour on a certain day. We would walk up and down for five minutes, during which time 'Cave Man', hidden in the doorway of the store, would give her the onceover.

Everything went according to plan. I caught a brief glimpse of 'Cave Man' crouching suspiciously in the doorway behind a shopper.

I could not wait to get back to school to receive his apologies and admission that I had, in fact, landed the most lovely girl in the world. He greeted me gloweringly and said: 'Well, I didn't think much of *that*.'

We wrote endless love letters. 'Got a 43 page letter from Betty this morning, which makes a total of 139 pages received so far this term.' She had left school and was considered 'grown up', which filled me with terror. I felt she was bound to meet someone else who was not just a schoolboy.

Love prompted me to try my hand at writing my first short story. It was, inevitably, romantic, and was entitled *Yesterday.*

It was promptly sold to the *Windsor Magazine* for £12.

This failed to create quite the sensation at Sherborne that I had expected. The Masters looked at me askance, and obviously wondered if this was 'a good thing'. It had certainly never happened before. Most of my contemporaries assumed that Roland had written it for me, and did not hesitate to say so. Actually, he had not, although he gave me a lot of help by some ruthless editing, and the excision of unnecessary adjectives. He begged me to read W Somerset Maugham and learn from him.

'If Maugham wants to say: "The man went to the corner and posted a letter," he writes just that. He does *not* say: "The unhappy man walked slowly and sadly to the windy corner and put the small, white envelope into the gaping mouth of the red monster which was to swallow it up and take it for ever away from him." '

Roland was a stern critic, but patient and, above all, constructive. I owe a lot to him, not least because he resolutely resisted using his influence in helping me get work. I think he was terrified of nepotism but, psychologically, he was absolutely correct. He was prepared to read, criticise and make suggestions. In all other departments I was on my own. For this I have always been grateful. I naturally started writing with an inferiority complex. For some years I had to put up with justifiably unfavourable comparison with his work, but when I finally did make a living I had, at least, the satisfaction of knowing that it was through my own efforts. This also enabled us eventually to collaborate on equal terms, extremely amicably, and with some success.

I was one of two boys chosen to attend the Duke of York's Camp at Southwold, during one summer holiday. I think it was part of an endeavour to make a man of me. I loathed the whole prospect, resenting the loss of a week of the holiday; but it turned out to be a very enjoyable time. The idea was to take fifty per cent of boys from public schools and fifty per cent of boys from working-class homes, shove them together and make them muck in.

At a concert in his honour the Duke of York, who was to become King George VI, made a speech. This was a courageous act, for he suffered from a severe stammer, and it must have been an agony for him. He was never entirely cured, although it later improved. Yet, in 1944, I was one of a privileged few to hear him give an impromptu speech when he spoke without one hint of hesitation.*

Practically the whole of the ensuing summer holiday was spent with Betty. We would lie for hours wrapped in an innocent embrace in a sandpit near Torcross; and so it continued until Christmas 1934. The first hint that the romance was over came when I noticed she was addressing her letters to me as 'Master M Pertwee' instead of 'M Pertwee Esq.' The 'Dear John' letter followed soon after.

I ate virtually nothing·for the rest of the holidays.

At Sherborne I broke a record of a kind when, in the School Certificate Examination, I achieved the lowest marks in maths, geometry and algebra accorded to anyone in the history of the school.

---

*Details of this are recorded later in this book.

21

This put paid to any hope of going to Oxford unless I could pass a simple examination called Responsions. I took the examination at Oxford and felt reasonably satisfied when I had finished the last paper. Anyway, it was said that only a half-wit ever failed.

I returned to Sherborne to report to Mr Boughey. There was a telegram, addressed to me, pinned on the door of his study. It consisted of one word: 'FAILED.'

I entered Mr Boughey's study. He asked how I had got on. I burst into tears.

Mr Boughey suddenly became a human being. He told me to sit down, and said it was not the end of the world. He left the school shortly afterwards, but asked me to visit him in his London flat, where he gave me tea and a nice, informative chat on the usefulness of French Letters.

When I left Sherborne, at the end of the Lent term in 1934, the new Headmaster, who did not know me as well as Mr Boughey, wrote:

'He has proved an efficient and cheerful prefect.* We shall miss him. I like him well, though sometimes his ambitions seem to me a little too worldly.'

My form master was not going to miss me, and he sped me on my way to those worldly ambitions with the words:

'You have been a failure here and you will be a failure all your life.'

Wait! I *think* his name was Harmes. If it wasn't, my apologies to Mr Harmes.

---

*I am one up on Coby here who later received the report: 'A thoroughly conscientious prefect. It is a pity he is so lacking in a sense of humour.'

Part 3

★★★★★★★★★★★★★★★★★★★★★★★★★★★★★★★★★★★★

Virginity Dropping

★★★★★★★★★★★★★★★★★★★★★★★★★★★★★★★★★★★★

ON LEAVING SCHOOL in 1934 I bought my first car, a bow-nosed Morris Cowley, newly-painted, new tyres, full set of tools, new hood, at the cost of £7. It was christened *The Green Bile*. The same car today is worth hundreds of pounds.

At the end of May I boarded a Heracles airliner bound for Paris, on my way to Tours to learn French.

The Heracles had a cabin like a first class railway carriage. It lumbered along at ninety miles an hour and took two and three quarter hours to reach Paris.

I stayed in Tours with a family called Chausson. There was no bathroom, and the lavatory had an unforgettable smell. Monsieur Chausson was a schoolteacher, who affected high stiff collars, and played the cello. He had five children and a rather pretty maid, who would willingly have joined me in bed, but I gave her no encouragement. I was still, for some reason, 'saving it'.

Tours can be added to the long list of my educational failures. The town was packed with other British men and girls. We had a great time, and hardly spoke a word of French. Monsieur Chausson seemed not to notice my lack of progress. I learned later that he hardly noticed me at all. In 1947, after the war, I paid the family a return visit, with my car loaded with presents. They were most polite, gave me lunch, accepted the presents graciously, and admitted that not one of them retained the slightest recollection of me.

One entry in my diary in July showed a certain prescience:

'Chancellor Dolfuss of Austria has been shot. I can see I shall be a brave soldier at the front before much longer.'

At this time the thought of another war did not terrify me. I remember telling Roland how lucky he had been in having a far more exciting life than mine. He had so much more experience to draw on——studying art in Paris, acting with H B Irving in Australia and, above all, fighting in the war.

I spent two months back in England during which we celebrated Granny's eightieth birthday at Torcross, and I rediscovered my mother.

For a long while I had known she was living not more than fifteen miles away, somewhere near East Grinstead. Suddenly, it seemed ridiculous that I should not meet her. It was not as if it had been forbidden. She was just never mentioned. I did some quiet detective work, made an excuse to Granny and Uncle Guy, and set off in *The Green Bile*.

She lived near Holtye in a lovely Elizabethan Manor House. What was then known as a trim parlourmaid opened the door and looked at me with cool enquiry. *The Green Bile* was not impressive and neither were my clothes.

'Yes?'

'I'd like to see Mrs de la Garde, if she is in.'

'Who shall I say wants her?'

'I'd rather not give my name, but I think she would like to see me.'

The maid's expression indicated some doubt about this. She withdrew and, about a minute later, my mother came to the door, slim, a little greying, with a sad, Madonna face and the same cool look of enquiry.

'Yes?'

'Do you recognise me?'

'No.'

'I'm Michael.'

For one moment I thought she was going to faint. She steadied herself, then kissed me, tentatively, nervously, as if expecting a rebuff.

I was to grow very fond of her, but I could never look on her as a mother, and she did not ask that I should. It was some years before I even called her that, but we had many happy times together before she died suddenly, too young, at sixty.

Granny and Uncle Guy were delighted at my initiative. I think they felt it was one in the eye for Dorothy, but nobody could prophesy Dorothy's reactions to anything. When I told her, she expressed immediate approval. Roland looked nervous, but he, too, took it calmly. Their only reservation was that Jon should not be told yet awhile, since he was going through a 'difficult' period, and it would be better if he was left without further complications until he had 'improved a bit'.

Still in pursuit of the French language, I left for Bayonne on 4th October 1934. I mention the date specifically for it was a red letter day. On the way, in a second class compartment of the Paris—Biarritz train, I lost my virginity.

In the train from Victoria I sat opposite an attractive, dark girl. Admittedly she was a bit 'past it'. (She was 24.) We chatted all the way to Dover, during which I learned she was half-Italian, half-Spanish, an atheist, married, divorced, and spoke five languages and had five Christian names—Ernestina, Maria, Luisa, Carmela, Caterina.

We shared a porter at Dover and another at Calais, which ensured we were in the same compartment again.

I stood her dinner at a little café near the Quai D'Orsay, which made a nasty hole in my pocket.

She was travelling to Spain, which meant she would be taking the same train south. We boarded early, lowered the blinds and lay full length on the two seats to discourage anybody else from entering. At this stage, the plan was merely to make sure we could sleep in comfort.

We talked for some time after the train left Paris. I found her views quite shocking. Her marriage had been a failure, and she now proposed merely to have affairs. I questioned the morality of this, but she was adamant. Sex was a normal, everyday thing and, if one felt like it, one should have it. I think she called it 'free love'.

It was more to test her sincerity than with any hope of success that I made my approach. The trouble was I did not know how to word it, and spent at least an hour mulling it over. Finally—and I can still blush when I think of the wording—I stammered biblically: 'Would you lie with me, if I asked you?'

She looked at me consideringly, with big dark eyes, then gave a little chuckle.

'Yes, if you want to.'

Suddenly, I did not; but it was too late.

I told her I had not done anything like this before and she said this did not matter. She had never slept with a virgin, so we were quits.

25

She was very gentle and sweet and after it was over——all of three minutes later——she gave me a long talk on every aspect of lovemaking, including the all-important preliminaries, which I had completely neglected. It was a shame she had to go on to Spain.

In Bayonne I stayed with a Protestant pastor and his family, who lived in a flat at the top of a gloomy, echoing building.

I learned French in Bayonne, but it was not a happy time. For a start, within one week of my arrival, I came out in a rash, like huge mosquito bites, all over my body. Since I had never seen anything like it, I immediately assumed that my sin of fornication on the train was reaping its just reward. Obviously I had syphilis. I lay in bed each night, quaking with fear, and waiting for my nose to drop off. I did not dream of writing home to seek Roland's advice. This was a pity. If I had, I would have learned that I, like every other member of the family, was suffering from an almost unique form of mange, caught off a Shetland sheepdog, which we had bought shortly before I left for France. The only known cure was sulphur baths, and I was cured within a week of my return to England.

I visited a brothel with some Frenchmen, who pitied my lonely and monastic existence. We watched three blue films made in about 1920, after which fifteen bare-topped girls paraded before us so that we could make our choice. As guest of honour I was given first pick, but told to hurry, since the films (which had made me laugh) had stimulated them enormously. Blushing, I said I did not want to do anything. They looked amazed. Didn't I fancy *any* of the girls? I assured them they were lovely, but I had made a resolution that I would never pay for sex. I left with my head hanging, and to the sound of derisive laughter.

Curiously enough, this is the one resolution I have never broken; but it did not impress my French friends. It merely reinforced their conviction that all English public schoolboys were queer.

Jon, meanwhile, was said to be 'improving'. Jon was always improving. No boy has ever improved as much as Jon did over the years. There was nothing people enjoyed more than to sit around saying how much Jon had improved. He improved to such an extent that he was allowed to meet my mother, and a fairly turbulent relationship developed between them. Within a couple of years she had joined the crowd, and was definitely seeing improvement in him, too.

He still had some curious ways. He was seen by an acquaintance getting off a London tube train, on two crutches, and wearing dark glasses. An old lady was helping him. If he gave an explanation, or ever admitted it, I cannot remember.

My writing career bogged down after its promising début. I sold a second short story to *Pearson's Magazine*, and thereafter collected nothing but rejection slips.

My only other paid work was as temporary secretary to romantic novelist, Denise Robins, answering readers' problems for a woman's weekly magazine. Denise was almost part of the family. She was thirty-eight and had already written seventy-six novels. She adored and admired Roland. He, while occasionally irritated by the amazing speed of her writing, secretly admired her incredible energy, and recognised her complete sincerity.

I can still remember him stabbing an angry finger at a proof page of one of her books, and reading it out to her.

'"Annabel looked at herself in a beautiful antique mirror, which was nailed to the wall." *Nailed!* If you insist on describing how it was attached to the wall, which is unnecessary, the damned thing would be *screwed*, not nailed.'

I loved Denise because she did not patronise me. Most people, knowing my ambition to follow in Roland's footsteps, would smile indulgently, metaphorically pat my head, and talk of the advantages of 'safer' professions. Not so Denise. Whatever her private feelings may have been, she offered me nothing but encouragement.

In 1965, I wrote the Foreword to her autobiography. Roland should have done it, but, unhappily, he died before it was complete. By then Denise had written one hundred and thirty-nine novels. Today she is on her one hundred and sixty-fifth, is still going strong and remains a firm friend.

Since I was obviously not going to be a successful writer overnight, I became an apprentice reporter on *The Tiverton Gazette*—circulation five thousand. Shortly before me, another young journalist had been there. His name was Reginald Willis and he subsequently became Editor of The London *Evening News*, one of the most durable and successful editors in Fleet Street's history. We became good friends years later and he published a number of my articles in The London *Evening News*.

The *Tiverton Gazette* taught me journalism from scratch but it also did pretty well out of me. I learned shorthand at a price which I considered 'not bad'. For private tuition five times a week the cost was 7/6d. Not bad!

Within a few weeks I was doing full reporting, including court coverage, and was the official film and theatre critic with the initials 'M P' at the foot of the column. I ran my own car out of my own (Roland's) pocket and received not one penny in expenses.

The Editor was a mild man named Morris, who couldn't roll his r's. Thus Mr Clapp of the front office was never known as anything but 'Mr Crap'.

My immediate boss was the sub Editor, Captain Young, whose claim to fame was having stood against Neville Chamberlain as an Independent candidate, and losing his deposit.

Captain Young prided himself on a brusque and bullying manner, which fooled nobody for he was the most inoffensive and kind-hearted of men.

My first contribution to the paper was the coverage of a funeral. The end paragraph read:

'There were a wealth of beautiful floral tributes. The funeral arrangements were satisfactorily carried out by J. Smith & Sons of Cullompton. Wigs were supplied by Strawson.'

The last line had unfortunately slipped over from a theatrical column.

It may have been this error (which caused a sensation) which prompted Mr Morris to make me his film and drama critic. I started out in traditional style, which meant I was kind to everyone.

'The more I see of the Dulverton Amateurs, the more I wonder and admire. The histrionic ability stored up in Dulverton is nothing short of extraordinary. This production of *She Stoops to Conquer* is a triumph.'

One firm rule—which also went for funerals—was that everybody, even remotely connected with the affair, must be mentioned by name.

This recalls a notice in a local paper for an amateur production of one of my plays, which started:

'The Swithin Players presented Michael Pertwee's *Night Was Our Friend* at the Town Hall last night and prompter Enid Lubbock had a busy time.'

After a few months of writing this kind of thing I asked Mr Morris if I could really criticise. To my surprise, and to Captain Young's horror, he said that I could write anything I liked. When the Captain demurred, Mr Morris gave him a lecture on the freedom of the press. To his great credit he stood steadfastly by this decision, despite storms of protest from Amateur Companies all the way from Uffculme to Southmolton.

One author-director, whose original play I had criticised harshly wrote me five pages of closely typed protest, which ended:

'I am afraid art is dead in Tiverton. As you know I fill a public position and am very closely connected with the church and other institutions in the Town. Were I Catholic I have no doubt I should be excommunicated. As it is, I find I am being very coldly received in certain quarters. Such is the power of the press.'

This made me feel very powerful.

Early in 1936 I learned there was a vacancy in the Auxiliary Air Force Squadron at Bristol. These squadrons were made up entirely of civilian weekend flyers. I was mad about flying, and here seemed a way to learn free.

I obtained an interview and went to Bristol.

The planes were two-seater Westland Wapiti Bi-Planes with open cockpits.

The first test was a flight to see how I reacted to aerobatics. I was given instructions on how to use the parachute, but as we were taxying for take-off, I gave the rip-cord a little tug to make sure I had the movement right. This coincided with the plane hitting a bump. I tugged too hard, and the parachute burst forth, nearly suffocating me. Within seconds it was streaming in all directions. We returned to base, and gathered the parachute into a huge bundle. The Sergeant in charge—from his manner I guessed he was a Regular—provided me with another parachute and suggested I leave the bloody thing alone.

This was a poor start, but I stood up to the aerobatics, and just managed to avoid being sick.

The next test was the important one—an interview by the CO. He was a severe man with steely eyes. He offered me a cigarette, but no ashtray. I was determined to create a good impression and surreptitiously tapped the ash into my jacket pocket rather than make a mess on his floor. He unbent towards the end of the interview and, as we went to lunch, said he hoped all would be well, and that I might soon be welcomed into the Squadron. At last, I thought, I had passed an examination.

I sat on his left at lunch. He was at the top of a very long table with the other members of the squadron on either side.

A mess waiter entered, carrying a large silver-plated dish on which was a mountain of sausages and mashed potatoes. He carried it high, balanced on one hand. As he wheeled round his foot slipped. The dish went flying and landed smack on the CO's head. It stuck there, like some comedy hat, cemented on by the mashed potatoes.

It was the funniest thing I had ever seen. I let out a roar of laughter and rocked back and forth about three times before I was aware of a complete silence. I stopped laughing and looked around. Not a smile cracked the face of any of the others. I looked at the CO. He had not moved. One steely eye was visible through a curtain of potatoes, and it was riveted on me.

Three days later I received a brief letter regretting that the vacancy had been filled.

The sad footnote to this story is that practically every one of those men was subsequently killed in action.

I was worried by my poor physique and fairly poor track record with the girls. This prompted me to write to Charles Atlas who advertised miracles with the weediest of bodies in a short time. He offered a complete weekly course plus, at the end, a certificate and six handsomely bound volumes on sex. The cost, when revealed, was so appalling that I decided to remain weedy.

This started a lengthy correspondence during which the cost came crashing down until it was about a quarter of the original asking price. Charles's final offer was to send the whole course under one cover plus, for good measure, a single handsomely bound volume on sex. This I accepted. I had filled in a very detailed form giving all my vital statistics, including my age—20, and was disappointed when the handsome volume turned out to be:

The Sex Life of the Man Over Forty.

At that time I imagined that most men over forty did not even think about sex.

I am now over fifty. I still think about sex and am still inclined to be weedy. Only last week I was looking longingly at the picture of a man, remarkably like old Charles, who was advertising something called The Bullworker; but I resisted it. He might have offered me *The Sex Life of the Man Under Twenty.*

When I left *The Tiverton Gazette* I (Roland) gave a banquet to the whole staff. I was presented with a timepiece, suitably inscribed. I do not think I can do better than to quote from the news paragraph which followed the event:

'The toast "The Guvnor" was given by Mr L A Clapp, and, in response, Mr C A Morris said he hoped that function might constitute the first of a number of annual events. Songs and stories were contributed by the majority of those present and the evening, which was characterised by delightful informality, was voted an unqualified success.'

My next unpaid job was at Gaumont British Film Studios in Shepherd's Bush. Michael Balcon was the executive head of production. Roland was writing a lot for them. I was to be a learner writer and they were unable to pay me anything since the British Film Industry was going through one of its periodic death-throes.

I was given a palatial office, recently vacated by a contract writer who had been dropped. I had a gorgeous redheaded secretary called Mary, and sometimes used another one called Winnie.

The Scenario Editor was Angus Macphail, who possessed a penetrating ability to detect weaknesses in story line, a fund of ideas to replace them, and an unquenchable thirst for alcohol, which he never touched before six in the evening; but you could set your clock by him.

I was put to work with a German expatriate writer, Kurt Siodmak, brother of the film director Robert Siodmak. Kurt had made his name with a film called *The Tunnel* about an Atlantic tunnel. We worked on a strange story which was designed to use three well-known characters of fiction—Doctor Nikola, Edgar Wallace's Mr Reeder, and another, whose identity I have completely forgotten. It concerned a jade Buddha worth millions of pounds.

One day I was dictating to Winnie, who proved to be slightly deaf, and not too hot as a typist. I dictated as follows:

'*CLOSE SHOT*. On the table stands a little Buddha, no bigger than a man's hand.'

On reading through the pages at the end of the session I found that Winnie had typed:

'*CLOSE SHIT*. On the table stands a little bugger no bigger than an iron stand.'

I had been at Gaumont for some months when I was summoned to the office of a Mr Alexander, who dealt with finance. He said they had been examining my position and had decided they must pay me something. He cut short my thanks, saying they were not offering much. It was five shillings a week. This I could not believe.

'You mean five *pounds* a week?'

'No. Five shillings. We've discovered that should you be injured while not on the payroll there might be serious insurance consequences.'

I declined the offer. At least, as an unpaid writer I could take a day off

31

when I felt like it. He warned this might mean I would have to go; but nothing more was said and I stayed until the early part of 1937.

That April I came of age. I had now been working diligently for some four years, but my total earnings during that period were something under fifty pounds.

Mr Harmes* looked like being right.

For my twenty-first my mother gave me a car, and Roland gave me a life insurance policy, which would produce £895 when I was fifty. My joy at this was slightly dampened on learning that, in future, he expected me to find the annual premium of £10. My fiftieth birthday seemed a lifetime away, and finding £10 a year when I had, so far, only averaged £12.10 seemed to herald ruination.

Joy, however, was unconfined at the discovery, around this time, that Betty was in love with me again. We had been meeting sporadically on a 'just good friends' basis, and then it happened. Blithely ignoring such minor problems as what we would live on, I took her in a punt on the Thames to pop the question. I did not get around to it, because I was violently seasick, and came ashore in a state of collapse. This may sound hard to believe, but I am an even worse sailor than I am a mathematician.

In discussing marriage I had not reckoned with Betty's father, who was a Scottish businessman with firm ideas about the correct way things should be done. When rumours reached his ears he made it plain that there could be absolutely no question of our getting engaged until I had formally asked him for his daughter's hand. I put on my best suit and nervously drove to their house in Buxton, where I was left alone with Mr Fergusson. There was a long pause, then I cleared my throat and made my little speech. He listened in silence, frowning, then asked how old I was (which he knew). I told him twenty-one. Now came the topic I had been dreading.

'What are you earning?'

'Er—nothing at the moment, actually.'

'I see. And what are your prospects?'

There was no point in lying. He knew the answer to this, too.

'Absolutely none.'

There was another silence, then he looked up, smiled, and nodded his head.

'That's all right,' he said. 'You have my blessing.'

He showed far more faith in me than I had in myself at this time.

---

*If it was Mr Harmes.

With Gaumont British crumbling, I left the studios to take another unpaid job, as a reader in the offices of Roland's agent, Hayes Hunter. I must be fair. I was, in fact, paid thirty shillings a week, which covered my fares, coffees and a few bunches of tulips for Betty, at 6d a dozen.

Film Rights Ltd were then operating from a dismal building in Whitcomb Street, which has since been pulled down. The offices were built round a well, which used to echo to the stentorian tones of Hayes Hunter bawling out his staff. They were all scared stiff of him. I was the only one he never shouted at. Perhaps he assumed that anyone earning only thirty shillings a week had so little to lose that he would not put up with too much shouting. Hayes was a big American, with big teeth and big horn-rimmed spectacles. He had a reputation for being a good and tough agent.

I worked as assistant to Alroy Treeby, a kindly Australian with a semi-American accent, which I think he had originally adopted to please Hayes Hunter.

During the summer I took a week's holiday to stay at Torcross. Here, in just six days, I wrote the draft of a complete three act play.

I did not know it then, but I was about to break the ice.

Part 4

Curtain Dropping (One)

★ ★

IN HIS AUTOBIOGRAPHY, describing how the play *Interference* was written, Roland said:

> 'It was through Harold Dearden that *Interference* came to be written. He was, at the time, a fashionable psychiatrist with a large practice, but his ambitions ran eagerly in the direction of writing.'

Anyone reading this book to the end will see that my life has often followed a pattern set by Roland's to an extraordinary degree.

I could repeat Roland's paragraph here word for word, substituting only the name 'Guy Beauchamp' for 'Harold Dearden', *Death on the Table* for *Interference*, and 'Manipulative Surgeon' for 'Psychiatrist'.

Guy Beauchamp had a flourishing practice in Harley Street at a time when 'osteopathy' was looked upon with deep suspicion by many people. The fact that he was also a qualified doctor probably assisted him. I knew Guy then only as a personal friend. The discs in my back had not yet started to slip with the monotonous regularity which today makes me one of his most frequent visitors.

Guy was fascinated by the theatre, and full of ideas. He approached me with an idea he had conceived for a comedy-thriller play, and suggested we collaborate. We worked out the plot line in our evening spare time. Not surprisingly, the play had a medical background. It was the story of an American big-time gangster, with a bullet lodged in his back, who came to Britain to blackmail a British surgeon into removing the bullet. The table of the title was the operating table on which the gangster met his death.

At the age of twenty-one a writer is fairly easily satisfied with his work, and what I had written during those six days seemed fine to me and to Guy so, on my return to London, I told Hayes Hunter about the play and asked if he would handle it. Hayes laughed loudly. Hayes laughed a great deal, when he wasn't bawling people out. He clapped me on the back and said everyone wrote a first play. He did not, however, offer to read it, so we sent it to another agency, Christopher Mann. There the play was handled by Aubrey Blackburn, who occupies the same chair today, and who has handled my last three West End plays.

Death on the Table was eventually accepted, without qualification, by Gardner Davies, who was then running Richmond Theatre, a first class shop window for trying out new plays.

Later, Hayes Hunter professed to be deeply hurt that he was not handling it. Perhaps he learned the lesson that, very occasionally, first plays are worth a glance.

The six months between March and August 1937 saw a fairy-tale transformation of my life. My first love was in love with me again. My first play was going into production, and my first original film script fell into the hands of Frank Launder, who was then a writer and Scenario Editor at Gainsborough Film Studios. He called me in for an interview. Later that same day I strolled nonchalantly into the house to inform a delighted Roland that I was about to sign a three-year film contract.

The salary was £3 per week for six months, rising to £4 for the next six months then jumping to £6, £12 and finally £20 for the last six months of the contract. Should they renew the contract for a further three years, I was promised £40 to start the second term.

I would not be a millionaire, but I felt like one.

When I joined them, Gainsborough Studios were having much the same kind of success as Ealing Studios had after the war, making reasonably budgeted pictures in an efficient manner. They had some talent working for them. Alfred Hitchcock made one there, and an up and coming young director, Carol Reed, directed one of the earliest pictures I worked on, *A Girl must Live*. Margaret Lockwood was one of the girls in it.

In charge of production was Ted Black, brother of the impresario, George Black. Ted was a quiet man, who wore quiet suits. His voice seemed to come from far back in his throat; but his manner was deceptive. He knew what he wanted and got it. It was whispered in the corridors that he was one of the few producers who could get his way with Hitchcock.

35

The studios were in Islington. You parked your car outside, whereupon a number of urchins would ask for sixpence to look after it. If you were foolish enough to refuse, they lit a bonfire under it.

At Gaumont British the children always demanded autographs of everyone leaving. I used to sign 'George Arliss' rather than go into a long explanation about being a nobody.

The urchins at Islington did not bother about autographs. They were a democratic bunch and would light a bonfire under anybody's car.

Will Hay was a big star in 1937, and many of his pictures were made at Gainsborough. He was a dedicated hypochondriac. Every day during the shooting of his pictures, a raffle would be held, with tickets selling at sixpence a time. You bought a ticket on which might be written: 'Headache', 'Flu', 'It's me old back', and so on. As Will Hay came on to the floor for the first takes of the day, someone would be deputed to say 'Good morning' and ask how he was. He always had something wrong and whoever held the winning ticket scooped the pool. The most unpopular ticket to draw was 'Very well, thank you'. It never won.

One of my first jobs was writing an outline for a Will Hay film, which was eventually to be called *Convict 99*. I was put to work with a young man called Jack Davies, who was a couple of years older than me. He had been contracted from outside, and was in the millionaire class, earning something around £15 a week. In my diary I described him as: 'A rather conceited man, who thinks he knows all the answers'.

I did not show him this entry until about five years ago and, since we had then been friends for some thirty years, he took it very well.

His family was steeped in show business. His grandmother was the first women to be fired from a cannon in a circus. His sister was the talented actress, Betty Ann Davies. He and I wrote several pictures and a play together after the war. His original film *Those Magnificent Men in their Flying Machines* was a huge success.

I was less happy when put to work with Val Guest and Marriott Edgar on another Will Hay subject. They worked as a team and wrote some very funny films. They were both in the big league, earning over £40 a week. Val sported racy clothes, an American accent and drove a large, American car. I was foisted on them with the twin intention of learning from them and helping with ideas. It took me about a week to discover that if I had any ideas, they evidently did not want to hear them. When I made a suggestion it was ignored, as if they had not heard me. It was like being sent to Coventry at school. The moment we left the office they became perfectly friendly and chatted amiably but, once back in the office, I appeared to become invisible and inaudible. I was acutely unhappy and unable to cope with the situation. It was bad timing that Ted Black chose this moment to ask me how I was getting on. I blurted out a somewhat incoherent description of the situation. He looked at me hard and said: 'If you ever hope to succeed in this business you must learn to get on with people.'

Fortunately, Frank Launder asked me the same question. On hearing the answer, he grinned understandingly, and invited me to join him in writing the screenplay of *A Girl must Live*. Everybody was very friendly after that.

The Crazy Gang were also making pictures there and making everybody's life an amusing hell. They would go to incredible lengths with a practical joke.

Once when they were rehearsing for a Jack Hylton stage show, Jack came into the theatre wearing a new and expensive suit. He showed it off to the Gang, who admired it. He took it off for rehearsal, and hung it in a dressing-room. During the day the Gang hired a tailor who came into the theatre and cut six inches off both the trouser legs, then repaired them and put on new turn-ups. At the end of the day Hylton's face was a picture when he put the trousers on. For quite a while he was completely mystified, as he could not believe that even the Gang would go to such lengths.

At the end of 1937 I was sent to Pinewood Film Studios to work on the script of a film for Tom Walls and Lilli Palmer called *Crackerjack*, which was a kind of Raffles story. I worked with two other writers, Basil Mason and A R Rawlinson, who was a handsome man in his forties, who became, and still is, a valued friend. He was another of those rare human beings who did not patronise or pull age. The following year we wrote a play together. His younger son would occasionally look in on us while we were working. At the advanced age of twenty-two I did patronise him mentally. He was only about nineteen and seemed immature to me. Good-looking, nice manners but not much push, I thought. He eventually had enough push to study for the bar while on very active service in North Africa during the war, and in 1970 became Attorney-General in Mr Heath's Conservative Government. We are now good friends, and he has the decency not to patronise me at all.

Both Basil and Dick were extremely kind about my contributions to *Crackerjack* and insisted I had earned a full screen-writing credit.

I took Betty along to the Press Show. The printed hand-outs gave the credits as follows:

Adaptation
BASIL MASON

Screen Play and Scenario
A R RAWLINSON,   MICHAEL PERTWEE

It was a proud moment. We waited eagerly for my name to appear on the screen. Up came the credits and away went my smile. My name had been omitted.

Next day I approached Ted Black, pointed out the omission and asked for it to be rectified. I got no change at all.

'Listen,' he said, 'Get this into your head. You are an apprentice. You contributed nothing. You were there to learn.'

This could have been justified, I suppose, but for something which happened a few weeks later. An option on my contract came up for renewal. To my dismay, I was informed that the Studios were not taking up the option. I was out. The reason? They were most dissatisfied with my contribution to *Crackerjack*, which was proving a box office disaster. It was a classic case of 'Heads I win, Tails you lose', and second only in injustice to my boxing match with Sainsbury.

I had Frank Launder to thank, yet again, for the last-minute reprieve which was granted. Frank was invariably kind and encouraging. I think he genuinely saw some talent in me, a view which was not shared by most others in the studio.

One thing I certainly learned at Gainsborough. You have to be tough to survive in the film business.

The year 1938 saw the realisation of my boyhood fantasies. On 24th January *Death on the Table* opened for a week at Richmond Theatre. Gardner Davies, who directed, did a first class job. The house was packed. The laughs were enormous, and a lady fainted at one shock scene. The reception was enthusiastic.

Most of the London critics came down and gave it rapturous notices.

'Vigorous inventiveness which holds the audience's attention continuously.'

The Times.

'Beautiful twists . . . London is very likely to see this splendid nonsense transferred.'

Lionel Hale.   The *News Chronicle.*

'A gem of cumulative ingenuity.'

The London *Evening News.*

38

At the end, the author Gilbert Frankau told me that if the play did not earn £50,000 he would eat his hat. As it turned out, he would have had an indigestible meal, but coming from such a distinguished writer it made me feel very good.

From the original cast of sixteen, (one could afford big casts in those days) five went on to appear in the subsequent West End production. They were Cameron Hall, who gave a justly acclaimed performance as a cockney hospital porter, Peter Coke, Tony Quinn, John Salew and Hugh McDermott, in his first stage appearance. He was our cook's nephew, and eventually made quite a name for himself.

We had no problems about a transfer. Most of the West End Managers sent representatives and there was a fight to obtain the rights. The only worry was to whom we should sell it.

Basil Dean secured the option. He was then one of the most important directors in London and his name carried immense prestige value. He went in with Howard Wyndham, Bronson Albery, O'Bryen, Linnit and Dunfee. It was a powerful combination.

We secured The Strand Theatre, with 9th March as the opening date.

The choice of Basil Dean had some unhappy consequences. For a start, it meant dropping Gardner Davies, who had confidently assumed that he would direct the play in the West End. It was the age-old show business tactic of playing safe, going for an established name. Gardner was bitterly disappointed, and rightly so.

In my opinion Basil Dean contributed little and, in some areas, lost a great deal from the original production. Certain arbitrary changes he made were a mystery to me then and remain a mystery now.

When I read Moss Hart's autobiography *Act One*, in which he wrote feelingly of his unhappy relations with Basil Dean during the production of one of his plays, it was an almost exact replica of my own frustrated emotions during the rehearsals of *Death on the Table*.

Our new leading man, playing the gangster, was Hartley Power, an American living in Britain, who had just closed at the same theatre after playing in *Room Service*. He was a fine actor, and gave a marvellous performance. Walter Fitzgerald played the British surgeon. He, too, was excellent.

With a much stronger cast and more time for rehearsal the play should have been a great deal better than in its original production; but somehow it did not catch fire. Each change seemed to dissipate the flow, reduce tension, slow the pace. I found myself continually arguing over apparently trivial points.

Guy Beauchamp was too busy with his practice to attend many rehearsals. So, in his absence, I was left to do battle alone.

In fairness to Basil Dean it has to be remembered I was only twenty-two, and quite inexperienced. He cannot really be blamed if he considered my opinion worthy of little attention. This did not prevent me expressing it with a regularity which irritated him profoundly.

I confided my worries to Roland, who advised a tactful and cautious approach. I was, after all, dealing with a man of immense experience. I agreed, but could only ask why I was being made to feel tiresome, difficult and argumentative, when I had found nothing to argue about at Richmond, in what had been a cheap and hurriedly assembled production? How was it that my ideas had not irritated Gardner Davies, who had always been prepared to listen, even if he sometimes did not agree?

I had, in fact, started off on the wrong foot when, not knowing Basil Dean was very superstitious, I asked where we might transfer, since we only had The Strand for a limited period? He gave an agonised cry, and forbade me to mention the future again. I would be lucky if the play lasted a week, tempting Providence like that.

The monumental row blew up over our 'juvenile lead'. We had dropped the actress who played it at Richmond. Dean produced a girl of his own choice. She was, I think, Australian. She had little experience. To me she lacked attraction, and, most important, talent. I told him she was unacceptable. He told me curtly that I would accept her and lump it.

I discovered the existence of something called 'The Author's Veto'. This gives the author the final yes or no on such arguments. I enlisted Guy's co-operation, and a letter was sent to Basil Dean by our agent.

After the dust had settled the girl quietly disappeared from the scene and her place was taken by an attractive and clever actress, Kay Walsh, who married a young film editor for whom great things were prophesied. He was David Lean. All things considered he has not done too badly.

I think the first night on 9th March 1938, was the most exciting experience of my life. Here was my Walter Mitty dream come true so much sooner than I could have dared hope.

The reception was absolutely tremendous. At the end the stalls actually rose and gave it a standing ovation.

Guy and I, in our tail suits, hovered in the wings straining our ears for the magic cry of 'Author'. It came, and we charged on to the stage.

Guy spoke first, and received resounding applause. He gestured to me, and I stepped forward. Here the dream went wrong. As I started to speak, they dropped the curtain on my head which brought me crashing to the ground. It was the biggest laugh of a laughter-packed evening.

The following day there was hardly a bad review. It was confidently predicted that we had a smash hit on our hands.

Basil Dean did not, I believe, watch the performance on the first night. This was another of his superstitions. He would pace up and down outside and only come in for the final curtain.

He came on the second night, however, which was a pity. It was a pity *anyone* came on the second night, because it was a disaster. There was a scene in which a hoodlum had to 'lock' several of the cast into a 'cupboard'. This was followed by a scheduled fifteen-second blackout, during which members of the stage management rushed on to the stage to carry out, invisibly, various secret tasks. Unfortunately, hitherto undiscovered, someone had fitted an operative lock to the 'cupboard' door. Without knowing it, the hoodlum, a Canadian actor, George Pembroke, actually locked the door, threw away the key and thus prevented the stage management from coming quickly on to the stage. It was not his fault, but instead of lasting fifteen seconds, the blackout dragged on for about two minutes as people tried to force the door, hissed at George to unlock it, or tripped over each other while searching for another way of entry to the set. The audience started to laugh, jeer and light matches.

The stage director, who finally saved the night by climbing through a window, was a young chap called Basil Dearden, who became a successful film director in the Ealing stable. He died tragically in a car accident in 1971. Following him through the window was the stage manager, a young Australian, Allan Davis, now one of the West End's top directors.

Basil Dean was white with anger and during the explosion which followed George Pembroke marched out of the theatre, apparently never to return. He was already marching down the Strand, when I pointed out there was no understudy to take his place. I was sent in pursuit, found him and led him back into the fold.

By the end of the first week several important figures from MGM came to the show, bringing the film star Paul Muni to see it. They entered into immediate negotiations and we sold the film rights for £3000.

The play received a remarkable amount of publicity. During the first week the Censor sent in a spy, who took exception to certain lines, which had crept in during rehearsal. Headlines in the papers proclaimed:

'Censor Swoops On New Play!'

One of the lines which had to be excised was when an American hoodlum misread a poem he was reading to his gangster boss, who was lying in bed in hospital.

'There are fairies at my bottom in the garden.'

Times have certainly changed since those days.

I still do not know why the play failed to fulfil its promise. An author can generally find some most convincing excuse for failure—the weather, the political situation, the location of the theatre; in fact, practically anything other than his own poor writing. I can personally produce some beauties over the years, but, in this case, there was no obvious explanation. The critics could hardly have been kinder. The public who came enjoyed it; but not enough of them came. It closed after a run of about five months.

It opened in America under the title *Come Across*. The reviews were as bad in New York as they had been good in London.

Walter Winchell, then critic of the *New York Daily Mirror* wrote:

'The 1938–39 season opened inauspiciously last night with *Come Across* described as a comedy-drama. It is a feeble attempt at melodrama, given to windy talk and dated thrillage. *Come Across* simply doesn't.'

My favourite review, which I still display on my office wall, came from the *New York Sun*, whose critic wrote:

'The new theater season toddled forth last night and executed a preliminary stumble at The Playhouse. . . . *Come Across* has two authors, Guy Beauchamp and Michael Pertwee, and the total manpower thus represented is considerable. The results unfortunately are not. I decided that the one thing worse than a bad play by an English playwright was a bad play by two English playwrights.'

The play closed in two weeks. Today it would have closed after the first night. It was disappointing. I had envisaged a triumphant visit to New York. However, I was only twenty-two, and it was something to have had a play produced in London and New York in the same year.

In England my name was being bandied about, and my agent had several enquiries from film companies. Gainsborough Studios were prepared to rent me out, sharing the spoils on a fifty-fifty basis, but their enthusiasm stopped short of giving me a rise. My agent received a firm 'no' when he suggested it. His efforts did, however, cause them to review my contract and, towards the end of the year, Ted Black summoned me and said he was pleased with my progress and that the studio was prepared immediately to alter the terms of the contract so that it ran for a total of six years, instead of three. This was wonderful news at a time of considerable insecurity in the film business. He jotted down the suggested terms. At the end of my first three years I would be earning £20 a week. The revised contract would stipulate a fourth year at £20 a week, followed by a fifth year at £30 a week, followed by the sixth year at £40 a week.

I suddenly realised I was being done. On signing the original contract I was told that should they hire me again my salary would immediately be doubled to £40 a week. Under the terms now suggested I had to wait *five* years instead of three to reach the same amount.

I told my agent, Alan Grogan, at Christopher Mann, who said it was a try-on. I should refuse point blank.

I did this. Ted Black took this blow very calmly and said, in that case, they were not interested in renewing the contract at all. Goodbye and the very best of luck. He wasn't bluffing either.

The next day I crawled back and agreed to his terms.

Granny died at the end of May, from cancer. I went down to Torcross and said a last goodbye to her. She looked like a shrivelled doll. In the end I think she was glad to go. Her only regret might have been that she did not live to see Betty and me married.

We were married in the Holy Trinity Church, Bromptom Road, on July 1st, with a reception at the Rembrandt Hotel. Dorothy made a nice gesture and allowed Roland and my mother to sit side by side in the front pew during the ceremony. Jon, now eighteen, was my best man. The author, Ian Hay, proposed the toast of bride and groom.

We honeymooned in a little hotel at Cagnes between Nice and Juan les Pins, where we stayed a month at the exorbitant price of £20 full pension for both of us.

Roland gave me the use of his car, and also a roulette system called Labouchère which won me enough to pay for the whole honeymoon.

Betty shed one quiet tear because the first thing I did on returning to our room at night was enter the roulette winnings in a notebook. She should, of course, have struck me on the head with it.

43

There was a splendid old French Count staying in the hotel with his young mistress. He had a Rolls Royce with a Chinese chauffeur. They never left the hotel, presumably for fear of being seen and recognised.

One night we found ourselves locked out of the hotel and nobody answered the bell. I climbed through an open window, and into a bedroom occupied by the Chinese chauffeur, who let out a strangled scream and hid beneath the bedclothes.

The next day I went to the Count and apologised. He looked quite blank. I said: 'Didn't your chauffeur tell you what happened last night?'

'No,' he replied. 'But then I haven't spoken to him for twenty years.'

The day we arrived back from the honeymoon Betty's mother died from a sudden stroke.

It was altogether a sad and unsettling time that autumn. War with Germany seemed inevitable. They were digging trenches in the parks. Everyone was talking ARP.

For years now I have been telling people that I was one of the wise few who immediately condemned Chamberlain's betrayal of the Czechs, and knew that he was cynically buying time. On reading my diary for that year I find that this is quite untrue. On the day he returned, waving his scrap of paper, I went to Buckingham Palace, where a large crowed had gathered. That night I wrote:

> 'I stood there in the rain and shortly afterwards he arrived amid huge cheering. Then a wonderful thing happened. A searchlight played on the balcony. Chamberlain, his wife, and the King and Queen came out to wave. I have never heard such cheering. I cried like a baby, as did everyone around me. How proud that man must be!'

Dick Rawlinson and I had finished our comedy *Chain Male*. (The spelling was a deliberate pun), which Gardner Davies accepted for production at Richmond. This time he was given a solemn promise to direct the play in the West End.

With the war crisis over we felt happier about our last act, which was smack up to date in taking place in a cellar converted into an air raid shelter. The relieved public might now be prepared to laugh at this.

We obtained an extremely good cast—Cyril Raymond and Joan Marion as the leads. Betty played the young girl opposite Ralph Michael, who was later to marry Fay Compton. There were Ambrosine Philpotts, Billy Shine and Charles Hawtrey, carrying on just as he now does in the *Carry On* pictures—and looking exactly the same, too.

I was getting almost *blasé* about first nights, and this one provided another rapturous reception.

To quote from the *Kinematograph weekly*:

> '*Chain Male* is by no less distinguished authors than A R Rawlinson and Michael Pertwee, scenario chiefs of British National and Gainsborough respectively. . . .'
>
> (I thought: 'Ted Black, please note.')

> '. . . A fine entertainment, well received—and congratulations to the two authors on both their work and the best first night speeches I have heard for some time.'

Yes, we had heard a cry for 'Author' and they did not drop the curtain on me this time.

At the end of the second act E P Clift, who with Alec Rea, was putting on a lot of West End shows, sought me out and made me promise not to sell *Chain Male* to anyone else until he had spoken to us again. After the audience trooped back to watch the third act, Dick and I danced a little jig in the bar. We were home! A transfer was assured because we knew our last act was by far the funniest of the three.

We were wrong. It was not. The public were still disinclined to laugh at Air Raid Precautions. The laughter significantly faded. E P Clift slipped out of the theatre without bothering to speak to us at all.

We had some good notices, but nearly all of them chided us for a bad last act.

My friend Lionel Hale (a friend after two great notices for *Death on the Table*) let me down badly.

> 'The curtain has not fallen on the first act before it is ominously clear that the plot is not enough. . . . It is a catch-as-catch-can affair and (a great pity) it does not catch.'

A great pity indeed. We did not transfer.

I still have Lionel Hale's programme on which he scribbled his notes. Those who like to wallow in nostalgia may like to read that advertisements in the programme offered modern freehold houses in Shepperton for £625. You could also rent houses on Cottismore Estate, Walton-on-Thames, for one guinea a week inclusive.

Several managements dickered with the play, but nothing came of it, and we decided we would have to re-write the last act.

During the week, actor Tom Walls, famous from Ben Travers' Aldwych farces, came down to see the play. We hoped he might be persuaded to act in it. My diary records that he behaved 'like an absolute bounder' and talked throughout the whole performance.

He was a marvellous actor, loved the horses and pretty women. Towards the end of his career a friend of mine asked after his sex life.

'I'm not as good as I was,' said Tom. 'But I'm getting cunning.'

So 1938 ended. I wrote in my diary:

> 'All my hopes have been fulfilled which is more than most people can say. I only hope that next year will prove as happy as this one has been.'

It did not.

I was invited on to the committee of the fledgling Screenwriters' Association, an organisation set up to fight for a better deal for screenwriters. It has now become The Writers' Guild of Great Britain, a fully-fledged trades union with considerable power, and a string of successful battles to its credit. I have since served it as Vice-President, and on the Executive Council.

In 1939 the association's aims were high but its power was non-existent. A P Herbert was made President. To celebrate this he wrote us a special little verse:

> *'The maidens who haunt picture palaces*
> *know nothing of psycho-analysis,*
> *and Sigmund Freud*
> *would be greatly annoyed*
> *as they cling to their long-standing phalluses (fallacies).'*

Dick Rawlinson and I re-wrote the last act of *Chain Male*, which was given a try-out by the Coventry Repertory Company. It achieved a remarkable amount of interest from West End Managers, several of whom dickered with it. Emile Littler was at the opening night and paid £100 to obtain the rights for London. The rest of the year was spent trying to find a suitable cast, but the play was finally put aside on the outbreak of war.

This was the first time I met Emile Littler and I was not to meet him again for many years.

In 1958 when my young daughter, Carolyn, decided to go on the stage she got the chance of an audition and came to me saying:

'I've got an audition with Emily Littler. Do you know her? What's she like?'

I am also reminded of another funny incident in the '50's, when Emile put on a musical which starred Sally Ann Howes, who was then unofficially engaged to Baron, the photographer. I could not go to the first night, but went to Baron's studio for the subsequent party. Actually, it turned out to be more of a wake, because the first night had been a disaster. In show business, if you have a disaster, you must find a scapegoat. On this occasion the scapegoat was Emile Littler. Everybody was blaming him for everything. It seemed he had done nothing right. Since I had not been at the first night I was unable to express any opinion, so sat quietly in a corner, drinking. A pretty girl came up to me and said: 'You're very silent. What's the matter?'

On the spur of the moment, and for want of anything better to say, I replied: 'What do you expect? Emile Littler is my uncle and I just don't like hearing him talked about like this.'

She walked away to hiss in somebody's ear. The effect was quite remarkable. From then on, throughout the evening, the odd person would approach me, chat of this and that and then say, confidentially: 'Mind you, I don't care what *they* say, but personally *I like* Emile.'

I have never told Emile this story, but if, occasionally, over the years someone has said to him that they didn't know he was my uncle this is the reason that he doesn't.

Suddenly, Ted Black started to smile when we met. He even called me 'Michael' on a couple of occasions, which was unheard of. At last I began to feel I was being accepted. This prompted me to pluck up the courage to ask for an extra week's summer holiday, without pay of course. He agreed most amiably. I left his office feeling as grateful as if he had given me a bonus.

I asked for the extra week because one did not have to be a prophet to realise this might be the last holiday for years, if not for ever. It was now clear, even to the most ardent supporters of the Munich Pact, that war was coming.

We returned to our little hotel in Cagnes for a blissful three weeks.

It was a perfect day when we left the Côte d'Azur to drive home, singing *J'attendrai* which was 'our' tune.

We climbed the mountains behind Cannes and looked to the other side, northwards, over Europe. We were then presented with the most heavily symbolic picture I have ever seen. Behind us all was blue sky and bright, warm sunlight. In front of us was a harsh, black line of cloud which might have been drawn with a ruler. Its blackness stretched unbroken as far as the eye could see. We stopped the car, and sat in silence. Neither of us spoke. Its message was ominously, theatrically clear. We looked back once at happiness, then moved on down the slope into the dark.

And so to war.

47

Part 5

Trouser Dropping (One)

BETTY'S BROTHER, ALASTAIR, myself and Bernard Quayle, a chum from Gainsborough, had all joined the Territorial Army together, not so much as an act of patriotism but as an endeavour to ensure that each of us would have two friends to turn to in the event of war.

We joined (London) Ordnance Field Park. RAOC quite oblivious of what Ordnance was.

On 1st September partridge shooting began——and so did Hitler, by invading Poland.

I called in to say goodbye to Roland who looked at me quizzically and said: 'You once said I was lucky to have had the experience of a war. Look, what I've laid on for you!'

He gave me his old wrist watch from the First World War, which had also served him as an identity disc. I had his name removed and my own name and number put in its place. I wore it throughout the war.

I reported to Wellington Barracks, Chelsea.

After a cursory medical examination, ('Open your mouth, say "Ah!" Drop your trousers, cough!') a corporal with beery breath piled several of us into a truck bound for Harrow. The driver did not know the way, so I directed him. It was deliberate masochism, but I made him drive through The Boltons and past our flat, which in a little over a year, had become a much loved home.

I cried. The others talked football.

Our 'barracks' was a large, newly-built factory. We were paraded in pouring rain to be handed four hairy blankets. A plump officer, Lieutenant Simmonds, who did not believe in killing by kindness but through pneumonia,

48

gave us a barking talk, saying we were to be billeted in nearby houses. He hoped—but clearly doubted—that we knew how to behave. We were now British soldiers and were expected to conduct ourselves like gentlemen. The man next to me whispered that this meant we should get out of the bath to piss in the wash-basin. At the time, I thought this was original, giggled audibly and received my first, sharp reprimand.

I was billeted, with four others, on a Mr and Mrs Lake, who treated us like honoured guests, made endless cups of tea and not once complained about anything in the six weeks we were there. You could not fail to behave like gentlemen with people as nice as that.

Bernard Quayle and Alastair arrived next day. Alastair wore a vast check cap and was dressed for golf, which he did not play. He looked even more incongruous than on an occasion when he mistakenly put on his evening tail suit for the Eton and Harrow match.

There was no army mess during the early days, so we ate excellent meals in a civilian canteen, run by an Italian family, a glowering, unfriendly lot. On the first morning Mr Simmonds marched in during breakfast, and bawled: 'Any complaints?'

The Italians looked resentful. 'What business is that of his?' they seemed to say.

I was in the canteen with about sixty others when Britain declared war. We listened to Chamberlain saying the words which shattered his dreams— and ours. There was no sound while he spoke. The Italians turned green, visualising imminent internment. Then it was over. We were at war. A soldier at the bar said: 'I'll have a cream bun, Miss.'

Nobody mentioned the war at all.

There had been no time to visit Gainsborough to say goodbye. One of my first actions was to write to Maurice Ostrer, head of the studio, bidding him a soldier's farewell and expressing the hope that, should I survive the war, my contract would be renewed. It still had four years to run.

This letter was not acknowledged and my salary was stopped, without a word, soon afterwards.

Some four weeks later, when in dire financial straits, I telephoned Ted Black to ask if he might wangle me a couple of free seats for The Palladium, he regretted this was impossible.

I heard no more from Gainsborough until the following December when I received a Christmas present of thirty shillings and an oddly worded letter asking for details of my army earnings. This, the letter stated, would be treated in the strictest confidence and 'might prove to your benefit and certainly not to your disadvantage.'

It certainly did not prove to my disadvantage because that was the last I heard of it.

If all this sounds a little acid, the acidity is intentional. I had not expected a hero's send-off, but a brief note from someone wishing me luck, even if accompanied by the news that they intended to stop paying me, would have been welcome.

As I have said, you have to be tough to survive in the film business. You also had to be tough to survive on a private soldier's pay of around fourteen shillings a week. On a couple of occasions, after various official deductions had been made, I found I actually owed the army money.

After so many years it is difficult accurately to describe the misery of those first weeks. I think, without knowing it, I was in a state of shock. It was the nightmare of dreaming one was back at school but waking to find it was true; only this was worse. School at least had a constructive purpose and you knew when it was going to end.

The previous two years had given me a sorely needed confidence in myself. I had proved the depressing Mr Harmes* wrong. I had not been a failure all my life. I was the youngest writer ever to have had a play produced in London and New York.

Now, suddenly, there was no rosy future. I was a number (7602536), wasting an active brain painting signs on bloody crates for fourteen shillings a week.

There was no hope of a commission, either, since I had not passed my Certificate A in the OTC at school.

Overnight, my hard won self-confidence evaporated, leaving nothing but despair. I found it impossible to speak to officers. If the occasion arose, I behaved like an awkward child of eight.

Nobody, except Betty, who had to bear the brunt of it, was aware of this desperation. Outwardly, I acted the cheerful schoolboy with the rest of them. I even had an old friend from Aldro, Phillips, to joke with.

Doubtless a lot of others felt as I did but, to many more, the army came as a welcome change. To me it was prison. To them it was security, a healthy life and three good meals a day.

I remember bumping into the actor, Jack Allen, who had recently married

*If it was Mr Harmes.

Collaborating with my father Roland on *The Paragon* (1948).

Ready to win the war. I became the only soldier in the British Army to be Mentioned in Despatches following acts of cowardice and disobedience.

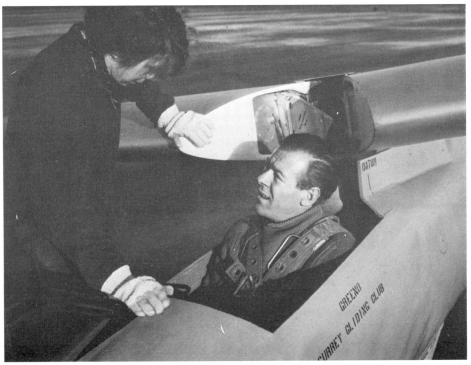

My gliding Instructor (or is it Instructress?), Ann Welch, giving me a going over after my first solo flight.

actress, Ruth Dunning, a good friend of ours. He was a sergeant in the Black Watch, stationed nearby. He looked every inch the soldier, bushy moustache, smart, confident, happy. As he marched up I thought: 'Oh, God! Here's another one who loves it.'

We chatted about old times. Tentatively, I asked him how he felt about it all. There was a tiny pause then he said: 'I cry myself to sleep every night.'

I could have kissed him. I was not alone.

Jon, meanwhile, had been 'improving' steadily for some time; but, after we had been at war a week, his reputation became a little tarnished. Uncle Guy voiced the hope that he was not going to be a shirker. This was unfair. In the last war Guy had not joined up until 1917, and then had only served in Ireland, where he was bitten by a horse.

However, Jon recovered ground by joining the Royal Navy on 9th September. I wrote: 'Good for him! A cushy job!'

Devotees of *Doctor Who* were nearly denied the chance of seeing him as its hero. His first ship was the *Hood*. He transferred just before its final voyage, which left only three survivors from a total complement of nearly eighteen hundred.

Ours was indeed a cushy job; but shatteringly boring.

We discovered the meaning of 'Fatigues'——another way of describing unnecessary work to keep you busy.

Our old Staff Sergeant, who lived in a world of army clichés, caught Alastair, Bernard and me with what must have been the oldest gag in his repertoire.

'Anyone 'ere like music?'

We stepped forward as one man and said we did. We spent the next hour moving a piano into a shed which was to be used as a chapel.

We discovered that Voluntary Church Parades were not voluntary at all.

I hated the first church service. The padre entered, followed by a spaniel dog, which gazed with rapt eyes at the pianist and miraculously stood up for the singing of the National Anthem.

The sermon sickened me. God was on our side and the enemy would get his just desserts. I do not believe that God should be allowed to take sides in a war. I privately believe that God should not allow war at all. When reviewing the subsequent carnage of six years, one is tempted to wonder what God was thinking about at the time.

We discovered the fixed routine of the rifle inspection, which was almost as solemn a procedure as the church service. The state of the rifles invariably proved a grave disappointment to all concerned. A procession would go round led by a captain, followed by a young 2nd Lieutenant, followed by the Staff Sergeant who, in turn, was followed by a Sergeant.

CAPTAIN. Very dirty butt plate, eh, Mr Wilens?

Lt WILENS. Definitely bad, eh, Staff?

STAFF. Shockin'. More elbow grease, me lad.

SERGEANT. Tck! Tck! Tck!

The sergeant's dialogue never changed although the 'Tcks' went up a couple of octaves on the day Alastair's barrel was found to house an earwig.

I discovered that my feet were still flat on our first route march, which left me crippled. As we sloped along, singing, we passed an old clergyman. His eyes filled with tears. He doffed his hat, and his lips moved silently in prayer. He must have thought we were off to the front. It was rather a shame that he was still there when we marched back.

I reported sick in the hope that I might be excused boots and be recommended for foot supports. There was no army medical officer, so we went to a civilian doctor practising nearby. His name was Doctor Gunter. I remember Doctor Gunter well because he was, without doubt, one of the nastiest men I have ever encountered. I meant to visit him after the war to punch him on the nose, but I did not get around to it.

Doctor Gunter obviously did not like the job which had been foisted on him. He hated his nice, neat surgery being invaded by a lot of dirty, sweaty soldiers.

Secondly, Doctor Gunter, did not know the difference between a Conscript and a Territorial. I hasten to say I am casting no aspersions on the Conscripts who, after all, made up the bulk of the British army, but the Territorials were all men who had volunteered for service.

Doctor Gunter, however, treated us like malingering scum, who had come to him with frivolous or non-existent complaints. Having dealt summarily and rudely with one or two others, he turned to me: 'And what do you think is the matter with you?'

I started to give him the past and present history of my flat feet. Before I could get to the question of foot supports he suddenly launched into a furious diatribe. The general gist was that men like me were a disgrace to the service and better out of it. He scribbled 'Medicine and Duties' on a scrap of paper and pushed me out. He did not prescribe any medicine, which would have been difficult for flat feet, but 'Duties' meant I must carry on as before, even though I could hardly get my boots on.

That was not the end of Doctor Gunter. He sent a letter addressed to the
CO stating I was a man who could make his disability as bad as I liked, that
I was perfectly fit for duty but, in his opinion, was trying to get myself out of
the army. He thought it would be a good idea if the army got rid of me since
I was not an asset to any unit.

Mercifully, the letter fell into the hands of a pleasant NCO in the front
office, who drew me aside to ask conspiratorially whether I really did want
to get out of the army. I told him that much as I hated the life I would hardly
have volunteered as a Territorial if my aim was to stay a civilian. He winked
and tore the letter up. Just to keep things straight, we reported the matter
to the orderly officer, a nice, young chap, who had already been labelled as
'human'. He excused me from wearing boots for a week.

One result of being excused boots came on the very next routine foot
inspection when Mr Simmonds paused to give mine a second look: 'A very
nice pair of feet. What's your name?'

I felt as flattered as a starlet whose bust has been admired by a film
magnate.

I discovered that the newly-flown barrage balloons looked very beautiful
in the September sunset. I was looking up at them when I walked into a lamp-
post, knocked myself cold and cracked my nose.

I did not report sick. I was terrified I would be sent to the unspeakable
Doctor Gunter, who might recommend a firing squad for causing self-inflicted
wounds.

I wrote a letter to Ian Hay, now Major General Beith, at the War Office,
to ask if there was any way of making the army believe I might prove to be
officer material, despite not having taken my Certificate A at school. He
wrote me a charming personal letter, but said there was nothing he could do.
I went to bed and dreamed that Mr Harmes* and Doctor Gunter were standing side by side singing: 'You'll be a private all your life.'

I discovered the discomforts of Guard Duties; two hours on four hours
off. Just as I was about to come off at 11 pm I heard someone approaching.
I yelled: 'Halt! Who goes there?'

A high pitched, falsetto voice trilled: 'Don't worry, dear, it's *Alastair!*'

I didn't worry but Alastair did because the orderly officer happened to
be walking nearby, which put Alastair on latrine duties.

In mid-October we moved to Aldershot. We shared a mess with an Officer
Cadet Training Unit. I shall never forget seeing actors Frank Lawton and

*If it was Mr Harmes.

53

Hugh Williams return from a route march, for they were officer cadets. My heart went out to Hugh Williams, so handsome and debonair on the stage, as he limped in. He obviously had feet like mine. It was nice to have them there, and I would occasionally sneak across and talk stage shop with them.

We had our first ENSA concert.

Someone, after Dunkirk, asked what had caused the collapse of the British Army and was given the reply, 'ENSA.' This was unfair. I saw a lot of marvellous shows during the course of the war, thanks to my old foe, Basil Dean, who ran it. This particular show starred Mai Bacon. She was introduced by a crusty, old General who said: 'I hope you'll all give Mae West a grand reception.'

He got the biggest laugh of the evening.

I learned to drive three ton trucks—to the dismay of one Aldershot lamp-post.

I spent a pleasant afternoon delivering a Jaguar belonging to an officer to his sister, who was a gorgeous girl. I lingered, chatting to her, for about an hour. When I left she tried to tip me half-a-crown, which deflated me. For a brief while I had felt human again. The next person to offer me half-a-crown was General Patton of the US Army, some five and a half years later, but I was a Captain by then, and took it in my stride.

We moved to Nottingham, where we were housed in a vast, empty factory. I smuggled in a lilo and a folding deck-chair which were much envied. An officer discovered them while on inspection.

'What do you think this is? The bloody South of France? I don't want to see that deck-chair again.'

I got rid of the deck-chair, but clung to the lilo.

Every morning in the factory we were rudely awakened either by an unearthly clanging from the central heating pipes or by a tremendous, reverberating fart blown by a man called Mac Davies. Everybody loved Mac Davies's morning fart, and it never failed to raise a cheer as well as the rafters.

I went to hospital with a streptococcal throat.

I went on Christmas leave, seven days of Heaven stretched to nine because we were due to go overseas.

The unit went back to Odiham near Aldershot.

Dick Rawlinson, now back in the army for his second World War, wrote to me about a branch of Army Intelligence called Field Security, which needed linguists.

I travelled five miles from Odiham to the Field Security at Mytchet, where

I was questioned about my political views, and given a test in French. I returned five miles to Odiham, reported to my CO who said: 'Pack your things and go back to Mytchet immediately. They've telephoned accepting you.'

In the space of three hours the RAOC had lost a private and the Intelligence Corps had gained a Lance-Corporal.

I was to go on a two weeks' crash course.

My first officer was a slight man with a lined, aesthetic face, an unsmiling mouth, iron grey hair and a mildly sarcastic manner. At first glance, I wondered why a man of his age had volunteered for army service. Had he been as old as I took him to be, Malcolm Muggeridge would be celebrating his centenary this year.

I remember little of the course except that we were treated very much as human beings. It was constantly impressed on us that we were important people with an important job to do.

Field Security was a branch of I (b), counter intelligence. It was made up of sections, consisting of an officer, a CSM, two sergeants and nine NCOs. All personnel had to speak at least one foreign language. Our job, on a low level, was counter-espionage, counter-sabotage, and making sure the units to which we were attached did not leave important documents hanging about. We were not very popular, often being confused with Military Police. This was possibly because, in the early days, we were known as the Field Security Police.*

Life became almost normal when I was allowed to live out with Betty in a room we found in Aldershot.

I did not finish the course. I must have impressed somebody, because I was one of the section hurriedly formed for an immediate and apparently important operation overseas. We were paraded before the Adjutant who said: 'I can't tell you where you're going but you are some of the luckiest young men in Britain. You'll be doing a job a lot of people would give their eye teeth for.'

I couldn't help wondering whether his idea of good luck and ours would coincide.

It was certainly a blow to Betty and me. We had counted on at least a

---

*If I am not very explicit about my work in I (b) during the ensuing years it is because it is still subject to the rulings of the Official Secrets Act.

month living out together, before I would be posted to a section. She packed her bags and left to stay with my mother in Berkshire.

We were piled into Bedford trucks and given a rousing send-off. There was no doubt in anybody's mind that wherever we were bound was a long way off.

We actually drove one mile to another barracks in Aldershot. Discreet questioning revealed that nobody knew how long we would remain there, but it could be for some time. It was the most dreadful anticlimax and, as I unpacked my kitbag, I thought of Betty in the train getting ever further away from me. She returned two days later.

We were stationed with an infantry battalion in the barracks—a Victorian monstrosity, with running cold water, which had been condemned in 1918. We mixed with some of the infantry and they, too, had all been told how lucky they were.

Three days later we were paraded and addressed by a brigadier, an enormous Scotsman in a kilt, who said: "It's been very nice knowing you; but, as often happens in the army, the whole damn shoot has been cancelled, and we're all going back to our units. No need to get down-hearted, though. The war will last for donkey's years yet. Goodbye, and the best of luck.'

We returned to Mytchet.

I never knew exactly what this operation was; but, years later, I was told it had been a scheme to send an invading force to the Northern tip of Scandinavia, to occupy some ore mines, which might have been very valuable to the Germans. If that is the case then we *were* very lucky—that it was cancelled.

Our section officer was Lieutenant Wilkinson, who scared us at first by looking very military, but proved to be a charming man.

My fellow NCOs were a mixed bag. They included Donald, who was short and fat, had been on the Stock Exchange and talked as if he'd owned it. Andy was another Scot, a schoolmaster, who seemed determined to prove what was meant by the term 'A dour Scot'. I did not like him until he accused me of being dour, from which moment we became firm friends. Archie was long, thin and drooping. Everything about him drooped including his moustache. 'Happy' came from Yorkshire and was not happy at all. He was small and thin and his hair stuck out in all directions. He hated the war and just

---

*Diaries were frowned upon on active service and without one to refer to I am forced to use Christian names and nicknames. This must also be my excuse for any subsequent errors in names, dates and places.

wished he was back in Yorkshire. Paul* was half-French by birth and three-quarters French in speech. He had a fund of English jokes, which only he understood.

In February we moved to Yorkshire, near Thirsk. Hints were dropped that we were again the luckiest young men in Britain.

Eventually, we packed up and left for the Clyde. Our section was split up, and I boarded the cruiser HMS *Berwick*. Nobody greeted us aboard, so we wandered about aimlessly. I found some steps, which led up to a small deck, from which I could see others of the section on another warship. I yelled a greeting, and then gave a fine imitation of Lord Nelson directing a battle from the bridge. I felt a gentle tap on my shoulder and turned to see a naval officer, who seemed to have more gold rings than I had eaten hot dinners. He was very polite in pointing out I was performing on a section of deck reserved for senior naval officers.

I removed myself hastily—too hastily. As I scuttled away my boots caught on the top rung of the ladder and I plunged head first to the deck below. I was revived some two minutes later with my first taste of Navy rum, which I detested.

I had now been in the army for six months, and had already been knocked unconscious three times without any assistance from the Germans—by a lamp-post, a cruiser's deck and a Geordie who had objected to being called a bastard.

There was no Scotsman in a Kilt to cancel this operation, but it was cancelled just the same. After a few hours aboard, and without any explanation, we disembarked and returned to our barn.

I have no idea what had been planned for us. I can only guess that Hitler's intention to invade Norway was known and that someone thought it might be a good idea if we got there first. If so, it seems he was overruled.

My next move was to hospital in Catterick with a bad case of pleurisy. I think they may have thought I was dying, for I was placed in a small ward by myself. I responded well to the M and B and, after a few days, felt better, but still extremely weak.

Hitler, meanwhile, invaded Norway.

Mr Wilkinson came to visit me. He closed the door, approached the bed in a somewhat furtive manner, drew up a chair, leaned close and said: 'I shouldn't be telling you this, but we're due to go overseas any minute now. Officially, you wouldn't be discharged from here for a couple of weeks, which means you'd be out of the section and back to Mytchet. I don't want to lose you, and I'm sure you don't want to lose us. I reckon I can wangle you out of here, if you feel up to it. What do you say?'

What can you say when someone talks like that? One side of me was immensely flattered to be genuinely wanted. An officer actually pulling strings to keep *my* services! What price Doctor Gunter now? But I had another side, and Doctor Gunter might well have nodded and said: 'I told you so' had he seen it. I must belatedly admit that I lied in my teeth as I summoned a gallant smile and told Mr Wilkinson to go ahead and wangle for all he was worth.

I did like him. I did like the section, but I loved England more and had a perfectly legitimate reason for staying safe and snug in her bosom, while they went off God knew where.

Mr Wilkinson gave my shoulder a friendly pat and went off to wangle so efficiently that, wrapped in a blanket and feeling like a wet blanket, I left hospital by car that very evening.

The ward Sister frowned blackly and said she had expressed strong disapproval. The trouble was she didn't express it strongly enough.

Part 6

Bomb Dropping

★★★★★★★★★★★★★★★★★★★★★★★★★★★★★★★★★★★★

BY THE TIME I returned to our barn I was feeling fairly philosophical. I had made my own bed and I had to lie on it. In fact, I was allowed to lie on it for several days. I was excused all duties and was treated like a VIP.

When the rest of the section heard the story they all said it was a damned good show, except for 'Happy' the Yorkshire lad. Poor 'Happy' had been a little less unhappy back in his beloved Yorkshire, but he viewed the immediate future with deep foreboding. 'Happy' listened to my story, then said I was a cunt—and he meant it. It was the first of only two occasions when I heard him express an opinion forcefully.

From Yorkshire we went to Dunfermline, near Edinburgh, where we froze under canvas. It was early April but a cold winter still lingered on.

We were allowed to write letters but they were now being censored.

When troops were in action, and normal mail was impossible, the army printed special cards which read:

    I am well. . . .
    I am not well. . . .
    I am wounded. . . .

On this the soldier put his name, rank and number, and marked the appropriate line with a tick.

Rumour had it that once the girls of the ATS and WAAF reached the battle area, they had a similar card which read:

    I am well. . . .
    I am not well. . . .
    I am worried. . . .

Our next port of call was Scapa Flow, where we boarded a luxury liner. (I think the *Empress of Britain*). It was her first voyage as a troop-ship.

Ours was an entirely French speaking section, with the exception of Mr Wilkinson, which I assume is why we were sent to Norway rather than to France. If there existed a Norwegian speaking section, it was probably on its way to Egypt.

I shared a large cabin with Andy and two others. The Duke of Gloucester had been one of its more recent occupants.

The other ranks ate their meals in the first class dining-room. We were served by stewards who, until the war, had hovered obsequiously over the tables attending to ladies in long gowns and gents in dinner jackets. The habit died hard. For the first day they served bully beef with all the right gestures, even dropping an occasional 'M'sieur' when caught off guard; but it could not continue, and by the second day they were chucking it at us with: 'Eat it while it's hot and for Gawd's sake don't mess the cloth. It's got to last.'

There were two other liners in the convoy and, all around us, sleek destroyers bouncing in the swell, throwing up frothy clouds of spray. During the first day two more liners and several more destroyers joined us. Every now and then, on the horizon, we could see the distant shapes of larger warships.

The only excitement of that day was the dropping of one depth charge by a destroyer and the dropping of one complete set of false teeth over the side by a soldier who felt sick.

We were four days at sea. One day the sea was so rough that I lay on my bunk praying we might be torpedoed. I really wanted to die.

They held a church service in the largest lounge to pray for our success. It was jammed to overflowing—and all volunteers. This was to have a curious sequel on the return trip.

We dropped anchor in a fjord bounded by barren hills with a scattering of snow on them. A Polish liner lay alongside us.

A solitary airplane seemed to sneak out from behind the hills. It took a look at us then dodged back out of sight again. An impressive barrage of anti-aircraft fire went up, including one shell from the single piece—date about 1890 by the look of it—which was the liner's total armament. It shook the ship from stem to stern and wisely was not fired again.

This brought everyone on the deck to see the fun. There was hardly a man aboard who had ever heard a shot fired in anger.

Seven more airplanes appeared briefly, keeping a discreet distance, but

60

disappeared as soon as the barrage started up again. Loud cheers echoed round the fjord. We were showing them!

Then a single airplane came over, flying fairly high, on a straight course. We watched, enthralled, as it sailed unconcernedly above the white puffs of the ack-ack shells.

I do not think that it occurred to anyone that it would bomb us. Officers had joined the men and were chatting and watching as calmly as if we were all at Ascot.

A huge waterspout shot up between us and the Polish ship and a second one straddled us on the other side.

Then, suddenly, the officers sprang into action, and started bawling orders for a general retreat below.

The raid lasted for three hours. The noise was tremendous. Nothing was hit.

But they were evidently worried about the safety of the liner. After several hours of utter confusion our liner was evacuated by all troops. Some were taken aboard warships. I found myself on the Polish ship. This hasty move caused a number of people, Mr Wilkinson included, to leave their kit behind. They were not to see it again.

The convoy sailed at dawn to steam south. At lunchtime the *Empress of Britain* gave a farewell toot on her siren, then set off alone in a westerly direction.

Towards evening we entered another fjord. Here were mountains standing black against the darkening sky. The sea was smooth as a lake. The water shone like mother of pearl. It was the most beautiful and peaceful sight.

So we came to the little town of Namsos. In the twilight it had the unreal quality of a picture postcard. Tiny wooden houses, with snow-covered roofs sloping at crazy angles. On a hillock stood a church, the only stone building to be seen.

The British papers had hailed our despatch to Norway as a crusade to save that country from the Nazi jackboot. We had expected a rousing welcome, with a few flowers strewn in our path. We were disappointed. The crowd which watched us disembark was silent, not showing a vestige of emotion, either friendly or hostile, like people who watch the Salvation Army parading on a Sunday, and showing about as much desire to be saved.

The infantry were packed straight on to a train to meet the Germans, who were advancing on the key town and port of Trondjeim to the south.

We were to stay in Namsos. We took over a house on the edge of the town, not too far from woods and the lower slopes of the nearest mountain.

The next day was warm as summer. With strict orders to hide if any German airplane appeared we spent most of the day diving for cover as sharp-nosed, sleek, black Heinkels flew low over the town on reconnaissance.

Two days later three thousand French troops disembarked with an efficiency which put our efforts to shame. I noticed the officers carried their own kit, which was unheard of in the British Army.

They were supposed to be billeted in the town, but their General categorically refused. His troops would not stay in the town. I acted as interpreter and asked where they intended to sleep? He replied cryptically: 'We have our tents.'

Everyone thought he was an idiot. They were wrong.

The next day, 20th April, we were baptised. I think we, in Namsos, were the first British troops to learn what Hitler's *blitzkrieg* bombing was all about.

Shortly after breakfast the church bell tolled. This was the standard air-raid warning. No one took any notice. It was the morning Heinkel on reconnaissance. A moment later came a strange whistle and a distant thump. Then, for six hours, the town was subjected to a ruthless, low-level bombing by high-explosive and incendiary bombs.

At this distance it is hard to remember things in their correct sequence. One is left with scattered impressions. First is the unearthly, screaming whistle of the bombs. Except for the brief attack on the ships no one had heard bombs before. Those had certainly not whistled, which gave rise to the rumour that these were fitted with some special device designed to scare the life out of the victims before blowing them to pieces.

It was soon apparent that they were not only attacking the harbour, but were determined to wipe Namsos off the map.

During this raid I discovered something about myself which has given me much comfort over the years and has also annoyed a number of women. In times of great stress, of fear, of anger, I fall asleep. It is some subconscious desire to run away and hide, to bury my head in the comforting sand of sleep. A woman cannot have a row with me in bed. The bigger the row, the quicker I fall asleep. Hitler's bombs had precisely this affect on me. Soon after the raid started I crept into a corner, closed my eyes, and went off to sleep. It wasn't deliberate. I just could not keep awake. When it became clear that I had neither suffered a heart attack nor was pretending, this created a deep impression among all ranks. When the first raid ended about three o'clock, there was a subtle change in everyone's attitude to me. Mr Wilkinson gave me a grin and obviously patted himself on the back for having yanked me out of hospital. This was the type of iron-nerved man the army needed.

Poor little 'Happy', who reacted poorly to bombing, kept repeating: 'How do you do it?'. I could not tell him.

As the last airplane droned away there was complete silence, as if the world had died. Then, gradually, as our ears came back to normal, we heard the crackling of fires, the occasional report of small arms ammunition exploding, then the joyful pealing of the church bell sounding the All Clear.

We emerged into the sunlight. About half the town was in ruins or ablaze. A stream of civilian refugees was moving towards the mountains in cars, on foot, on bicycles. Some pretty girls went on skis.

It is always easy to criticise after the event but I did not understand then, and do not understand now, the mental paralysis which seemed to grip the officers assembled in that house. The town had no anti-aircraft defences. It was only half-demolished, so the Germans would return. We now knew why the French General had elected to stay under canvas in the shelter of the pinewoods. The civilian population had got the message, and the survivors were moving out *en masse*.

Yet no one in the house did anything but sit and discuss how nasty the previous six hours had been.

This discussion was interrupted by the second raid, which lasted four hours. It was heavier, more concentrated, then the first. They flew lower, in threes, realising there was no anti-aircraft to trouble them.

I only slept for about an hour this time. 'Happy' woke me with the news that we were shortly to be burned alive. The houses all around us were blazing fiercely.

Even then nobody ordered an evacuation. At the end there was no joyful pealing of the church bell. The church was a blackened shell.

Now, at last, it occurred to someone that it might be a good idea to retire into the woods. Ours was one of *eight* houses in the entire town which had not been demolished or set on fire. I consider we were undeservedly lucky to be alive.

We gathered up small items of personal equipment and went outside. It was an awe-inspiring sight. Huge fires raged everywhere. Worse even than the screaming of the bombs was the sound made by those flames——a strange, rhythmic wailing which rose and fell. Fire music. My childhood nightmare come true. Flames do make music. Ask anyone who was at Namsos on that day.

We were told to split into small parties and make for the woods. The gloomy looking Archie, the despairing 'Happy' and myself left together. Archie was humping his full kitbag. I took my hand-driven Viceroy shaver, my precious lilo and a sleeping bag, which was something else I had smuggled over against army regulations.

We three were among the last to leave, and were only about halfway towards the shelter of the trees when the third raid started.

They spotted our uniforms immediately and started to machine-gun us from about three hundred feet. We had to run up a steep, slippery snow path. At the summit we were still two hundred yards from the trees, when three airplanes came at us. Archie waved a sad farewell, straddled his kitbag and used it as a toboggan to disappear down a precipitous slope. 'Happy' fled along the path taken by the others. I decided to take my chance across some virgin snow, which appeared to give quicker access to the trees. It was a great mistake and now another, more routine, nightmare came true.

Everyone, at some time, has dreamed they are running from danger and their legs become leaden and will not carry them. I had not gone five yards before I realised why no one had trodden the virgin snow. It was like walking through a bog. With every step I took my leg sank into the snow up to my crutch. I then had to drag it out before taking another pace forward. I reckon I was doing about two yards a minute, and there were at least two hundred yards to go.

A silver bomber spotted me and made me his target. I do not know how much Hitler spent in actual hard cash trying to blow up one lance-corporal; but it must have been a considerable sum. With his first run the bomber dropped a stick of bombs, which were absolutely accurate so far as the line was concerned, but the first landed about sixty yards behind me and the second about sixty yards ahead of me. The rest exploded in the woods. I had managed to advance about ten more yards before he returned and tried his machine-guns. He was a poor shot and miles off target. He made a return trip and whipped up the snow about fifteen feet away to my right. I now decided that rolling was better than walking and achieved a higher rate of progress. I was still rolling when he made his final pass and missed again.

Then a miracle occurred. It started to snow and, in seconds, the sky was blotted out.

I crawled, rolled and ploughed my way towards the haven of the trees and finally tumbled, exhausted, into a hollow beneath a tall pine.

Here I found 'Happy', with a sprig of pine fastened to his tin hat (camouflage, he explained). He pointed towards another tree and said he wanted to kill the French soldier hiding there, because he kept on running into the open every time an airplane passed overhead.

I asked the Frenchman why he did it. He shrugged and said he hoped that one of the airplanes might be from the RAF and where was the *sacré* RAF?

This was a question which, during the ensuing month, was raised over and over again in ever shriller tones; unreasonably, of course. The RAF had nowhere to land, but it is difficult to be reasonable when you are being bombed all day.

We re-formed in the woods and marched south towards a town called Steinkjer ('Stinker', naturally). We marched because there was no transport and thus had to abandon the warm polar kit which had been issued to us. I stuck grimly to my lilo, flea-bag and razor. I blessed them in the coming days.

Steinkjer, like Namsos, was on a fjord and, like Namsos, was bombed and burned to ashes before our eyes.

Our GOC was General Carton de Wiart, VC an odd, fiery character with one arm and a patch over one eye. He was completely without fear and had the greatest contempt for anyone who showed any sign of nerves.

We now had attached to our section a corporal, Pat, who had lived in Sweden as a golf professional. He was an extraordinary fellow, with no army training, who was apt to call officers 'Old boy'. He was also entirely fearless. General Carton de Wiart loved him, no doubt sensing a kindred spirit. It was their initial meeting which forged the bond. Pat discovered an unexploded bomb, a small one. For some reason he thought Carton de Wiart might like to have a look at it. He marched into the GOC's office, carrying the bomb and said: 'Look what I've found!'

As soon as the officers present saw what he was carrying they scattered, yelling for him to get the hell out of there and get rid of the bloody bomb. Not so General Carton de Wiart, who summoned them back and said: '*This* is the sort of man I want around me.'

From that moment on, Pat was never more than about a yard from the GOC's elbow, and was rushing around issuing orders to all and sundry regardless of rank. He must, for a brief while, have been the most powerful corporal in the British army. He finished up with a house, a car and a batman of his own.

We left Steinkjer in flames, with the Germans advancing on to the southern bank of the fjord, and one of their cruisers pooping off at us to speed us on our way.

We sheltered for a while in a barn. We chose poorly, because it was near a cross roads, which the Germans bombed and strafed all day.

We had to threaten to kill 'Happy' who kept repeating: 'Well, we'll all be dead by morning.'

He did, however, provide us with a good laugh, and brought off his second coup in frank speaking—the first having been to call me a cunt, for voluntarily discharging myself from hospital. (I had by now come to think he had been perfectly right about that.)

He was dozing when a brigadier entered the barn and peered out at a German airplane, which seemed about to hit the roof. The noise of the plane woke 'Happy'. He saw the brigadier, from behind, peering out of the window. He jumped to his feet, rushed across the barn, tapped the brigadier on the shoulder and pulled him round: 'Don't be a bloody fool!' he said. 'If they catch sight of you, we're done for.' The brigadier froze, mouth half-open, but 'Happy' had not finished. 'I'm just going to the WC. It's outside on t'other side of the barn but I shall crawl *underneath* all the way so as not to make footprints. *That*'s the way to behave.'

He gave a knowing nod and departed. The brigadier said not a word. He was too stunned. I think our section broke a record that day. I am sure no lance-corporal has ever spoken to a brigadier like that, and got away with it.

The brigadier retreated before 'Happy' crawled back from his pee. When we told him what he had done, he turned a shade whiter than his normal white. Then, after a brief silence, he looked positively cheerful.

'Never mind,' he said. 'We'll all be dead by morning.'

The battle round Steinkjer was now rapidly becoming a rout. The Germans had crossed the fjord and were advancing fast.

There was no Field Security work to do. We just sat in the barn, waiting to die with 'Happy'.

At five o'clock one morning a Scottish captain entered the barn seeking a volunteer, who could drive a lorry, to go in search of a petrol tanker, which had been abandoned by the roadside some miles away. It was to be rescued, and used to refill all vehicles as they retreated towards Namsos. My experience in the RAOC made me the obvious choice, so I volunteered.

I found the petrol tanker not far from Steinkjer, and drove it back on the Namsos road. On a narrow stretch, with a steep precipice on one side, I had to go near the verge to get round a wrecked car. The side of the road gave way. I was thrown violently sideways, hitting my head. When I pulled myself together, I found the lorry stuck at an angle of forty-five degrees over the precipice. There was no hope of moving it.

I trudged back to the crossroads and found my Scottish captain, who was extremely nice about it and told me to return to the tanker and fill the passing transport from there. I gathered, although he did not say so, that a full retreat had been ordered. I armed myself with a couple of buckets and returned to the tanker.

I must digress and write a few words about the army's tiniest decoration. This is 'Mentioned In Despatches'. I had, as a child, met veterans of the First World War who had been mentioned in despatches. It conjured up an exciting picture of a grim-faced motor-cycle despatch rider driving through a hail of shells with a message reporting some act of heroism. I am not at all sure that in my dream at Aldro in which I saved Mr Heath's life in the trenches that I was not mentioned in despatches in addition to winning the VC.

The perceptive reader will already have guessed that I was mentioned in a despatch. I think it was through an act of calculated cowardice.

I spent the entire day with my two buckets, filling up the oddly-assorted stream of vehicles retreating from the Steinkjer area. I even gave some petrol to a lovely girl, who was motoring in the wrong direction. I pointed out that she was going towards the fighting line but she smiled, shrugged and threw me an orange and a piece of chocolate.

The troops crowded into the lorries looked in a pretty sorry state, all of them dirty, quite a number wounded.

Towards nightfall the stream visibly slackened. I could now hear small arms fire quite clearly.

I filled up a lorry carrying Mr Wilkinson and a number of our section. 'Happy' gave me a goodbye wave and a look which definitely said that word again.

My Scottish captain arrived in a large, American car he had scrounged from somewhere. As I filled him up he said: 'You'd better catch the last lorry, and see you don't miss it.'

'Yes, sir.'

He drove away about a hundred yards, stopped and reversed to where I stood.

'Wait a minute,' he said. 'How are you going to know which *is* the last lorry?'

This was a good question to which there was no answer. As I pondered what to reply, images went chasing through my mind. I would miss it, deliberately. I would wait until the last possible moment and then, alone, walk towards Namsos. For a few hours, perhaps for four or five days, I could stroll along, watching the airplanes go over and for a brief, blissful period would not be bombed or machine-gunned. I would sleep in farmhouses, and be given nice Norwegian meals by friendly farmers and their motherly wives or lovely daughters.

I suppose the whole thought process lasted about three seconds, then I straightened my shoulders and said: 'Don't worry about me, sir. If necessary I'll follow on foot.'

He took out a piece of paper and a pencil.

'All right, Corporal,' he said. 'What's your name and number?'

I think this must have been the reason I was 'mentioned'. I can recall no other occasion in which I displayed either heroism or cowardice to account for it.

As it turned out, my plan failed dismally. I returned to the barn to retrieve my flea-bag, lilo and razor, then as I started on my way, singing, I was picked up by an angry looking major, who would not listen to my excuses and forced me into his car.

I rejoined the section at Brigade Headquarters which was dispersed round a sizable farm. Here, following my display of pseudo-devotion to duty, I committed an act of disobedience for which I suppose I could technically have been shot, since we were on active service. Looking back, I still wonder how I found the nerve to go through with it.

It was decided that all other ranks must take a bath. It was certainly ten days since anyone had done so. The thought behind the order was, no doubt, correct but the method of carrying it out was not.

The farmyard contained a water tank, some three feet deep, with a diameter of about six feet. This was filled with water, into which the entire complement of troops were ordered to bathe, six at a time.

I do not know how many troops had bathed in the same water before my turn came. It must have run into hundreds. The water was shit brown in colour with the consistency of a medium grade motor oil. Its odour even beat Monsieur Chausson's lavatory in Tours.

Six men clambered out. Six of us were ordered in. Five went in but I just stood there feeling sick. The sergeant major in charge yelled at me to get in and look quick about it. Something snapped, I shook my head and said: 'No.'

A silence fell over the whole area. The five men in the bath stood erect, naked, looking at me.

The CSM repeated his order. I shook my head again. The silence became electric. Not a man in the farmyard moved. Even the German airplanes seemed tactfully to have left the area.

Then came the words: 'Are you disobeying my order?'

'Yes.'

The next moment I was under arrest and hurled into a small storeroom without a window. The door was slammed and locked. I sat there on a crate, trembling, shaken by the enormity of what I had done. I know I realised that I had, in one stubborn moment, wrecked any hope of a productive military career. The army was not a reasonable institution. There was no logic in its rules and regulations. There were those who gave orders, those who obeyed them, and an idiot few who disobeyed. An order is an order. No argument. A soldier commanded to commit virtual suicide by charging an enemy machine-gun post doesn't stop and say: 'No, this is stupid.' If he does he gets shot by his own side. What could be said in defence of a man who refused to take a bath? It was hopeless. I was doomed.

I was marched in before some officers—'Lef-Ri-Lef-Ri. Halt! Cap off!'

The CSM recited my crime in stentorian tones. I was asked what I had to say for myself.

I had progressed considerably since eight months before when the mere sight of an officer struck me dumb. In this case I was assisted by the conviction that nothing I said would make the slightest difference to whatever punishment they handed out; so I spoke my mind. I claimed I was perfectly clean, had washed regularly in snow and was open to any inspection they cared to make of my body. I said that the water would not only have made me dirtier, but was a hazard to health. Finally, with a gulp, I pleaded that, before coming to any decision, they inspect the water to see whether they themselves could contemplate taking a bath in it.

After a certain amount of muffled whispering I was marched out again, and once more locked in the dark storeroom.

About half an hour later I was informed I was free to go and that no charge was being made against me.

It seems that on occasion the army *is* a reasonable institution. I still have no idea how this miracle occurred. Perhaps my Scottish captain was lurking in the background and waved his despatch. Perhaps Mr Wilkinson spoke up for me. Perhaps they did inspect the water and ask themselves what they would have said had General Carton de Wiart ordered them to take a bath in it.

I noticed, the next day, that the water was changed after about every twenty baths. I kept well out of the way of that CSM, who had a hungry and frustrated gleam in his eye.

As a rider to this episode Mr Wilkinson, with an odd but perhaps deliberate sense of timing, chose this week to inform me that he was recommending
me for a commission, if and when we ever returned to Britain. To be
recommended for a decoration for an act of cowardice and a commission
for an act of disobedience in the space of less than a week must be a unique
achievement in the annals of the British army.

About ten days and innumerable bombings later the end came. We were
back in Namsos. Alongside the wreckage of the jetty three ships flying the
tricolour waited to evacuate us.

Before I went aboard, a lone Norwegian standing on the quay, said: 'You
come. Our country is destroyed. You go. I cannot understand.'

Who could blame him?

French and British troops were piled together in a stinking, airless hold.
There was no room to lie full length, no food, and precious little water. We
were allowed on deck only in allotted numbers. Someone said it was because
the ship lacked ballast, and might capsize.

I was on deck as dawn was breaking—the most beautiful I shall ever see.
Ahead lay the night; behind lay the mountains, with their fringe of snow, lit
with a delicate pink glow, which darkened slowly into a deep, blood red. The
sea, smooth as glass, shimmered green and opalescent. It was hard to look at
such beauty and realise the desolation we were leaving behind. Suddenly, the
blood red of the mountains became a symbol of a little nation bleeding,
friendless and alone.

Such was the end of a crusade which failed before it ever started.

In 1941 I wrote a book, a kind of worm's-eye-view of the first eight months
of war, which included what I saw of the Norwegian campaign. It was accepted
with enthusiasm by Heinemann, but had to go through various channels of
censorship first, starting at the Ministry of Information, whose telegraphic
address at the time was 'MINIFORM', if anyone wants to know. They handed
it to Military and Naval Censorship, who made a number of important cuts,
providing their own substitutions such as the word 'Town' for 'Aldershot',
presumably in case the German High Command learned that Aldershot was
a garrison town. The Navy went further and substituted 'Warship' for 'Destroyer' in case the Germans should guess that destroyers were sometimes used
on convoy duties. Other major deletions were any mention of Harrow,
Nottingham, and the fact that once, as a private soldier, I had used the
Southern Railway Line to go on leave.

This over, the Ministry of Information wrote a letter which included the
following:

'As to the subversive remarks on some officers, particularly in view of the fact that the writer was then in the ranks, I think he may be thankful I have cut them. Had they appeared there might have been rather unpleasant disciplinary action and it was certainly conduct to the prejudice of good order and military discipline. The book now goes to PR (O). Room 019. WO for the *mere formality* (the italics are mine) of permission to publish. It will not have to go to MI 11. Good luck to it.'

I never found out who read the book in Room 019. WO but he banned it in its entirety. It was never published.

The voyage back to Britain in the hold of that French ship was extremely prejudicial to good order and military discipline. It was sheer hell and I am surprised some people did not die from suffocation.

We were transferred to a British liner for the final stages of the journey home.

Once aboard they held a Service of Thanksgiving for our safe return. In contrast to the packed congregation on the outward journey, who had all prayed hard for God to look after them, only myself, two other NCOs and three officers attended to give Him thanks for listening. There must be a moral in this somewhere but it escapes me.

In truth, it was a totally demoralised body of men who sailed into port, so mentally crippled that they could hurl abuse and boots at an innocent RAF man in charge of a barrage balloon on the quay, who had the temerity to give us a cheerful wave.

I can think of no one less suitable to have greeted us on our return than the Chief of the Imperial General Staff, Field-Marshal Lord Ironside. It needed a man of extreme tact and great humanity to make any impression on the miserable body of half-starved men who were paraded on the quayside. Lord Ironside was not that man. He marched down the front line stopping at every fifth soldier and said: 'Looking fit; very fit indeed; much fitter than I thought. Yes, very fit indeed.'

He never varied the dialogue. I do not know if he wrote his own script, but whoever did, his subsequent pep talk was a masterpiece of intempestivity. It was so excruciating that I only recall his final words:

'Remember, you were not driven out of Norway. You were *ordered* out, and you came out with your tails up.'

A wreck of a soldier, wearing no boots, standing next to me, said, quite audibly: 'Tails up? We never saw a fuckin' woman the whole time we was out there.'

Part 7

★★★★★★★★★★★★★★★★★★★★★★★★★★★★★★★

Other Rank Dropping

★★★★★★★★★★★★★★★★★★★★★★★★★★★★★★★

THE GERMANS INVADED the Low countries on 2nd May.

Betty was in France with an ENSA play.

Aunt Decima was doing her bit in Paris.

They were both safely evacuated.

I went to OCTU in Colchester to learn how to become an officer and gentleman. I cracked two ribs horsing about in a barrack room on the night they rang the church bells, when it was rumoured the Germans had started their invasion. I was propped up in a concrete pill-box, armed with a rifle, which I could not have fired. I would have been unable even to raise my arms in surrender.

I realised I would fail the final examinations. Reading a compass and maps defeated me. I prayed I might sit next to somebody who would let me crib. I had been thrashed at Aldro for cheating in an examination, when I had been completely innocent. I rationalised that, if I cheated in this examination, it would even the score. I need not have worried. An NCO with access to the papers sold the questions to everyone with five shillings to spare. The only problem was how not to do too well.

I was commissioned into the Intelligence Corps, and sent on a Field Security course in Matlock, Derbyshire.

After the course I was posted 'Home Duties'. This meant indefinite leave at home until a posting was found. There was a story of an officer so posted in the First World War, who remained happily at home for three years, quite forgotten. After I had been five weeks in Buxton with Betty, I began to wonder if this was happening to me. There was only one rule about Home

Duties. You had to inform the War Office of any contemplated change of address. We decided we would like to visit Devon. I notified the War Office of our intended change of address and, by return of post, received a form entitled: *'Joining Order'*. It was dated 22nd November 1940, and informed 2/Lieut MHR Pertwee, Intelligence Corps, that he was appointed IOIbNID, the appointment to carry the acting rank of lieutenant while so employed. He was to report immediately to G2IbBTI, Northern Ireland, for further instructions.

2/Lieut MHR Pertwee had received rapid promotion to lieutenant, but he wished he had kept his pen shut.

After that, I made a resolution never to interfere with fate again. I would just accept what came my way, and hope for the best. It was a resolution to which I adhered, with one exception, and which I never regretted—except in the case of the one exception.

Belfast could not have been a more comfortable posting. After the first few weeks, I lived as near a normal married life as was possible in time of war. Betty joined me, and we lived out in a series of pleasant rented houses and flats at ridiculously cheap rentals. It was a pleasant, social and indolent existence, which lasted three years. Considering that England suffered the horrors of the Blitz, and Belfast only had two major air raids, we were very lucky people indeed.

Roland finally split up with Dorothy. He had to wait until he was fifty-six to find someone who gave him complete happiness and devotion. I had known Kitty for ten years, and had even nursed a secret crush on her when I was sixteen. Later, after the war, when I saw a lot of them it was remarkable to see the complete change in him as he settled down to twenty years of blissful domesticity.

Coby qualified as a doctor, joined the army and subsequently took part in the Burma campaign, as MO to the West African Rifles. It must have been an unpleasant experience, but his letters did not reveal much. One, which I still keep, read:

'Having a wonderful time. Wish you were here.
Played bridge last night and won 1/4d.'

Within a year of being commissioned I was promoted to captain.

On 19th October 1941, my daughter, Carolyn, was born in a Belfast nursing home. The local doctor who attended Betty during the prenatal months, delivered the baby, made regular visits afterwards, and also attended her during a subsequent operation, charged us exactly £5 and apologised profusely for submitting a bill at all.

Since Carolyn turned out to be not only very pretty but the kind of daughter every parent dreams of having—and rarely gets—I can now permit myself to say that I thought, at first glance, she was an absolutely hideous baby. She was very red, very spotty and screamed her head off.

I was on duty as orderly officer the night she was born. In the report book, which I suppose still exists somewhere, was written:

'Captain Pertwee reported the birth of a daughter. No further action recommended.'

They held a short story competition for all ranks in Northern Ireland. James Bridie was the judge. I was the only professional writer to enter the competition, so it was difficult to see how I could lose. The stories were submitted anonymously.

I did not win, and in his comments, which accompanied the return of my manuscript, James Bridie's opening paragraph read:

'If this man ever hopes to earn any money from writing he should . . . etc.'

I could not even comfort myself by saying Bridie did not know what he was talking about, because I had always been one of his most fervent admirers.

I wrote a film story designed for Will Hay, which interested Mick Balcon, who was then running Ealing Film Studios. While on leave in London, I had a meeting with Mick, Angus Macphail, still his scenario editor, and Bill Hay. Everyone liked the story except Bill Hay, so that was that. I had renewed contact with Mick, which was to prove valuable. He later asked me to write a treatment for a film entitled: *Soldier From the Wars Returning*, based on a novel by Jerrard Tickell. Roland was to write the screenplay, but they thought that someone with current war experience would be useful on the basic story. They were pleased with what I did and even paid me extra money for some re-writes.

After this, Mick Balcon personally wrote to me, saying that, when the war ended, I need have no fears about re-starting my career. If I was interested, he would gladly offer me a long-term contract at Ealing Studios.

I have never been more grateful for a letter, and am still grateful. In one glorious moment the nagging worries about the future were swept away. I do not know if Mick was consciously aware of how much this would mean to a man in my position; but he knows now.

While on leave in London I met up with Richard Greene, the actor, later "Robin Hood" of TV fame, who told me the Cinema Unit might need writers, and suggested I call on Carol Reed, now a captain, who was stationed—of all places—at the Ritz Hotel.

At the door of Captain Reed's suite I was met by a portly and extremely scruffy looking NCO whose uniform looked as if it had been borrowed from somebody else. A closer inspection of his face revealed him to be Peter Ustinov.

I found Carol Reed in bed with a mass of papers laid out on the counter-pane. We had a chat, but I did not pursue the matter.

On the same leave, Guy Beauchamp took me along to see a dress rehearsal of Noël Coward's *This Happy Breed*. Noël Coward was one of his patients. I was honoured and impressed to meet The Master for the first time—and even more impressed by him after the final curtain, when he came up to Guy and said: 'Well, dear boy, and what did you think?'

'Awful,' said Guy. 'Dreadful, Noël. You can do better than that.'

Coward merely gave his charming smile and said: 'Oh, dear! I'm sorry you didn't enjoy yourself.'

He was always one of those admirable few who could take criticism without any apparent rancour.

During an army exercise near Belfast I incensed the general commanding a British division by disguising a rather pretty NCO as a girl with enormous tits, who infiltrated his Headquarters, and gained audience with the general himself, to pour out a sad story of rape by one of the troops under his command. The general was most sympathetic and promised appropriate action. Before leaving, 'she' left a 'bomb' on the General's desk. He and his entire staff were presumed by the judges to have been wiped out. I was forbidden to go near him again on pain of being wiped out myself.

In 1942 I was posted to Armagh, where Betty and I had a flat. We employed a maid called Mary, who used to steal quantities of food. Rather than lose her I discovered her hiding place and used to steal half of it back, before she could get it out of the house.

I received a visit from the Chief of Police who told me that, as an Intelligence Officer, I should sack Mary immediately, since she was a dangerous IRA suspect. I found this difficult to believe of a woman who had once asked: 'What is Stalin?'

The Police Chief was evasive about the evidence against her and, beyond the fact that she was Roman Catholic, produced nothing concrete. I told him I would think about it.

The next day Operation 'Torch' came to fruition when the US forces invaded French North Africa. It was a thrilling day, a turning point in the war. I rushed up to Mary and said: 'Mary! The Americans have invaded North Africa!'

Mary looked at me closely. She was always anxious to please. Finally, she said: 'Is that a good thing?'

That afternoon I told the Police Chief I had no intention of sacking Mary. He was displeased.

While the Russians turned the tide, North Africa was conquered, and Italy wisely changed sides, I merely retreated from Armagh and returned to Belfast.

It was obvious, with the invasion of Europe coming, that a young officer of my age could not expect to sit out the rest of the war in Ireland.

Together with a number of others I was flown to London at the end of 1943 for an interview regarding some more active employment.

It was a chatty, informal interview. I gained the impression they were looking at personality more than anything else. At the end, the spokesman of the Board asked if there was any particular type of job I would like to do? It seemed a silly sort of question, which demanded a silly answer, so I said: 'Yes. I'll take the section working at Monty's invasion headquarters.'

Everybody had a good laugh at this one and said: 'Who wouldn't?'

A few weeks later, early in 1944, I was posted to Montgomery's invasion headquarters at 21st Army Group.

Moral—silly answers sometimes get results.

Part 8

★★★★★★★★★★★★★★★★★★★★★★★★★★★★★★★★★★★

Cough Dropping

★★★★★★★★★★★★★★★★★★★★★★★★★★★★★★★★★★★

IF THERE WAS one thing General Bernard Law Montgomery disliked it was people coughing while he spoke. I learned this soon after joining 21st Army Group Headquarters, when he addressed the entire staff in the theatre opposite St Paul's School, which housed our HQ. He walked on to the stage and waited until there was complete silence; then he invited anyone who felt like coughing to have a good cough there and then, because he wished to hear no more once he had started speaking. Several people dutifully made rasping noises.

He pointed out that every officer present had been hand-picked as the best available at his allotted job. Therefore, so far as he was concerned, there were no fixed hours of work, no definite time to come in or knock off. If there was work to be done which took twenty-four hours of any day, he would expect those concerned to work for twenty-four hours. If, on the other hand, there was nothing to do, then there was no need to come in at all. A lot of nonsense was talked about dress. Dressing smartly, according to regulations, did not make a man work harder. If anyone felt like turning up in a polo neck sweater and flannel trousers he was welcome to do so. (Within a matter of days several people did.)

His talk included none of the famous clichés on 'hitting the enemy for six', but was all sound, reasoned common sense. I left that theatre deeply impressed.

My first job started rather frighteningly, when I was informed I had been selected to go out on an operation alone. With some relief I learned that this merely entailed attending a surgical operation on an officer, who had been

77

with Monty in the desert. He had been wounded and, shortly before the attack at El Alamein, had undergone an operation. On being given the anaesthetic, he had sat bolt upright and blurted out some highly secret information about the forthcoming attack. He was now at 21st Army Group and was 'Bigoted',* which was the code word for those who knew full details on the coming invasion of Europe. He also had to have another operation.

My task was to attend the operation and make sure that as few people as possible were within earshot while he was given the anaesthetic. He, and everybody else, was scared stiff that he would repeat his performance.

He was definitely twitchy as he lay in bed prior to the operation. But, after a preliminary shot of some kind, he relaxed considerably and was smiling as he was wheeled into an ante-room outside the theatre. Here I got rid of everyone except for the anaesthetist and a jolly sister. The anaesthetist told him not to worry. He smiled and said he was not worried any more. The anaesthetist gave him a shot of pentothal, whereupon he sat bolt upright and yelled: 'Cherbourg! Cherbourg! Cherbourg!"

Then he fell back unconscious.

The doctor gave me a look and the hint of a wink. I turned to the sister, intending to warn her to forget what she had heard.

'There!' she said. 'All that fuss, and he didn't say anything, did he?'

It has always amazed me how the secret of 'Overlord' was kept, considering the number of people, 'Bigoted' or otherwise, who must have known enough to make a shrewd guess, and the number of people who knew or guessed, who could not resist telling their wives or girl friends.

I may even have been personally responsible for stopping full details being spread all over London, after an almost farcical balls-up in the strict security precautions which surrounded the room in which full details of the whole operation, except the date, were laid out. I should certainly have been held responsible had I not been present to take instant action.

At St Paul's School there was a hall complete with stalls, dress circle and a stage; nicely proportioned, beautifully panelled. This was The Place. The whole floor of the stage was taken up by a huge map showing the Normandy landing area. Around the walls hung the logistic details. There were also maps showing the planned line of advance from the initial landings through D + 1, D + 2, etc.

*Before discussing any Top Secret matter concerning the invasion you always had to preface your conversation with the question: 'Are you Bigoted?'

One minute alone in that hall would have been enough for the most amateur spy to have taken in the whole plan.

The doors were locked. One of my NCOs was always on guard. No one entered without being vetted.

On this particular morning two things went wrong. My NCO absented himself for a few moments from his position at the door. At the same time, someone came out of the hall and *left the door open*.

This coincided with an army of cheerful London charladies, who came to the school each day to 'do', marching up the stairs with mops and pails, ready to start their work. The first of them saw the open door. They had no idea what was inside, but here was a door which had always been locked to them. Inside was a room that must therefore need 'doing'. They had probably been longing to get at it for weeks. The first of them pushed the door wide and led the way in.

At this moment, by sheer good luck, I arrived. I gave a yell which stopped them in their tracks. I leapt up the stairs, pulled the first woman back, pushed her out, slammed the door and leaned against it with my heart thudding as if I had run a four minute mile.

I attended all the periodic high level conferences in the hall. I do not know that I was really entitled to, but I did so from the start and no one threw me out.

I have no idea what the Americans thought of Montgomery at this time. Later disagreements were widely publicised, but his own staff had complete faith in him.

His enormous popularity with the troops was already well established. They worshipped him. He had a way of reaching the ordinary soldier which is unsurpassed. I saw an example of this myself.

It was during one of the conferences attended by Winston Churchill and Sir James Grigg, the Secretary of State for War. I was inside, listening, rapt as always. Outside stood one of my sergeants, who was told there was an urgent phone call for Sir James Grigg. He opened the door and entered, looking for Grigg. Unfortunately, I was across the other side of the hall, and could not assist him. As he entered, a bevy of senior brass rose and waved him away. Someone very important was saying something very important. They always were. The sergeant wavered slightly, but stayed on course. This caused a further barrage, which finally unnerved him and brought him to a halt.

Then one man rose, walked right across the hall and said: 'Yes, Sergeant? What can I do for you?'

It was Montgomery. The sergeant gave his message, and Grigg went off to take his phone call.

After this, so far as that sergeant was concerned there was only one man with 'any bloody sense' in the hall and that was Monty.

Fifteenth May was the occasion of the biggest conference of all. It was, in effect, a verbal dress rehearsal for the invasion.

I stood at the door vetting each person as they entered. There were very few exempted from the necessity of showing their card. Among these were Montgomery, Eisenhower, Winston Churchill, Field-Marshal J C Smuts and His Majesty George VI. I should add to this list the name of H G Stoker, a charming actor who had returned to the Navy and, I think, was a commander. As he was feeling for his pass I could not resist saying: 'Don't worry, sir. My wife appeared with you in a play before the war.'

'Good gracious!' he said. 'That is an odd way of getting into a conference like this!'

Churchill had been ill again with pneumonia. We all thought he looked very frail. There was only a short flight of stairs up to the hall, but he paused on every one of them. He was not prepared to admit it was to rest, so he took the opportunity of chatting to someone each time he stopped. Afterwards somebody said he doubted if the old man would live to see the end of the war.

The doors closed. I took up my discreet position, and spent some of the most riveting hours of my life as the whole of 'Overlord' was rehearsed. By midday it was over except for the final speeches.

Montgomery spoke first, incisive, supremely confident. Clearly he had no doubts about success.

He was followed by Air Marshal Sir A T Harris, who put in some passionate propaganda for using the full might of his Bomber Command, leaving one with the impression that he felt not enough use was contemplated for it.

Then came Eisenhower, who impressed with his utter determination to show the world that this was not an invasion by two nations, but by one unified, integrated force. He looked ahead to victory and beyond: 'It is my view that there will never be another world war in which our two nations do not stand, side by side, together, from the very start.'

In contrast, Field-Marshal Smuts proved something of an anticlimax. He was, after all, addressing an audience of men who had spent months, some of them years, planning every move of this vast operation, and who knew exactly what they were up against. His theme, however, was that no one should underrate the Germans, that victory would not be handed out on a platter, that there would be much hard fighting before the battle was won.

Then came Winston Churchill. I shall never forget the sight of that bull-dog figure, holding a gigantic cigar, standing on the invasion map, legs astride, one foot on Caen the other on Bayeux.

His speech was at times humorous, at times aggressive, sometimes almost indistinct. At one moment his voice would thunder and the next be trembling with emotion.

Of poor General de Gaulle who was, hypothetically, battering on the door demanding to be let in on the secret, he said: 'I have every sympathy with General de Gaulle and his violent tantrums but let us conquer some of his country before we start squabbling about how it is to be governed. Yes, let's give them a bit of land to govern first.'

He could not resist a swipe at those who opposed his favourite theory—that too large a percentage of troops was in support, and too small a percentage in the actual firing line. He begged those responsible to think again, even at this late hour, and try to reduce the numbers behind the firing lines. He even quoted in outraged tones, that two thousand men alone were working in Army Records. As if sensing hackles rising in certain parts of the hall, he paused, gave an impish grin and waved the cigar: 'But here I go again, throwing my weight about on matters for which my constituents did not elect me.'

He gave unstinted praise to the American war effort and was surprisingly modest about the British contribution.

'We will give what we can but we must remember that, when we have done this, the United States will bear the brunt.'

Finally, he spoke with emotion of those who would help to win the battle but would not return.

'Many young men will fall, too many; but through their unsurpassed vigour and courage we shall prevail. God bless you! God *help* you all!'

A surprising number of hard-bitten officers found it suddenly necessary to blow their noses.

Then came the climax. As Churchill sat down, Eisenhower rose again: 'I do not think,' he said, 'that it would be right to conclude these proceedings without hearing a few words from His Majesty.'

There was a silence. I thought my heart had stopped. I am sure that this was unrehearsed and that the King had not been warned of this. My mind flashed back to the Duke of York's camp, and to that other speech so carefully prepared, so painfully delivered.

Then the King rose and stepped on to the stage, a lithe figure in Naval uniform looking very sun-tanned. He turned to face his audience. He looked calm, sure of himself.

Then he proceeded to speak, without a note and without stumbling over a single word. It was as if he had never stammered in his life.

I can only think that at this historic moment, standing in uniform, surrounded by the best brains of two armies, he felt happy, at home and among friends.

Everyone trooped out, leaving only two behind——Montgomery and Churchill, deep in private conversation. I brought Churchill an enormous whisky and Montgomery a small orangeade while they continued to talk. Churchill smoked two cigars that morning——a large one and a small one. I still have the butts of both of them.

Later, I personally conducted Churchill to the lavatory. He chatted pleasantly all the way. It was one of the most memorable journeys of my life.

There followed a banquet and I decided to risk attending that, too. Once again, no one threw me out.

At the end, the majority of those present had to queue for coffee. I joined the queue but each time I advanced, some more senior officer came up behind me, and I would give him my place. In this way I kept finding myself at the end of the queue. As I stood there a bulky figure wearing a rather unusual American uniform approached and looked me over. Then he fumbled in his pocket and produced half-a-crown.

'Are you the guy who's collecting money for coffee?'

I assured General G S Patton that I was not.

Shortly before the invasion, 21st Army Group moved to a big country house near Portsmouth. The weather was appalling, and faces grew progressively gloomier as it worsened day by day. The Nissen hut I lived in was struck by lightning and, since there was no pause between the flash and the explosion, we thought we had been hit by a bomb.

The night of Eisenhower's agonising decision, whether to risk the invasion or wait another eighteen days, was unbelievably oppressive. No one spoke unless it was absolutely necessary. There was only the sound of the bloody wind which never seemed to let up.

There was a great sigh of relief as the more cheerful weather forecast came in and the decision was made to go.

Every soldier was handed printed messages from Eisenhower and Montgomery to speed them on their way.

Montgomery's included the following:

With Valerie French at a premiere——we were grimly inveterate first nighters.

The 'TV star' signs autographs. Fame was transitory. Within a couple of years, from such letters as '*Please may I have a photograph of your person*' it came to '*Aren't you old Whatsisname?*'

The family I fathered—'*The Grove Family*' (1955), first of Britain's many TV soap operas. (*Centre*): Grandma (Nancy Roberts); (*left*): Mum (Ruth Dunning); (*right*): Dad (Edward Evans). Back row (*l to r*): Christopher Beeny, Sheila Sweet, Peter Bryant and Margaret Downs.

A Contented Creator surrounded by some of his celebrated 'Yakity Yak' girls (*1956*). Far left is model Jean Clark; next to her, actress-to-be Shirley Ann Field.

'The time has come to deal the enemy a terrific blow in Western Europe. . . .
To us is given the honour of striking a blow for freedom which will live in history;
and in the better days that lie ahead men will speak with pride of our doings. . . .
Good luck to each one of you. And good hunting on the mainland of Europe.'

A long night of droning airplanes and no news.

The following morning about a hundred war correspondents arrived, with
tongues hanging out and pencils poised, to hear what Monty had to say.

They looked frustrated when they were led into a village school to be
addressed by the Chief of Staff. They were a funny sight, crowded into a
small classroom, many of them crouched over desks designed for four year-
olds.

When the Chief of Staff had finished he told them that General Montgomery was prepared to have a brief word with them—and brief it turned out
to be.

They assembled on the lawn of the house where Monty was quartered.
Monty appeared, relaxed, eagle-eyed, wearing corduroy trousers and a grey
pullover. Silence fell. He looked at them for some moments then said:

'I don't think I have anything to say to you—nothing at all. Things are
going pretty well. *I'm* sleeping in the garden. I wouldn't be doing that if it
weren't, would I?'

A lot of them looked bitterly disappointed, Personally, I thought it was the
most cheering thing I could have heard. I do not believe one of them reported
it.

Monty never behaved according to accepted rules. He was often accused
of playing to the gallery. No doubt, on occasion, he did, and most effectively.
He was also said to be unnecessarily aloof, cutting himself off from all social
contacts with those around him. He certainly did that too. As soon as he
reached the beachhead he withdrew from the HQ and lived by himself in a
caravan guarded by a few special troops and by one of my NCOs, who stayed
at his side for weeks to supervise his security. He lived this way because he
was entirely dedicated to the winning of the battle. He had no other interest.
I am sure he never thought about anything else, thus any social contact would
have been an intrusion. He ate and slept because that was necessary. For the
rest, it was the battle and nothing else.

This seems as good a place as any to print the text of a letter addressed to
General Montgomery from Mr T Bandcroft, of 67 Canada Crescent, North
Acton, which fell into my hands. I do not recall if it ever fell into Monty's,
though I think he would have enjoyed it.

'Sir, I think something should be done to stop the criminal incompetence of our General Staff. For years now we have had retreats and setbacks all over the world because our Military Idiots are still using the Battle of Hastings technique. The only way is to ask for a spare Russian general to take charge of the invasion. If only we had one Vatutin. God help our poor boys under the Sandhurst boys.'

I paid my first visit to the beachhead a few days after the invasion, in handcuffs; that is to say I was handcuffed to a terrified French collaborator who, following interrogation, was being flown back to certain death.

I flew in an Anson from Southampton accompanied by some officers from the War Office. We ran into shocking weather, flew in solid cloud and came out of it to find ourselves among the cables of a balloon barrage, well below the balloons. The pilot wisely decided to return to Southampton. This manoeuvre was missed by the red-tabbed officers who had been dozing. As the plane started a bumpy descent towards Southampton airfield they awoke with loud cheers and cries of 'La Belle France!' and were deeply moved.

We were luckier on our second attempt (I suppose the wretched prisoner did not think so) and landed in a field near Bayeux.

I had a few precious minutes to rush into the town, which had miraculously escaped much damage, to buy butter and Camembert, which were in plentiful supply.

I stopped the first soldier I saw carrying what looked like a Camembert: 'Is that Camembert?' I asked.

'No, chum, Fromidge. That's what you ask for. Fromidge.'

I thanked him, and found some on my own. Roland and Kitty were very grateful, but I had to change my groundsheet which stank to high heaven.

I left permanently for the beachhead on 30th July, armed with an army issue English-French phrasebook which contained the following gem:

'Merde alors!'——'Oh, bother!'

We were transported across the channel in large LSTs. You had to drive your vehicle up a ramp into their jaws. Two cars ahead of me drove straight into the water and were lost for ever, but we got aboard all right.

We landed at Arromanches, using the prefabricated harbour which was now working superbly, despite its initial battering by the weather.

I had sent one of my NCOs——Denys Clarke——as an advance party to find us accommodation. He was an insurance broker in civil life, and has handled all my insurance affairs since then. Actually, the arrangements he had made for us nearly cost him a lot of future business. Scorning canvas, which was the fate of most of the HQ, he had found us a little stone farm-house in a field. It suited us perfectly. I had a pleasant room with a comfort-able bed to myself.

That night one of the few German airplanes to dare show its nose over the area circled round for about fifteen minutes before dropping a bomb about a hundred feet away. The entire ceiling came down on me, badly cutting my nose. My only genuine war wound.

No one was seriously hurt but eight cows died in the field.

Ivor Novello, Diana Wynyard, who was then married to Carol Reed, and Margaret Rutherford came out to perform the thriller *Love from a Stranger* in the open air on a stage so small that the furniture had to be miniaturised. There was a grandfather clock which stood about three feet high. Ivor Novello obviously revelled in playing a sinister role instead of the matinée idol, but he had a rough ride. As if it had an evil mind of its own, the tiny grandfather clock elected to keel over practically every time Ivor had something sinister to say. Thus, in the middle of a speech, he would have to break off and lunge at the clock to prevent it falling.

Then, as the play reached its climax, about one thousand heavy bombers flew over to knock hell out of the Germans' communications. They knocked hell out of the play, too. After a few minutes of vain endeavour, the actors gave up, and waited until the last bomber had gone. As they prepared to re-start, a joker at the back yelled: "Urry up, Ivor! They'll be comin' back in a jiffy.'

Ivor gave a tired smile and ploughed gallantly on.

I had a chat with Diana Wynyard afterwards. They all felt rather deflated and a little hurt that, at the end, no senior officer had risen to express a word of appreciation.

Almost exactly five years after I joined the army I received orders to leave the safety and comfort of 21st Army Group HQ and attach myself to the Guards Armoured Division.

Paris had now fallen and Monty's troops were streaming west towards the Belgian frontier, headed by the Armoured Division. We chased after them and, on the third day, I was given a map reference where I might find the HQ of 30 Corps. It may have been my continued inability to read a map which brought us to a village, where the only visible inhabitant told us we would find the soldiers in a wood a mile further on. What he neglected to say was that they were German soldiers, who did not want to surrender yet.

We were probably the only British unit to retreat in disorder during those halcyon days; but, as our entire armament consisted of eleven revolvers and an unassembled Bren gun, we were probably wise to do so, since they had machine guns and a mortar.

This led us to the barn in Gondecourt where, as I have already told, Roland had billeted all those years before. I sat there, looking at his watch which had been on his wrist, and spent the night writing him a letter.

We caught up with the advanced troops as they liberated Brussels.

I still cannot think of the liberation of Brussels without a lump in my throat. It seemed that every inhabitant of the city had turned out to welcome us, except for a few dedicated patriots who were hurling grand pianos out of the windows of collaborators. The population had clearly been preparing for the day because every one of them waved an allied flag. The whores, lissom, blonde and lovely climbed aboard the jeeps and tanks and presented specially printed cards, with specially reduced prices. Every tank, every jeep, every truck carried a crowd of wildly cheering men and women. Our speed through the street averaged about a quarter of a mile an hour.

During a hold-up I saw a pale, thin young man looking at me with sad eyes and unsmiling face.

'What's the matter?' I asked. 'Aren't you happy.'

'I am happy,' he said. 'It is the first time I have seen daylight for three years.'

They came out of their shops with their arms laden with gifts of food, drink and chocolates. A few lucky ones who stopped near jewellers' shops, found themselves the owners of new watches.

I went out on the city, just walking around. I must have been kissed a thousand times, about twenty-five per cent by men. The whores became a bit of a bore. When one extremely pretty girl approached me and asked if I would have a drink, I gave her a curt 'no'. Her face tautened as if I had slapped her. She turned, walked away to sit down beside a respectable middle-aged couple, her mother and father, and whispered that there was at least one ill-mannered British officer in town. I felt terrible.

I met that first evening, two families, who are still my friends today. Every officer and man who stayed any time in the city was 'adopted', often several times.

My immediate superior at 21st Army Group had been Donald Loudoun, a barrister in civil life and who is now a London Magistrate. He had been in charge of the airborne Field Security Section but, to his fury, had been found medically unfit just before the invasion.

COUGH DROPPING

On my second day in Brussels I located him at the Grand Hotel. He had been put in charge of Intelligence I (b) in Brussels. He informed me that my section was to stay in Brussels and work with him. My 'action' with the Armoured Division was over. They, poor chaps, went on to Antwerp and some very heavy fighting.

I was delighted at the prospect of staying in Brussels. I did not feel any sense of guilt, since I hadn't pulled any strings. I was still sticking to my decision to trust to luck. So far it was a system which had worked remarkably well.

I commandeered a luxury apartment in the fashionable Avenue Louise. I acquired a handsome Oldsmobile, abandoned by the Germans, and went out to celebrate with a pretty girl from the FANYs who drove for another 'I' department. Her parents had been on their honeymoon with mine. She later produced a photograph of the four of them together. The Oldsmobile was stolen while we dined and discussed what a small world it was. The next day I acquired an even better La Salle which I drove for a year.

The car thieves were very busy in Brussels. So many army vehicles were lost that it became a punishable offence to lose one. One of my officers found the secret. He bought a padlock and chain and chained the rear wheel to a lamp-post. The first night he tried this he came out of a restaurant to find the wheel still chained to the lamp-post but the jeep was gone. They had jacked it up and put on the spare wheel.

Donald Loudoun set up his HQ a few doors from me, in a deserted building which had housed a night-club.

A week after the liberation I collapsed suddenly with pleurisy for the second time. I was carried into the car and driven to a nearby hospital. Large numbers of wounded were also arriving from the front near Antwerp. I was in great pain and could not sit straight, but I felt a fraud at the sympathetic 'Ohs and Aaahs' from the crowd of ladies who stood at the hospital gates.

The hospital was overworked, understaffed and somewhat disorganised. I had been two days there and was still in a lot of pain when an MO told me that since I might be occupying a bed for six weeks it was back to hospital in England for me. I enquired when they contemplated moving me? He said the next day.

After he had gone, I lay back and thought about things. Six weeks back in England had its attractive side; but it undoubtedly meant losing my section who I think liked me as much as I liked them. It meant losing what was both a pleasant and fascinating job. It meant losing Donald Loudoun, a

87

good friend, as my superior. It meant a new posting, which might be something boring back in the British Isles or something unpleasant in the Far East.

I mulled it over all night and then, at dawn, quietly dressed and discharged myself from hospital. I took to my bed in Avenue Louise. I doubt if they even missed me.

Thus I deliberately chose to alter the course of my army life. If I had stuck to my previous decision I should have allowed myself to be taken back to England and trusted to luck once again; but I did not and, quite possibly, by this action I altered the whole course of my life.

A lot of men lost their lives during the war and a lot of men also lost their wives. In our own mess of about twenty officers there was formed an exclusive little club entitled: 'The Coccu's Club'. The sole qualification for membership was that the applicant's wife had fallen in love with someone else and wished to terminate the marriage. Subsequent reconciliation did not mean that the member had to resign, unless he specifically requested to do so.

The club membership grew with startling rapidity. A few of us sat back and smiled condescendingly. It was just six months after I had arrived in Brussels that the smile was wiped off my face and I was welcomed to the club.

Once again my life and Roland's had followed astonishingly similar lines. One began to wonder where it would end.

One of the men who lost his life was an old school friend of mine from Sherborne, named Wright. Shortly after the liberation I heard he was in the city and sought him out in the hotel which his unit was occupying. It had been evacuated a few days earlier by German troops.

I found him in a bedroom which had been converted into an office. In their hasty retreat the Germans had left all their office equipment behind.

We chatted, had a drink and arranged to meet again.

I left the hotel and was walking away, when I heard an explosion. It seemed to come from the hotel. I went back to find a scene of confusion. An officer had been killed by the explosion of a booby trap in one of the rooms.

It was Wright. Minutes after I had left the room he had evidently opened a drawer containing a booby trap and been killed instantly.

I drove back to my office in the Avenue Louise, and just sat at my desk and shook.

About four hours later I received a telephone call from Lt-Col. Niall

MacDermot, who was Donald Loudoun's immediate superior at Montgomery's HQ, which had now moved into Brussels. He asked if I had heard
about the explosion at the hotel. I told him I had not only heard of it, I had
been there, and was lucky to be alive. Wright could easily have opened the
drawer while I was in the room with him. He cut me short. He did not want
to hear about my escape. His point was—what had I done about it?

The answer was nothing. I realised, suddenly, that I had neglected to
carry out a single one of the tasks for which I had been so carefully trained,
both as NCO and officer, for the past four years. I had no excuse, for I had
been there. I should immediately have ordered the evacuation of the hotel.
I should have instituted a search. I should have reported instantly to Loudoun
and 21st Army Group that the Germans had left booby traps behind. Warnings should have been sent out to every military unit in Brussels to be on the
alert.

I had done nothing but sit at my desk, mourn poor Wright, and think
of my own lucky escape. I had not acted as a trained soldier, but as a very
fallible human being. It was deplorable. Naturally, I was given hell. I am
surprised I was not sacked on the spot. I deserved it.

Niall MacDermot was a barrister in civil life and became a Labour MP.
He also proved to be a most forgiving superior officer.

The work in Brussels was as varied and exciting as the social life was
wearing and exciting.

One of my tasks was the preliminary interrogation of agents, who had
been parachuted into the zone. These were dropping like confetti all over the
place. It was assumed that Admiral Canaris was just shooting them off by the
dozen to please Hitler. In the main they were a miserable and inefficient
bunch, with little chance of getting away with anything; ill-trained, of low
intelligence and even lower morale. They were mostly traitors, dropped into
the country of their origin, having been more or less press-ganged into service.
I could never fathom why they agreed to do it, since it was obvious to the
meanest intelligence that Germany was losing the war. I asked one Belgian
spy why he had done it and his reply was: 'I'd have been sent to work in a
factory if I hadn't agreed.'

One agent was spotted parachuting down about eight miles outside
Brussels. Within minutes, the area was cordoned off and we were searching
it; but he struck lucky and landed near a railway line. He walked down the
line and reached Brussels, where he booked himself a room in a hotel, using
a false name and papers. He had, in fact, got away with it. The search was

called off. What we did not know was that to make better speed into Brussels he had buried his radio transmitter in a ditch near the spot where he landed. The next night he went back to retrieve the radio. He could have returned straight to Brussels, safe and sound; but what did he do? He decided to go and have a drink in the nearest café. A sharp-eyed British officer noticed mud on his boots and put two and two together. He was promptly arrested, complete with his transmitter, which he carried in a canvas bag.

This was an average example of the grade of intelligence displayed by the agents who fell into our hands.

We also found that their instructions, having landed, were of a most general and cursory nature, such as reporting the amount of damage caused by V1s, as if that mattered.

Some spies were retained by British Intelligence and used for various purposes. Others were handed over to the Belgian, French or Dutch authorities. Most of them were shot.

All of them arrived at my office with enormous sums of money which I would dutifully count and lock up until I handed them over with the money and personal possessions. I can only guess what happened to the money once it fell into the hands of the Belgian, French and Dutch investigators. Tempting though it was, I never helped myself to a penny. When the war was over I had reason to be thankful that I had not.

Some months after my demobilisation in 1946 I received a personal letter from an officer, supposedly a close friend, who was still serving in Intelligence in Brussels. The letter concerned an agent who had passed through my screen and had subsequently been executed. It read:

'Dear Michael,
The widow of J Hendricks, who was a prisoner in your charge is demanding the return of the sum of 125 Belgian francs, a Bible and a devotional object which were in his possession when interrogated by you and which I understand you took off him. Would you kindly return the money and the two other items at your earliest convenience otherwise I fear there may be unpleasant consequences.'

I wrote back:

'Dear Jim,
Regarding your letter. I note that this was a DO letter.' (DO meaning it was a personal rather than official communication). 'May I ask whether your Colonel was aware of its contents?'

90

He replied that his Colonel had *not* been aware of the letter because, as a friend, he wanted to deal with the matter on a friendly and unofficial basis. To this I replied:

'Dear Jim,
Since we are writing on a friendly and unofficial basis kindly take the 125 Belgian francs, the Bible and devotional object and shove them up your arse.'

My friend Jim seemed to resent this suggestion almost as much as I had resented his ineptly worded and offensive letter. He now informed his Colonel and then wrote an official letter demanding either an immediate return of the objects or a satisfactory explanation of their disappearance. Failure to comply would, he said, lead to unpleasant consequences.

Angry, but with a clear conscience, I went down to the Legal department of the War Office, where I gave a *resumé* of the situation, adding that, had I been so inclined, I could have emerged from Brussels with a fortune. The major to whom I spoke looked horrified and exclaimed: 'You can't come to us! We're the people who would be court-martialling you!' Then he looked around, lowered his voice and added: 'Tell them to stick it up their arse!'

I told him I had already done that. Then he shrugged and said that if I had a clear conscience there was nothing to fear in the long run.

So I wrote back to Brussels expressing my eagerness to co-operate fully in investigating this grave matter and would even welcome a court-martial; but reminded them that I wished to call as witnesses *all* my former NCOs, together with my CO, Donald Loudoun, Niall MacDermot, Montgomery's Intelligence Chief, Brigadier Williams, and a number of others who might have something to say about my character.

I heard no more, and the only result was that my old friend Jim joined the exclusive little list of people, headed by Doctor Gunter, whose noses I would willingly have punched in the event of our meeting again.

My worst experience with a spy came at Christmas in 1944, when Field-Marshal von Rundstedt made his do or die attempt to win the war for Hitler, leading to the Americans' heroic defence of Bastogne.

The Germans had infiltrated a number of English (American) speaking agents behind the lines to report on troop movements. They were reportedly well-trained and hard to spot. We were supplied with a list of questions, which had to be fired at anyone suspected of being one of these agents. The type of question, to which an immediately correct answer was expected, was:

91

Question: 'What is Bing's surname?' *Answer*: Crosby.'
Question: 'If Bing and Bob met Dorothy, what would they be making?'
Answer: 'Lamour.'

There were about twenty questions, simple to a genuine American, difficult for a phoney.

At the same time we knew that a German Parachute division was waiting up in Northern Holland to descend on Brussels to link up with von Rundstedt's armies. The code word for the arrival of the airborne attack was 'Milk'. All units had been warned to be ready, fully armed for street battles, should the message 'Milk' be received.

On Saturday 23rd December we held our Christmas party and milk was definitely *not* on the menu, a copy of which I still have. I note that Vins blancs were supplied by Captain M Pertwee, and Vins rouges (Bordeaux '42) by courtesy of the Wehrmacht. A night-club owner, Johnny de Granada (of whom more later), was one of the guests, and he supplied a dozen bottles of champagne. Donald Loudoun, now Major, was the guest of honour.

In the midst of the celebration, when the champagne was already finished, the Military Police brought in a man whom they had picked up acting suspiciously. He was, or seemed to be, an American. He wore one of the largest stetson hats I have ever seen and his pockets were stuffed with dollar bills. He was coldly resentful about being arrested. I gave him a quick, preliminary interrogation. He claimed to be a technician who was going to work in the Antwerp docks. He had arrived the day before in Paris. I asked him how he had arrived and his answer was enough to convince me that he was a phoney:

'By flying boat.'

A flying boat to Paris! Leaving the rest to continue with the party I repaired to the interrogation room with the prisoner, taking with me the soberest staff sergeant I could find. I dug out the questionnaire and fired the first question: 'What is Bing's surname?'

He looked at me with cold, grey eyes, and said: 'That's your problem.'

I warned that failure to answer correctly could have serious consequences, then tried again. He failed to answer; or refused to answer, any one of the questions correctly. Even a heavy blow with the butt of a rifle on his toes did not encourage him to co-operate.

I was still persisting with the questions when a flushed NCO lurched in waving a piece of paper.

'Code word "Milk,"' he gasped. 'It's come!'

At that moment the air-raid sirens started to wail. The parachutists were evidently landing.

The party came to an abrupt end, and the entire section were propped against the windows with guns at the ready.

The Staff Sergeant, who had assisted in the interrogation came to me, revolver in hand and said grimly: 'The prisoner? Shall I shoot him now?'

I told him 'no'. He was to be locked up but should be shot the moment street fighting started. He looked disappointed, and locked the man up.

Half an hour later there was still silence, but no 'All Clear'. Donald Loudoun then suggested that he and I go up to HQ, see Niall MacDermot or Colonel Williams to find out the exact situation. We drove to HQ where we discovered that it was a false alarm. The code word had been sent out in error. We laughed with relief, stopped for a drink and a chat, until I suddenly remembered the prisoner. I knew that at the slightest sign of trouble he would get a bullet through his head. I drove back like a maniac but he was still alive, sitting calmly in his locked room.

The following morning I interrogated him again, and found him a completely changed man. Only then did I realise that he had been drunk the night before. He was a man who outwardly held his liquor well. He was a genuine technician. He had arrived by airplane and not by flying boat. He had a badly bruised foot, and he was going to complain personally to General Eisenhower and to the President of the United States.

There was nothing I could do but apologise and add: 'By the way, I saved your life last night. One of my men wanted to shoot you on the spot.'

He paled visibly.

'Jesus!' he said. 'I'll never drink again.'

Our work included flushing out collaborators. To assist in this we used a certain amount of unofficial civilian help. One of these was a pianist and night-club proprietor, Johnny de Granada, who owned a little night-club called 'The Jockey'. At this time there was still a curfew in Brussels, and any establishment remaining open after midnight risked a raid and immediate closure. In recognition of Johnny's assistance I managed unofficially to let his club stay open as late as he wanted. As a result, my evenings cost me absolutely nothing for about a year. I shudder to think how many cases of champagne I consumed at no cost whatsoever. When I re-married in 1952, and the news was published in the papers, Johnny wired me from Brussels offering to come over, at his own expense, to play at the wedding.

93

All kinds of people turned up at The Jockey. I was there one night when I spotted Noël Coward who, for some reason, was wearing snow-boots.* I joined him for a drink. He knew Roland and I reminded him we had met at the dress rehearsal of *This Happy Breed*, with Guy Beauchamp. In the course of the conversation I mentioned that Guy and I had written a play together, which seemed to surprise him. I told him the title and said it had been on at The Strand.

'Oh, dear!' he said. 'I missed it. I must have been out of town.'

It was only later, when thinking over our conversation, I realised he was never out of town for more than a few weeks, which might indicate an immediate assumption on his part that the play had not lasted very long; but he certainly did not mean it that way. He was a man of impeccable good manners and to me, on a very slight acquaintance, enormous charm. I still wish I had asked him why he was wearing snow-boots in a hot night-club.

The mention of boots reminds me that in The Jockey I first met another man I was to see a lot more in the coming years. He was Arthur Christiansen, the Editor of the *Daily Express*.

He was tubby in those days, with a red complexion and twinkling glasses. He had just returned from the front and claimed, with how much justification I do not know, to have been the first British civilian to have set foot on German soil since the war. He was furious with the chambermaid at his hotel who had diligently cleaned the boots he had been wearing, which were caked with German mud which he had been saving up to take back and display to his friends in England.

Chris is the only man I have seen actually drinking champagne out of a shoe. True, it was his own shoe and the occasion was a weekly luncheon of the Thursday Club in London; but it was a splendid sight.

Chris had a fund of stories about life on the *Daily Express*. He first came to work in London having made a reputation for himself on the Manchester edition. Lord Beaverbrook summoned the Editor of the London *Daily Express*, Beverley Baxter, and said he had decided to bring down the young Christiansen to act as a kind of co-Editor. At this Baxter said:

'If you do that I have no other course but to offer my resignation.'

'Your offer will be accepted,' said Beaverbrook.

'In that case,' said Baxter, 'I withdraw the offer.'

*Coward was in Brussels to take part in a show with Geraldo's band, Frances Day and Will Hay.

In March 1945 British troops at last hung their washing on the Siegfried Line, while Donald and I brought off a double by celebrating the simultaneous break-up of our marriages. I wangled a brief but ineffectual leave in England. The marriage was, to all intents and purposes, over.

I found, during this period of acute unhappiness, that I wanted to understand rather than to hate. I obtained no comfort from the violent reactions of those close to me, who loved me. Their intentions were of the best but their angry reactions did not help. I needed someone who would be able to talk about it rationally, with knowledge and with understanding, who would be able to explain how and why. It is easier to bear with an illness if you know what that illness is. The same goes for unhappiness. I felt that it would be easier to live with it if I could stop asking: 'How has this happened to us? *To me?*'

There was one obvious candidate to play this role—my mother. She and Roland had apparently been very happy. I had never heard her say a word against him; yet she had fallen in love, left him and abandoned two young children in the process. From her I could be sure of getting it straight and without frills.

I went so see her and told her my story.

Her face went grim. Her mouth set in a hard line.

'How could she?' she said. 'How could she do this to you?'

She was no different from any of the others. If anything, she was more bitter in her denunciation.

My meeting with her had one good result. On the way back to London I did manage to laugh for the first time in a long while.

On reflection, I suppose the answer is that we all make special rules for ourselves. The sins we condemn in others are not sins if we commit them, because human nature's innate dishonesty enables us to find excuses for anything we do.

When I look back on some of the inexcusable things I have done, I realise that I felt no real sense of guilt because, in the majority of cases, I have not been found out. A feeling of guilt comes if you are conscious that your action has hurt someone you like or love, and not in the actual commission of the crime. This raises the sobering thought that a person can go right through life and be described by all who know him as a saint, whereas, in reality, he may merely have been clever.

I returned to Brussels feeling mercifully numb.

I have to say, too, that there could have been no better place in which to nurse a broken heart. There was still a fund of goodwill towards the British and an inexhaustible supply of soft shoulders to lean on.

In June I was promoted to Major, which staggered me. I was promptly moved from Brussels to the ghastly ruins of Cologne, where I became Area Security Officer in overall command of various Field Security Sections.

I found an undamaged house in the suburbs of Cologne, at Junkersdorf. The unit comprised myself, my batman, one other officer and a few NCOs.

The officers had their mess downstairs and the NCOs had one upstairs. We procured two German maids, who served all ranks at mealtimes. At first they spoke not a word of English, but the NCOs soon took them in hand. After a week, Elizabeth, who suffered from hot flushes, produced my food with a flourish and proudly cried: 'Bullshit, Herr Major!'

I took the bullshit without comment. She put down the plate, made a little curtsey, then left the room with a respectful: 'Fuck you very much.'

It was a good joke but the English lessons ended.

Germany's will to resist also ended and its armies surrendered. The war in Europe was over.

A few weeks later I saw Monty, now a Field-Marshal, for the last time, when he addressed about a hundred of us in a village church.

Even in victory he was allergic to coughing. On this occasion the wretched offender was actually strangled within earshot of the whole gathering. Just as Monty started to speak, a goose outside let out a hoarse screech. Monty stopped talking. The goose stopped screeching. He tried again and the goose screeched again. After three false starts Monty glanced meaningly at a young officer, who rose and left the church. Moments later there came one, last protesting screech. The young officer returned and gave a nod. Monty started up again without further interruption.

He gave a fascinating review of the battles, and told one amusing story which I do not think has ever been published. During the final days of the German collapse a British brigadier personally captured the German Field-Marshal, Milch, who started to throw his rank about. The weary brigadier seized the Field-Marshal's baton and struck him over the head with it. Afterwards he felt somewhat guilty and reported what he had done to his General, whose only comment was: 'Have you still got the baton?'

The brigadier said he had, and the General told him to hand it over. The General, in turn, reported the incident to Monty, whose only comment was: 'Have you still got the baton?'

The General said he had, and Monty told him to hand it over. Shortly afterwards Monty went to Buckingham Palace to report to the King. During the course of his conversation he told the King the story of the baton. The King's comment was: 'Have you still got the baton?'

Monty did not relate what happened after that.

Cologne was a shambles. There were four hundred habitable houses out of a total 400,000. The population emerged from holes in the ground to queue for half a day to buy one cabbage; but they were decently dressed, clean and invariably polite. A gentleman would always rise to give his seat to a lady in one of the few trams which were still running.

The black market flourished. When buying a dog for a girl friend in Brussels I was asked the equivalent of £25 in cash or just two pounds of coffee.

Everyone's ambition was to scrounge a Leica camera. Unfortunately, in Cologne, they were unobtainable. The Americans had got there first and a half-track had driven up and down the few usable streets while a GI with a loud-hailer had threatened instant retribution to any German who did not surrender his Leica instantly.

The German population was desperately short of the barest necessities for survival. It was impossible not to admire the discipline of a nation who had put up with so much. It was also difficult to like them. Far too many people rushed round to claim that their cousin was Jewish. I received a daily shoal of correspondence from incarcerated suspects all claiming to be innocent of any crime.

'Never a Nazi was I and I have two sons who I easily infected with my pinion.'

One man I grew to admire was the first Mayor of Cologne, thin, grey, with the face of an old eagle, and a manner which discouraged any personal approach. He had to receive me any time I cared to call, to give him orders or voice some complaint. Only once in all our meetings did he briefly unbend and discuss matters other than the business which brought me there. He was preoccupied about the eventual rebuilding of Cologne, and had worked out it would take twenty trains a day for twenty years to remove the rubble before reconstruction could begin. He therefore proposed that the ruins be left as a monument to the futility of war and that the new city be built around the rubble in a semi-circle from one bank of the Rhine to the other. He was wrong about this. The city was rebuilt miraculously quickly. He also recommended a cellar where I might find some good wines. He was right about that.

He had no excuses for Germany's war crimes; but this did not stop him fighting inflexibly for what he considered to be the good of his people. He was, perhaps, too inflexible and was eventually removed from office to make room for someone more amenable. Konrad Adenauer had the misfortune to be ahead of his time. He was not cut out to be a yes-man.

The eight months I spent in Cologne were comfortable, boring and de-moralising. The work was routine. The Germans gave no trouble. We unearthed a German General hiding under an assumed name. He had been in the Berlin bunker and had brought out Hitler's will, shortly before the end. He was, I believe, the last person in allied hands to see Hitler alive.

Time hung heavily with little to do in one's spare time but listen to The American Force's Network endlessly playing *I'll Get By*, *Sentimental Journey*, and the Pied Pipers singing *Dream*. Every now and then the programme would be interrupted by a sonorous voice which announced: 'Re-member! Penicillin fails once in every seven times!'

So far as I was concerned, it would not have mattered if penicillin failed every time, for ours was the one branch of the army which dared not fraternise while the 'anti-frat' regulations were still in force.

During this period an unfortunately worded directive on Non-Fraternisa-tion was issued by SHAEF Headquarters. It uttered dire warnings on the penalties arising from fraternisation with German women and ended with a paragraph which announced that members of the allied Womens' Services would be arriving in Germany as soon as possible. It was not intended the way it read, but it caused tremendous resentment among the higher echelons of the ATS and WAAF.

There were always the odd weekend trips to Brussels, and I took a leave in the Ardennes rather than return to England. During this leave the United States dropped their atom bombs and the war was over.

It was inevitable, I suppose, that this longed-for news should come as an anticlimax. Instead of joy there came the full realisation that I would be returning home to a home which no longer existed.

In October, I discovered that people in my position could obtain a month's compassionate leave. I took advantage of the army's compassion to go to London, see Mick Balcon and fix the terms of my future contract. I also made arrangements to keep on my little flat in Gilston Road, on which I had kept a tenuous hold throughout the war.

I met up with Jon, now completely improved except in health for he was in the process of being discharged from the Navy on medical grounds.

On my return to Cologne I found that once again someone in the army loved me. They offered to make me a Lieutenant-Colonel if I would agree to serve another year at least. It was nice to be asked. I would have liked to call myself 'Colonel', but I unhesitatingly refused.

On 1st February 1946, after six and a half long years, I walked eagerly into Olympia, to emerge carrying a brown raglan overcoat, a grey flannel suit, a pair of black shoes, a dubious looking tie and a quite appalling hat.

I was free.

Part 9

Wife Dropping (One)

A SENSE OF anti-climax persisted throughout 1946. To start with, victorious Britain was a dreary place in which to be victorious—ration cards, petrol coupons, queues and that dreadful word 'austerity'. Belgium had been Heaven in comparison.

My divorce petition was not heard until ten months after my demobilisation and the case developed into a rollicking farce.

A good-natured girl friend of Betty's had to give the essential evidence concerning the adultery. My counsel asked her to describe what she had seen. She hesitated, looked at me, then burst into tears and denied she had seen anything at all. This blew our case sky high. The judge nearly ruptured himself trying to contain his laughter, which was caused, I think, by the look of stunned horror on my counsel's face. Having regained control, the judge asked counsel if he would care to have a brief adjournment? Counsel said he would like nothing more. We adjourned to a corridor to ask the witness why she had suddenly changed her mind. She said she had not been able to bear the unhappy look on my face. I thanked her very much, but pointed out that I was bringing the case and wanted it to succeed. It could not succeed without her evidence. It took several minutes to persuade her that she was in no way injuring me by telling the truth. She then returned to court and gave her evidence.

Only one hurdle remained; my own appearance in the witness box to identify Betty's handwriting in a letter expressing her wish to terminate the marriage. I was handed a paper. My counsel, his suave self again, asked if I could identify the handwriting. I was unable to do this because they handed

100

me a *typewritten* copy of the letter. This had the judge going again. My counsel almost lost his wig as he whirled on my lawyer to hiss furiously. The lawyer began to shuffle a heap of papers, muttering that he had it some-where. He was still shuffling and muttering when the judge lost patience and granted the decree *nisi*.

I was given the custody of Carolyn, but requested that she be allowed to stay with her mother. This was not an easy decision. In effect. it meant sacrificing the role of father and relegating myself to that of a friendly uncle, who would be visited a couple of times a year; but she was only five and I have no doubt that the decison was right. During the years which followed we never indulged in a battle for her affections and she grew up apparently unaware of any estrangement. She illustrated this herself, when travelling in a train with me at the age of six. The other occupant of the apartment was an old lady, who gave her a sweet and asked her name.

'Carol,' she said. 'And aren't I lucky? I've got two Daddies, but Mummy only sleeps with one.'

As a rider to this remark (which failed to make me laugh at the time), the Head Mistress of her public school later told me that she was the only child she had encountered from a broken home who appeared to have no psycho-logical problems whatsoever.

There were other factors which made 1946 a depressing year. During the eight months in Cologne I had not written a word. When I joined Ealing Studios as a contract writer I found it difficult to work with enthusiasm. For the first time, writing was an effort and not a pleasure—and it showed. I laboured on a number of projects without achieving anything which satisfied me or anyone else. By the end of the year I had serious doubts about my own future.

I gained one adaptation credit on a picture called *Against the Wind* which dealt with British sabotage in German occupied territories. T E B ('Tibby') Clarke wrote the final script. Our leading lady was a slim, attractive red-head, who at that time spoke quite incomprehensible English—Simone Signoret.

Tibby Clarke wrote many successful pictures; *The Blue Lamp*, *Passport to Pimlico*, *The Lavender Hill Mob*, and others. He later received an OBE for his contribution to the British Cinema. We became close friends, and he would occasionally spend the night with me in London. Once I forgot to leave a key out for him and he was arrested trying to enter the house through a ground floor window. When the police discovered who he was they put him up in a cell in Chelsea Police Station and he got a much better breakfast than I would have provided.

I suppose my most positive achievement of the year was the forging of new friendships, many of which have lasted to this day.

One of these is Monja ('Danny') Danischewsky, who had been Mick Balcon's publicity chief, but had now turned to writing and producing. He was to make the Ealing film of Compton Mackenzie's *Whisky Galore*.

Through Danny I met Compton Mackenzie several times. He was the youngest elderly gentleman I have ever known. It was almost impossible to persuade him to go to bed at the end of a party. I vividly recall one story he told. He was sitting in the Café Royal, dining alone. Near him, leaning against a pillar, was a waiter. A second waiter approached the first waiter, looked surreptitiously all round, then whispered confidentially: '*Well . . .* He's eaten it.'

Compton Mackenzie said he had never stopped wondering what 'it' was.

Some of my new friendships were made round the poker table. We had a regular school which, more often than not, played all night. Members of the school included Harry Watt, who made the film, *The Overlanders*, Bobby St John Cooper, the cartoonist, who invented Tate & Lyle's famous Mr Cube, Thornton Freeland, the American film director, and his actress wife, June Clyde, Vasco Lazzolo, the artist, and Guy Morgan, a journalist who had moved on to screen-writing. Guy had been on the *Daily Express* during the crisis leading to the abdication of King Edward VIII. As the crisis reached its peak, the whole staff of the paper were crowded round a wireless set listening to the news. Guy, who was late with some copy, sat alone working at his desk. Someone ran past him shouting: 'Abdication!'

A few moments later another man ran past shouting: 'The Duke of York!'

Guy looked up from his copy and said: 'What came in third?'

Danny was the keenest and worst poker player I have encountered. His trouble was an incurable curiosity. It was impossible to bluff him, for ne paid to see every hand. I suggested he should write a book about his poker experiences, which should be entitled:

'*I CAME . ... I SAW . . . FUCK!*'

I played a lot of poker at this time. I joined Crockfords Club, where I played almost every day, I generally lost, but it was a useful training ground. Terence Reese, the bridge champion and a great player of all card games, became a good friend. He gave me the best lesson I ever had at poker, which has served me well over the years. It was in one line: 'Poker is not what you win. It's what you don't lose.'

Danny came to me as a lodger. He had rented a house in Somerset and could only visit his family there at weekends. I enjoyed having him. It was impossible to remain depressed in his company, and my morale was at a low ebb. To add to my general depression I had developed digestive trouble, and acute sinusitis. This meant I was always taking pills or putting drops up my nose. This prompted Danny to write me a little verse.

> 'Pains in his tummy,
> and stuff up his nose.
> He shall have mucus
> wherever he goes.'

Danny liked gracious living, but he did not find it with me. He hated my daily lady who 'did' in a rather desultory fashion. I once found him in the bathroom glowering at the bath. He shook his head sadly, and said: 'Abandon soap all ye who enter here.'

Occasionally, Brenda, his wife, came to stay. She was discouraged, too, when the old gas heater blew up in her face with a shattering explosion. I jumped out of bed and rushed in to see how she was. I don't know whether she was more shaken by the blast or by the fact that I was stark naked.

Brenda is inclined to faint in hot places. One night at a dinner party in a restaurant she keeled over in a dead faint and laid her head in a plate of fish.

'Don't worry everybody,' said Danny. 'Brenda's motto is: "There's no home like plaice."'

Undoubtedly, the most important of several women in my life was my landlady, Mrs Ivanov, who lived on the ground floor below me. She showed her sympathy in a most practical and generous way. She provided me with breakfast at 1/− and lunch and dinner at 2/6. On Sundays she brought the breakfast up on a tray, and willingly made it for two when the occasion arose.

Danny*, himself from a White Russian Jewish family, loved Mrs Ivanov. He was present on the day she burst into the flat, beaming happily, and said: 'Today is my lucky day. For long time I have not had any cock; but I just meet a nice man in the street who promises me all the cock I want.'

I was stunned, but Danny was able to explain the Russian's inability to

*See his own autobiography: *White Russian, Red Face.*

103

pronounce the long 'o'. She was referring to coke which, like everything else in victorious Britain, was in short supply.

Danny, despite his background, is the most English of men and has always yearned for the life of the English country gentleman. He has now achieved this ambition and works from a delightful house near Farnham, Surrey. Its only drawback is a herd of the fiercest pigs I have ever seen, who inhabit his back yard and attack almost anyone without provocation. Danny, however, appears to be immune.

'The reason,' he says, 'is that pigs do not eat Jews.'

A gloomy 1946 ended with one of the coldest winters ever recorded. My central heating failed through a renewed lack of 'cock'. One day I decided to stay in bed just for warmth. I had a little portable gas fire with one bar. I put this on a chair beside the bed, close to my face, and fell asleep. I was awakened by the telephone. Before I could answer it, I was violently sick. While I was asleep there had been a gas cut. The fire had gone out. The gas supply had then resumed, and the unlit fire had continued to give out gas. But for the telephone I should undoubtedly have died, and everyone would have thought I had committed suicide.

1947 improved. I discovered an old novel entitled: *Israel Rank*, which I was sure would make a film. I gave it to Mick Balcon to read. He expressed some doubts, but suggested I write a film treatment and submit it to him. When he read my treatment his doubts were dispelled, and arrangements were made to buy the film rights of the book. One snag arose, which nearly put paid to the whole project. The author's widow insisted that any film made must be called *Israel Rank*. Since the story concerned a half-Italian, half-Jewish mass murderer, and since J Arthur Rank, who owned the studios, was neither half-Italian nor half-Jewish, it was obvious that this was not a tactful title for an Ealing film. With some difficulty the lady was persuaded to change her mind. The title I eventually found for it was *Kind Hearts and Coronets*, which was to prove one of Ealing's most successful films, with brilliant performances by Sir Alec Guinness, who played all the murder victims, male and female. It also proved a heart-breaking experience for me. Having 'sold' my treatment I started to write the screenplay, working with Henry Cornelius,* its producer.

Corny had apprenticed with Alexander Korda, who, he told me, never completely conquered the English language, having particular difficulty with

---

*He later made the successful *Genevieve*.

double negatives. Once, when a junior employee, Corny had been summoned to Korda's office. He knocked on the door, received no answer, but walked in. Korda was there, behind his desk. He pointed a stern finger and said: 'Boy, not to don't knock before I not tell you not to don't come in. Go!'

Corny was a lovable man, with twinkling eyes behind thick spectacles, who possessed a sly sense of humour. We got along well on a personal level, but found it difficult to agree about how *Kind Hearts and Coronets* should be treated. It developed into a long drawn out, friendly but wearing battle, with Angus Macphail, the scenario editor, and myself on one side, and Corny on the other. His problem——or perhaps I should say my problem——was that Corny would psychoanalyse everything to what I thought to be an extreme degree, considering we were writing a comedy. We argued for a whole day over a scene (*circa* 1910) in which two old gentlemen in a train discussed the dangers of the new-fangled automobile. Corny did not like the scene and finally insisted it be cut from the script because, he said, two men who disliked cars would not risk travelling in a train.

We battled on, enjoying ourselves in the process, and gradually started to see chinks of light.

Robert Hamer then arrived upon the scene. He was to direct the picture. He was a man of considerable talent, who made a big mark with his picture, *It Always Rains on Sunday*, which broke new ground in the British cinema.

Robert Hamer had a problem. He hated me. I use the word 'hated' advisedly. He despised me as a writer, and detested me as a person. We only had to be in the same room and he would start to twitch. When he could bring himself to talk to me he would stare up at a corner of the ceiling as if I had taken off and landed there. The truth was, he could not even bear to look at me. I do not know the reason. I doubt if he knew himself. It was something chemical, beyond his control. I have occasionally had the same kind of reactions myself about the most inoffensive people. I did not feel the same antipathy towards him, but I soon realised that any hope of working with him was out of the question. I therefore quietly withdrew from the scene.

Robert Hamer and John Dighton wrote the screenplay together. When it was completed, the studio sent it to me for comments, also asking me what screen credit I considered I should have.

I thought the screenplay was first class; everything I had always hoped it would be. I was so impressed that I swallowed my somewhat bruised pride, and wrote a personal note to Robert Hamer, congratulating him. He replied by return saying that he was touched that I could find it possible to write

105

such a generous letter. It was a gesture, he said, that he would never forget.

I also wrote to the studio giving details of my contributions to the script, and pointing out that it was through my original treatment that the subject had been bought. I said that I would leave the actual credit to their discretion and would be happy to abide by their decision.

This letter was shown to Robert Hamer. He thereupon circulated a memo to *all* departments stating that my sole contribution was nearly to have caused the subject to be shelved. In his opinion I had earned no credit at all.

Someone showed me this memo. I then wrote again, saying that rather than cause Mr Hamer's blood pressure to rise to bursting point I would gladly forego any credit.

My name did not appear on the screen but, many years later, I was pleased that, in his autobiography, Mick Balcon gave me credit.

Angus Macphail had been a firm ally throughout. He was, I think, almost as interested as I to discover what made Hamer twitch. Since they were good friends he made several attempts to discover the cause but did not succeed.

Angus and I kept in touch until he died. He was constantly amusing although a perilous after-dinner companion.

Danny once invited him to dine with an elderly couple. The husband was something big in the silk world. Before the evening started Danny begged Angus to watch his step, since his guests might be easily shocked. Angus behaved impeccably throughout dinner, and well into liqueurs. He stretched over backwards, even if tilting slightly, to show interest in the subject of silk, and kept asking for more details of the wondrous workings of the silk-worm. By nine o'clock he was still at it.

'Do go on, Sir! Please go on! Absolutely fascinating!' He drew out his cigarette case, proffered it to the old gentleman and said: 'Have one of my arseholes.'

Astonishingly, the old gentleman did not react at all. Afterwards Danny conjectured he must have thought Angus had said: 'Have one of my Three Castles.'

I wrote a thriller play in three weeks called *Night was our Friend*.

I gave it to Mick Balcon, who was enthusiastic and said that Ealing would arrange for the play to be presented in the West End. They would buy the film rights, and Margaret Lockwood would star in the film version. It sounded too good to be true—and it was. Margaret Lockwood refused to do it. She had recently made a film called *Bedelia*, in which she played a murderess. My story gave her a somewhat similar role. She felt, quite reasonably, that it was a mistake to play two similar characters in quick succession. At this, the whole scheme collapsed.

The day I received this sad news I went to the Screenwriters' Club, where I had a good deal to drink. I told the story to a man I had never met before, and finished with the line: 'And now that bitch Maggie Lockwood has refused to do it!'

He listened courteously, which is more than I would have done in his place, for he turned out to be Maggie Lockwood's husband.

Night was our Friend was subsequently given a tryout by Windsor Repertory Company. It was directed by John Counsell with his wife, Mary Kerridge, and Allan Cuthbertson playing the leads. It was a first class production, and went down well with the audiences. Alan Dent, critic of the *News Chronicle*, described it as: 'Never for more than five minutes anything but engrossing.' He confidently predicted it would move to the West End.

The play did everything but move to the West End. It was made as a film with Michael Gough and Elizabeth Sellars and was directed by Michael Anderson, who was later to make some big pictures. It was shown on television with the young Jill Bennett starring. It played in every repertory company in England, and, after twenty-five years, still brings in a tidy annual sum from amateur companies.

Mick Balcon was given a knighthood. From the many hundreds of congratulatory telegrams and letters it was typical of him that there was only one which he made public——from a young man who had worked at Ealing, and looked forward to returning there when his period of Army National Service was completed. This was during the time of the Palestine 'troubles', when the British were playing the villains in their efforts to control illegal Jewish immigration.

The writer of the letter congratuled Mick, who is Jewish, on his knighthood and looked forward to returning to Ealing: 'After I've knocked hell out of those bloody Jews.'

At lunch, a day or two afterwards, we were speculating on what the young man would do if, sitting in his desert tent, he suddenly remembered Mick was Jewish. Would he volunteer for a suicide mission, or quietly hang himself then and there?

Mick remained philosophical about the latest threat to his people, 'I'm not worried,' he said. 'The poor chap has very bad eyesight.'

Part 10

★ ★

J Arthur Rank Dropping

★ ★

AFTER ABOUT EIGHTEEN months at Ealing Studios I decided to give up the security of J Arthur Rank's weekly pay-cheque to go freelance. It was an amicable parting. Mick would have been happy to keep me on, but I had not become attached to any of the various teams of producers, directors and writers, which were being formed. I also realised that I was still not cut out to be part of an organised body. In a sense, Ealing was a school where I was not my own master.

I left with absolutely no prospects, and to the dismay of my agent, Al Treeby, of Film Rights. Hayes Hunter had died, and Al was now running the writers' department.

Shortly after I went freelance, Al informed me that Herbert Wilcox, then a top producer, was looking for someone to adapt the Joseph Conrad book *Laughing Anne* for the screen. The book had already been sent to a number of established writers. Al, however, managed to persuade Wilcox to let me read it. I knew that my chances of landing the job were practically nil. I had little experience and nothing to recommend me. Therefore, having read the book, I sat down to write an outspoken commentary on its manifold faults as a film subject. When he read this, Al, a timid man, who hated offending anybody, said it would be a great mistake to let Mr Wilcox read anything so critical. It would merely ensure that he would never look my way again.

I told him to send it just the same. I had nothing to lose and was constitutionally incapable of saying I liked something if I didn't. Al sighed, said it would be on my own head, and sent it off.

A week later he called to say that Herbert Wilcox wished me to write the treatment and was prepared to pay me £100 a week for so doing.

I think I must have been the only writer to have given a completely frank appraisal of the subject. Honesty sometimes pays. I wrote the treatment. Herbert Wilcox was most kind about it, but the picture was never made.

Roland suggested that we collaborate in writing a play. The difficulties of a father-son working relationship are almost a cliché and presumably will continue to be difficult until some future society ordains that all old gentlemen over the age of fifty will be painlessly put down for their own good. One is bored by hearing of the keen young man with the bright new ideas who enters the family business only to be sat upon by the old maestro who knows it all and just does not want to listen.

There was nothing of this in my working relationship with Roland. If I have to search for reasons I think there were two. First, I did not collaborate with him until he suggested it. Thus I was able to start with the feeling that he had enough respect for my professional ability to make writing with him a worthwhile proposition. Secondly, the very thing which, sadly perhaps, had been lacking between us helped to make collaboration easier. There had never existed the normal father-son love-hate relationship. Love had been an alien word in our upbringing. Any overt expressions of affection were invariably laughed off or ignored. On an emotional basis we were almost as much strangers as I was with a mother whom I had hardly known. It was only through working together that the long-buried affection gradually and belatedly started to blossom.

If there is any credit to be handed out for the successful collaboration it must go to Roland, who never once pulled rank on the basis of age or experience. If there was any division it was that almost automatically I had my way in any discussion about what young people would say and he had his way with the older characters.

The only disagreement I remember, which caused a few hours of irritation, was when, at the age of sixty, Roland learned from me that you do not write: 'There was not a living *sole*.' but '. . . living soul.' He had written 'sole' for forty years and refused to take my word that the expression referred to the human soul. He was quite prepared to argue about it, too.

'Do you write "A soul person."? Of course you don't! Yoy write: "A sole person." Therefore when I write: "There wasn't a living sole." I am, in fact, writing: "There wasn't a living sole person." and am just leaving out the word "person."'

It took a bridge session at the Garrick Club, when he put the argument to

W Somerset Maugham and Alastair Sim, to persuade him that he was wrong.

I do not know how I have the temerity to record this, since I have only just learned, after thirty-seven years of writing, from my twenty-eight year-old secretary, that the word is 'arbitrary' and not 'arbitary'. I did not even have an argument to put up in my defence. She only had to produce the *Oxford Dictionary*.

My first collaboration with Roland was in writing a play, *The Paragon*.

It was a melodramatic, well-constructed piece about a blind man, whose only son has been reported killed in the war, but who is, in reality, a deserter. The son returns to the house in search of money. The story shows how the blind man gradually pieces together the evidence that his son is alive.

The Paragon broke one record in being the first West End play to be written by a father and son. We sold the film rights before clinching the West End deal. The play was presented at the Fortune Theatre by Alec Rea and E P Clift. The blind man was played by Walter Fitzgerald, who had been in my first play before the war. Others in the cast were Rachel Kempson*, Hugh Burden and seventy-four year-old Arthur Wontner.

As we walked into the foyer on the first night Roland found himself face to face with W A Darlington, the critic of the *Daily Telegraph*, who said: 'Roland! Oh, dear! You are the last person I want to see just before criticising your play. Anyway, how are you?'

'I shan't tell you,' said Roland.

Roland and I sat in a box with Kitty and a girl friend of mine. All went smoothly until poor Rachel Kempson missed an entrance cue. Two actors were left on the stage desperately ad-libbing for nearly two minutes.

Roland suddenly lost his head. Muttering profanities, he started actually to climb out of the box, with the evident intention of jumping on to the stage. At this moment Rachel Kempson entered and the play continued.

Reflex action can make people do strange things. On one occasion in a melodrama an actor had to make a dramatic exit, after telling his wife he would never darken her doors again. He made his speech, marched to the door and found it would not open. He panicked and, instead of walking off through the wings, fell to his knees and crawled out through the fireplace.

The Paragon was strong, dramatic meat, and received a tremendous ovation. Roland and I both made a curtain speech. Roland said that people

---

*Sir Michael Redgrave's wife and mother of all the Redgraves.

often asked how two writers collaborated on a play. He would like to say that in this case his son had written every other word.

The reviews were enthusiastic.

'Gripping . . . Good enough to make us look forward to the next effort of Pertwee *pére et fils.*'

Beverly Baxter. The *Evening Standard.*

'A play of dramatic and emotional strength.'

A E Wilson. The *Star.*

'The firm tread of theatrical success.'

The *Times.*

'It grips and stimulates.'

Harold Hobson. The *Sunday Times.*

In the course of an excellent review, W A Darlington wrote:

'To see a father and son taking an author's call together is a touching and unusual spectacle.'

The only sour note was struck by Leonard Mosley in the *Daily Express*, who concluded a lukewarm review with the words:

'The writers were Roland and Michael Pertwee, who looked murder at each other only when one tried to grab the other's curtain speech.'

This was so palpably false that I forsook my rule never to complain to a critic, and taxed him about it. He swore blind that the offending paragraph had only appeared at it did through bad subediting of his piece.

Queen Mary came and told us she enjoyed every moment. Ivor Novello came five times, so he had no need to tell us how much he enjoyed it; but the public did not come. The takings were poor and the play lasted five months.

It broke records with subsequent amateur productions. It is still performed today.

With *Death on the Table* and *The Paragon* behind me, I was beginning to learn that critical acclaim does not necessarily ensure financial success.

This prompts me to put down a few reflections on criticism and critics.

In 1969 I received reviews for a play which were so good that I carried some of them around in my wallet. Harold Hobson went so far as to compare me favourably with Feydeau. The play had only a modest run.

Two years later I wrote another play, which gained me my worst press in over thirty years. It not only displeased the critics, it appeared to enrage some of them. The *Daily Express* summed up the general feeling with the words:

> 'I find it absurd that anyone bothered to write it, that people agreed to perform in it and that customers managed to sit through it to the end.'

This play played to near capacity on its first full week and, within one month of its opening, broke the all-time box office record for the theatre on two consecutive weeks. It was my first solid, smash hit.

The British* playwright can therefore derive some satisfaction from the knowledge that a bad press need not kill a play, any more than a good press ensures success.

Writers could save themselves much needless anguish if they could force themselves to look on the critic merely as one individual who is paid to express his opinion.

The critic does not necessarily represent public taste; neither does he write his reviews to suit the type of person who reads his newspaper. Most critics strongly defend their right to give an individual opinion, regardless of whether their readers are likely to agree. Many people regret this, feeling that the critic should be a trusted guide. It is highly probable that the critics' determination to express their own personal views may be a contributing factor to the public's tendency to ignore what they say; but it would be unfair, indeed, to deny them the right to say it.

Undoubtedly, there are times when a critic (like any writer) thinks up a telling phrase, tucks it away and uses it at the first available opportunity. I think it was James Agate who, criticising Laurence Olivier's first appearance as Romeo, wrote:

> '"Romeo, Romeo, wherefore art thou Romeo?" And I heartily agreed.'

One is tempted to believe that he may have had this stored away for some time before he used it.

A popular misconception is that most critics are personally biased, frustrated writers, who cannot wait for the opportunity to break authors' hearts. This must be rubbish. A critic may have to see five plays in a single week. He would have to be an extreme masochist if he really hoped to hate all five of them.

---

*As opposed to America, where a bad press can close a play after one night.

Everyone loves a good press and dislikes a bad one. I do not believe writers who claim to be immune. After a first night, I stay up until dawn to buy all the papers. It is human nature to prefer praise to criticism; but it does pay to take a balanced view of both.

It should never be forgotten that, although the writer himself buys all the papers, the average member of the public buys only one.

To the author, each play he writes is his child on whom he has lavished time, effort and love. He should, however, remember that, to the critic, the same play is merely a casual acquaintance, whom he meets once, either likes or dislikes, and then, in most cases, promptly forgets. The critic's involvment is as brief, impersonal and uncomplicated as that.

I have little time for writers who welcome good reviews, but lead protest marches down Fleet Street when they get bad ones.

Fortunately, for my peace of mind I have never suffered from this particular form of paranoia. I frame my worst notices and stick them on my office wall, because they are generally more amusing than the good ones.

I can honestly say that I have only twice been really irritated by critics. The first occasion was by Milton Shulman, then reviewing films who, after severely castigating one of my pictures, went on to praise Alastair Sim for producing 'some extremely funny moments by abandoning the script and relying upon the wit he can engender in a lifted eyebrow and a shrugged shoulder'.

I am sure Mr Shulman could not have meant to suggest that Alastair Sim periodically stopped the action, faced camera, then lifted his eyebrows and shrugged his shoulders just to get a laugh. True, there were two sequences without dialogue, but carefully written and worked out, in which Alastair Sim performed brilliantly, using his eyebrows and shoulders to great effect; but he was not abandoning the script. He was following it and interpreting it in his own inimitable way. I may be misjudging Mr Shulman, but his criticism could be taken to imply that scenes in which an actor gets laughs without the assistance of dialogue must automatically be credited to that actor. If this were true, the writers of silent movies would have had a hard time.

The second occasion for irritation was caused by Ronald Bryden, the dramatic critic of The *Observer*. As he had every right to do, he slammed a musical comedy of which I had written the book. (His criticism, which was wittily brief and to the point, can be found later in this book.) Some weeks later writing in the magazine *Plays And Players* on the subject of the Critics' Votes for the 1967 awards he wrote:

113

'One can only be delighted at the trend which produces such plays as *Rosencrantz* and *Guildenstern Are Dead* and *After The Rain*, and fills The Aldwych, National and Nottingham Playhouse, while *The Four Musketeers* withers.'

Here Mr Bryden was inaccurate in expressing his personal delight, since the musical was then playing to excellent business. This was one of the rare occasions when I felt tempted to write a letter of protest, but since the man who wrote the lyrics for the musical was Herbert Kretzmer, drama critic of the *Daily Express*, who was equally incensed, I left him to make the protest.

Soon after the war Jack Davies and I had renewed our friendship. I joined him and Dorothy, his wife, on a holiday in France. Also with us was their young son, John Howard Davies, who had become a child star in *Oliver Twist*. He was a lovely little chap, quite unimpressed by stardom. Not once did he refer to the film during the two weeks we were together. He went on to make two more films but I do not think acting ever appealed to him much. He is now a big name on the production side of television.

Jack was at this time the film critic on the *Daily Sketch*. We teamed up in our spare time and wrote a small picture called *Trouble in the Air* for George and Alfred Black, the sons of George Black, the impresario, and nephews of Ted Black, my old boss at Gainsborough. The picture was made at Highbury, which was then the headquarters of something called 'The Charm School', aimed at discovering budding stars. One day on the set I met Ted Black for the first time since I had joined the army. I shook him warmly by the hand and, noting a blank look in his eye, reminded him of my name. He smiled and nodded.

'Of course!' he said. 'Didn't we meet before the war?'

I had clearly made a big impression at Gainsborough.

George and Alf, who had taken over from their father, were producing a number of spectacular stage shows.

Jack and I later worked on another film for them, designed for The Crazy Gang. We used to work in the evenings at George and Alf's top floor office near St James's Street. One night, about nine o'clock, we heard a spine-chilling scream from the floor below.

In an office below we found the lady caretaker lying on the floor in hysterics. She had surprised a burglar opening a safe. We gave her a brandy. The police arrived and departed. George and Alf went off to the Prince of Wales to see about their night's takings. Jack and I remained in the office, working. We then decided to give the Blacks a shock when they returned. We opened

Afloat (or nearly) on location for the film *The Naked Truth*, with producer Mario Zampi and Shirley Eaton: this was the film that made Peter Sellers a star.

With Diana Dors on a balcony of the Carlton Hotel, Cannes, during the 1956 Film Festival. We were both also acting as newspaper correspondents while Diana's husband daubed moustaches on a pretty rival's poster photographs.

At another premiere with the lovely Helen Cherry, wife of Trevor Howard, and my co-panellist on the TV show 'Guess My Story'. Film producer Marcel Hellman is on the left.

A publicity photograph taken while Jerry Lewis directed, and I watched shooting on my film One More Time which starred Sammy Davis, Jr., and Peter Lawford. They failed to amuse but at least Jerry wore some very funny hats.

drawers, strewed papers on the floor and spilled some red ink on the blotter. As soon as they returned Jack was to lie on the floor with a paper knife apparently stuck in his back. I was to slump across the desk, with my head near the pool of red ink. We heard footsteps and took up our positions. The door opened. Then came a piercing scream, followed by the thump of a falling body. It was not George and Alf who had arrived, but the caretaker, who had come upstairs to thank us for our assistance. It was a disastrous joke and it took about ten minutes and half a bottle of brandy to revive her.

This picture was not made either; but we had a lot of fun writing it.

I wrote a film in which the young juvenile star was a pretty teenager named Petula Clark. Not long ago I heard her say in a television interview that she wanted to forget the films she made at this period of her life, so, because she is a very sweet girl, I won't give the title. I suppose I only met her about three times during the production of the film. About twenty years later when she was a hugely successful international star I found myself standing beside her outside the White Elephant Club in Curzon Street. We were both waiting for a taxi. There was absolutely no reason why she should remember me, so I said nothing. After a few moments she moved over to me and said: 'I wonder if you remember me? My name's Petula Clark.'

As I said — a very sweet girl.

I wrote the screenplay of *The Paragon* which, as a film was entitled *The Silent Dust*. The producer was N A Bronsten, who made a comparatively brief impact on the British cinema. He said he was in a great hurry so I completed the job in a month, working night and day. I delivered it to him and he seemed highly satisfied. I went for a week-end to Paris to recuperate, leaving on a Saturday morning and returning Monday morning. On my return, I found that, during the week-end, he had hired Richard Llewellyn* to write a completely new script in two days. He presented it to me on the Monday and asked me what I thought about it. I read the script, which may have been excellent but which bore little or no relation to *The Paragon*. I said that if that was what he wanted he was welcome. The director, Lance Comfort, went further. He said if that was what Mr Bronsten wanted then Mr Bronsten would have to find another director. At this Bronsten picked up the new script, put it in the wastepaper basket, and that was the last time he mentioned it.

*Author of *How Green was my Valley*.

115

The picture was made in 1948 with Nigel Patrick, Stephen Murray, Derek Farr, Beatrice Campbell (Nigel Patrick's wife) and that grand old actor, Seymour Hicks. He was required to ride a bicycle in the film, but could not manage it, so he was provided with a tricycle. The dialogue director was Wallace Douglas, who taught Seymour Hicks how to ride the trike and even doubled for him in the more energetic shots. Wally and I were to get together far more closely in years to come, when he directed some of my West End plays.

The film was fair but did not slay them at the box office. It did, however, kill the American stage production of *The Paragon* stone dead. We had sold the Broadway rights to the Shubert Brothers, who presented it for a week in Wilmington prior to opening at The Golden Theatre, New York. It received good notices in Wilmington, and played to satisfactory business for four days.

An agreement had been made not to release the film until six months after the Broadway opening; but someone jumped the gun and, during the Wilmington week, the film was premiered in New York. The Shuberts let off a combined snarl and closed the play instantly.

Variety headlined the news:

"FILM PREMIERE SNAFUS 'PARAGON' LEGIT DEBUT."

It also snafued my long-awaited trip to America.

Jack Davies and I wrote a comedy play entitled *How are the Mighty*, which was about the collapse of Hollywood's most publicised happy marriage.

I dealt us one cold hand of poker to decide whose name should come first on the credit. I looked at my cards and was embarrassed to find I had dealt myself a full house of kings. Jack laid down four aces.

The play was rejected by most of the West End managements and had to wait two years before John Counsell directed it at Windsor, with Peter Graves, Patrick Cargill and a young girl named Geraldine McKeown, who had previously only played small parts. Even then she stood out as a star with a delicious, inborn sense of comedy timing.

The *Sunday Chronicle* reported that several London managements, which had previously rejected the play, were having to join a long queue fighting to get the rights. They lied and the play was not heard of again.

Just after we had written the play, and were hopeful of an immediate West End production, we asked Al Treeby to send it to Nigel Patrick, for whom it would have been an ideal vehicle. A week or two later Al called up to say that Paddy Patrick had asked him to tell us he absolutely *adored* the play, would have given his eye teeth to be in it but, most unfortunately, was committed elsewhere. He was, however, sure that the play would be a smash hit whoever finally played the part.

The script which had been sent to Paddy was returned to us. Inside we came across a personal note written by Paddy to Al Treeby, which the kind-hearted Al had forgotten to remove.

It read:

'Dear Al,
    Me no likee.
       Love,
          Paddy.'

Part 11

★ ★

Foreign Operator Dropping

★ ★

THE YEAR 1948 saw the start of a new outlet, writing for a variety of European-based film producers. This provided several trips abroad, some amusement, much irritation—and very little money.

The first of these was Raoul Levy, a Frenchman, who had made a small thriller film in France, and now wished to branch out into the international market. He was staying at the Savoy Hotel when he asked me to meet him. He approved of me and I approved of his suggested idea. He quoted me a figure higher than anything I had yet received, and told me to join him in Paris the following week. He casually asked me to pay his bill at the Savoy, which he would repay when I arrived in Paris. We shook hands and that was almost the last I saw of Raoul Levy and positively the last I saw of my money. When he had become a millionaire, and was papering his walls with Picassos, having launched Brigitte Bardot to fame, I waited until he was in exalted company at the Carlton Hotel, Cannes, to approach him and remind him in a piercing voice that he owed me fifty pounds for hotel bills at the Savoy. He roared with laughter, clapped me on the back, said I was absolutely right, and still did not pay.

Otto Siessens was plump, jolly, and full of charm. I had met him in Brussels after the liberation and he had promised he would employ me after the war. He was as good as his word, and I am still not sure whether I am glad or sorry. He whisked me off to Madrid to write a picture.

Otto instantly disappeared from Madrid, leaving me in the hands of a father-and-son production team—Antonio Gomez, who was small, grey and nicely mannered, and his son, Paco, aged about twenty-seven, who was even

118

smaller and looked as if he had just died. He was, at the time, enjoying—
and I mean enjoying—singularly bad health. According to his mother, who
was always with us, it was his liver. He was allowed to eat no fat at all. He
shuddered at the very thought of fat. When brought a plate of specially ordered
plain boiled spaghetti, he would pick up a jug of water and pour the contents
all over the spaghetti. If a bubble of fat appeared in the water he would hiss
triumphantly and send the spaghetti back. If it showed no trace of fat, he
wouldn't eat it anyway, because the water had rendered it inedible. He had a
very beautiful wife with hot eyes, who kept telling me the English were cold.
This made me feel like the spaghetti after Paco had poured water on it.

They all spoke five languages, often at the same time; but our common
language was French. I thought of them always as Gomez *père* and Gomez
fils.

Gomez *père* and *fils* never kept an appointment. Occasionally one of them
would turn up alone and cancel a meeting because the other was not available.

We did meet at mealtimes, but they had a firm rule never to discuss
business while eating, since this was considered bad for the health. There
wouldn't have been much chance to discuss business anyway because, apart
from Gomez *fils*'s antics with the water jug, Gomez *père* and Gomez *mère*
also kept forbidding each other to eat. Their livers, too, were apparently in
poor shape. Despite this, every morning, everybody told everybody how much
better they were looking.

It was not long before I found myself a prisoner in my hotel. I could sleep
and eat and drink—so long as it was in the hotel; but I could not go out
because I had no money. My money was always coming 'mañana' but somehow never did. They were, they said, waiting for Otto. For a few precious
days I was able to get out, by poncing off a Brazilian girl friend from London.
I used to take her out to dinner—and she paid. Mercifully, before she left
Madrid, Gomez *père*, who had a kind heart, came up with a pittance and I
was able to repay her.

Otto Siessens reappeared after a month, and gave me a sound dressing
down for not telephoning him about my money troubles. This would have
been difficult since he had not told me or Gomez *père* and *fils* where he had
been. However, he produced a little cash so I did not argue about that.

I completed the script in England, sent it off to Otto and awaited his
reactions and my money. Neither was forthcoming and numerous letters failed
to get a reply.

Months went by; then Gomez *fils* appeared in London, looking better. He had put on about two pounds and weighed at least six stone. He had come to discuss another film. I said I was not prepared to discuss another project until I had been paid for the first one. He expressed horror and surprise; (my letters to him had evidently gone astray, too), then stunned me by immediately paying about two-thirds of what was owed. Hardly had he slipped away from London, when Otto Siessens suddenly appeared, rather like the Demon King in a pantomime—and just as angry. He was in a towering rage and, somewhat illogically, threatened *me* with legal action for daring to accept money from Gomez *père* and *fils*. It was, he inferred, a diabolical plot to jeopardise his copyright in the subject. I told him I did not give a damn who paid me, and would unhesitatingly accept the rest of what was owed to me from Gomez *père* or *fils* if they offered it. Otto immediately paid me about fifty per cent of the residue.

My next foreign assignment was for a very frail producer, Igor Kolinski, who suffered from permanent and painful flatulence. I was to write a screenplay from an original story by the well-known French film director, Julien Duvivier and screenwriter Charles Spaak, a brother of the Belgian statesman, Paul-Henri Spaak.

I stayed in Paris for a month and got on well with both Duvivier and Spaak, who were both experienced professionals. Duvivier was also important enough to afford to be absolutely beastly to Igor Kolinski. From first to last I did not hear him address a civil word to Igor. Strangely, this seemed not to affect Igor at all. He never answered back and just went on belching quietly. Perhaps he took it out on me instead, because, before many days were out, I found I was again a prisoner in my hotel. No money was coming in. With Duvivier's blessing, I locked the door and remained in my room with the entire script and refused to come out until some cash was pushed under the door note by note.

Later, I flew out to Tenerife where the film was being shot. There was an impressive array of talent. Duvivier directed. Herbert Marshall, George Sanders, Agnes Moorhead, Patricia Roc and the French actor, Dalio, headed the cast.

I arrived to find a state of open warfare between Duvivier and Kolinski, who was also being sniped at from the rear by the Spanish end of the film.

After a few days we moved to a beautiful hotel, lying on a tropical-looking bay, cut off from the nearest village by a mountainous road. It was an idyllic setting. The water was phosphorescent and, when swimming at night, it twinkled all around your body like millions of little stars. Here we were nicely bunched together to continue the major war, and several other minor skirmishes of a more personal nature.

I was at this time about a third of the way through a long, on-and-off engagement to a very lovely English girl, who joined me out there, enabling us to add to the sound of battle by venting our insecurities one upon the other.

Bart Marshall had brought along a pretty young wife — an ex-starlet, Boots Mallory. He had changed very little from the days I admired him in *Interference*. He was still ruthlessly British after years in Hollywood, and full of nostalgic longings to go back to see Chelsea beat Arsenal. I spent most of my time with them, because they were quiet and companionable and reserved their own battles for the night, when they had some beauties.

George Sanders had also brought along a new wife. She was one of the sexiest and most attractive girls I had ever met. She was darkish, with a well-rounded figure. Her name was Zsa Zsa Gabor, and she was very jealous indeed of George; so jealous that she publicly accused my beloved of making eyes at her beloved. This was unfair, because my beloved never took her eyes off me for long enough to allow me to look at any other woman for more than a second — which was one of our major problems. Since my beloved was not in the film business and did not have to keep anybody happy except me, she gave Zsa Zsa as good as she got and they had a slanging match which I think they both enjoyed enormously.

Igor Kolinski did not enjoy it, because he wanted to keep George Sanders happy; so he blamed me. I went to George Sanders and apologised, but he could not have cared less. He grinned and went on playing his guitar. He also possessed a very pleasant singing voice and used to entertain us every evening.

Before returning to England, I received a letter addressed to 'The Genial kinematographical and theatrical author Sr Don Pertwee'. The letter started with the words: 'I am a great admirer of the work you are about to do.'

I do not know whether this fan ever saw the picture. I did not. If it was ever shown in Britain, I am not aware of it.

It was shown in America. I saw a review of it in *Variety*. The first thing I noticed was that I had not been given credit for writing it. The screenplay credit went to Julien Duvivier and Charles Spaak. I was very glad about this when I read the review.

Not long after this, dear old Otto Siessens turned up in London again, and asked how much I wanted for writing him a full script in one day. This was such an astonishing request that I quoted a rather low sum. With un-characteristic generosity he offered to double it if I would really do the job in a day. I took benzedrine and worked for just over 24 hours without stopping. Otto stood over me, every now and then giving me a kick when I looked like dropping off. He thanked me very much, took the script and disappeared, still owing me money. Subsequent letters to him evidently went astray.

In September 1950 I was reading my *Sunday Graphic* when I came across the following paragraph which made me sit up with a start:

> 'Michael Pertwee is off to Cannes at the Aga Khan's invitation. They'll discuss the possibilities of writing a film based on the Aga's life. And who can portray the Aga? They do say Paul Muni khan.'

This was news to me. The *Sheffield Telegraph* went a little further:

> 'The Aga Khan, spiritual leader of eight million Moslems, said at Deauville today that he had consented to a film of his life being made with scenario by Michael Pertwee. "I shall not be in the film personally; neither will the Begum," he said. "But I am being consulted about the production. I agree with what is to be done."'

A few days later I received a call from Geneva from a producer I had met during my wanderings, René Anglade, who explained the mystery. I was to fly straight to Cannes, put up at the Carlton, ring the Aga Khan at his villa and get straight down to work. The money would be big, since I would be required to follow the film to India and Africa. René Anglade would be in Cannes.

I hung up, packed, and caught a plane to Nice that same day. I booked in at the Carlton and, to show willing, called the Aga Khan before I had even unpacked. I was put on to a secretary. I announced that I was there and ready to start whenever His Highness felt inclined.

There was only one problem. The Aga Khan was not there. Neither was he expected. He was in Paris, and from Paris was shortly moving elsewhere. René wasn't there either. I managed to trace him in Geneva, called him and demanded to know what he was playing at. He told me not to worry. The Aga must have changed his itinerary. Fly straight to Paris, he said, and contact the Aga there. He would give me a great time in Gay Paree.

Luckily, I had not unpacked my case. It was only when I was excusing myself to a rather frightening looking man at the Carlton reception desk, that I remembered that I had not brought any money. There had been no time for travellers cheques and, after all, René was to have met me with all I needed.

I managed to scrape up enough to pay for the telephone calls, and to buy a third class rail ticket to Paris. I did not, however, book into a hotel in Paris. I was getting cagey. I went into a public call box and called my friend the Aga Khan from there.

I was connected with another secretary. The one at Cannes had been polite. This one was not. He did not know what I was talking about, he said. His Highness had certainly not given me, or anyone else, permission to work with him, and there was absolutely no point in my trying to get an interview. He hung up.

Since I was now completely broke, I thought this would be a good time to look up Gomez *père*, who was reportedly in Paris, Raoul Levy, who lived in Paris, and Otto Siessens, who had an office in Paris. They all owed me money and, even if they did not fully pay up, one of them would surely bail me out to the extent of a trip back to London.

By one of those odd coincidences, which keeps making me say what a small world it is, I spotted Raoul Levy sitting at Fouquets on the Champs Elysées. (He had not yet become a millionaire.) He made an appointment to meet me at his flat. I kept the appointment but he, predictably, did not. I tried Gomez *père*, but it seemed he had left town. Lastly, I invaded Otto Siessens' office where I was met by a man who looked exactly like Gomez *père*. This was not surprising, since he turned out to be Gomez *père's* elder *frère*, who worked for Otto. Gomez *frère* said he thought Otto was out, but would go and look. He went into an inner office then returned to say that, as he had feared, Otto was not there. I left a fairly uncivil message and walked into the corridor where I saw a figure slipping hastily into the lift. The doors closed before I could discover whether it was Otto, his twin brother or someone who looked exactly like him.

After that I dropped the foreign operators. To be fair to them, they also dropped me.

Part 12

Titubation Dropping

A FEW IGNORANT or dirty-minded people looking at the chapter heading may hope this describes how I entered the pornographic film market. Having skated discreetly over masturbation, the writer devotes a whole chapter to titubation.

Titubation, as anyone should know, is, in fact, fidgetiness, especially caused by nervous irritation. Otto Siessens and his ilk caused me titubation. The public who did not come to see *The Paragon* caused me titubation. The failure to get going at Ealing had caused me titubation.

I was enjoying writing again; I was busy; I was in reasonable demand; I was making money, but I still suffered from titubation.

In brief, I needed a solid success; something which would be both praised and profitable.

This finally came through Mario Zampi, who was to become a close friend.

Mario was Italian and intensely proud of it. He was a small man, quick of temper, quick to forgive. He never entirely conquered the English language, but had a better understanding of British comedy than any producer I have met. He was not a great director, but he possessed an infallible nose for what was funny and what was not. He was not particularly constructive in providing new ideas but, if he felt something was wrong, he was nearly always right. In a long association I only once came anywhere near having a fight with him. I felt he had gone back on something he had agreed to and, when he denied it, jokingly called him a liar. He jumped to his feet, thumped the desk and roared:

'I only lie to one person in this world and that's my wife.'

Mario had been one of the founders of Two Cities Films and, before the war, had produced the film version of Terence Rattigan's *French Without Tears*.

When Italy entered the war, he was interned, along with Charles Forte and most of the Italians in Britain. Their first prison had been in London, just off the Fulham Road. Many of the internees had money. They had the choice of some of the best chefs and pastrycooks in London and, as a result, they ate like kings. Upstairs was the British mess where their gaolers ate bully beef, dished up by an army cook. At every meal, with his mouth watering, the British orderly officer had to enter the prisoners' mess and ask: 'Any complaints?'

There were seldom any complaints. He would then walk upstairs and eat whatever the army cook had thought up for the day.

Mario was made the prison Camp Commandant. It was to him that the British Commanding Officer suggested it would save manpower if they all mucked in together and only had one kitchen and one menu. Mario black-mailed him into issuing some extra rations. Thereafter, the gaolers ate almost as well as the prisoners, which probably prevented a mutiny in the British army.

Mario found it hard going after the war and was looking for a comeback. He made it through an original idea of Jack Davies's, which Jack and I had been throwing around in our spare time. On meeting Mario I told him the idea and he bought it on the spot.

The picture was *Laughter in Paradise*. It starred Alastair Sim, Fay Compton, George Cole, A E Matthews and Joyce Grenfell. It was a riotous success with the public and was the box office hit of the year. Beyond the lonely voice of Milton Shulman, it received nothing but praise in every newspaper in the country.

It was not set up too easily. Alastair Sim was in great demand and was a hard man to please. Mario decided to approach him by the back door— *via* me.

I had just been elected to the Garrick Club, where I joined Roland as a member. Patrick Hastings had proposed me and I think Laurence Dunne, the London magistrate, seconded. Alastair Sim was also a member. Mario asked me to have a chat with him on an unofficial basis. Alastair promised to read it, but doubted if he was available, even if it proved a good part for him. I waited a week before I lunched at the club again. Alastair was sitting

125

at the far end of the long table. When he saw me he waved and mouthed: 'Very good indeed, but not for me.'

I had not expected him to accept; so, when we met for a drink afterwards, I did not pursue the subject. I accepted his refusal as final and chatted about other things. He then started talking about the story and all the things he had liked about it. Gradually, as he talked, he visibly warmed to the idea. By the time we went our separate ways he asked me not to tell Mario that he had refused it, as he would like a little more time to think. Eventually, he accepted. I am sure if I had pleaded with him to reconsider, he would never have played the part.

I also played in the picture, half-satisfying a secret desire to be an author-actor.* I was a randy bank clerk, who made a pass at a girl and got his face slapped. Mario had the time of his life with this shot, as if determined to teach me a lesson about wanting to act. On the first take the girl gave me a gentle slap. Mario said it was not hard enough. He gradually built up the slap until she was hitting me with all her strength. He shot the scene twenty-seven times. The next day I looked as if I had gone fifteen rounds with Joe Louis or Ivor Sainsbury.

Jack was still working on the *Daily Sketch* so I spent the pre-production days with Mario. We were still searching for a girl to play the young woman's role. Mario asked me to come to Ciro's Club where there was a dancer in the floor show who was very beautiful. He wondered if we might take a chance on her. We saw the show and I agreed with him about the girl. We brought her up to the office and talked with her. She was breathtakingly lovely with big gazelle eyes, a generous mouth—the kind of girl you could not stop looking at. After she had gone I said we must use her. Mario offered her the part which she turned down regretfully; something to do with her personal life. We cast Beatrice Campbell in the role. Hardly had we done this, than the girl reappeared to say she had changed her mind. She would like to play the part.

This was impossible, but Mario gave her a one-line bit, playing a cigarette girl in a night-club. Her only words were: 'Who wants a tiggy?'†

As a result of seeing her speak these four words ABC signed her up on a seven-year contract.

---

*This had been another Mitty dream.

†Memo to Jack Davies. It was my line.

This is how I jointly discovered Audrey Hepburn.

Another who played in the film was the character actor, Ernest Thesiger. He had a great sense of humour. With obvious enjoyment he told me he had been stopped by a lady in an underground station who said: 'Excuse me, *weren't* you Ernest Thesiger?'

I heard another story about him, though I cannot vouch for the truth of it. He was in Moscow on a theatrical tour. He went into one of the public conveniences and, finding himself alone, wrote on the wall 'Burgess loves Maclean'.

I wrote an original film story, *Interrupted Journey*. It was a thriller concerning a man's nightmarish experiences after causing a rail crash through pulling the communication cord. In the end it turned out to be a dream.

I was washing my car one day when my next door neighbour stopped to chat with me. He was Robert Garrett, who had just set up an independent film production company in partnership with Anthony Havelock-Allen. Tony had been a partner with David Lean and Ronald Neame in the immensely successful *Brief Encounter*.

Bobby Garrett casually asked if I had any original ideas for a film, as they were looking for one to put into immediate production. I gave him *Interrupted Journey*, which they bought the next day for the largest sum I had yet received.

Richard Todd, Valerie Hobson (Tony Havelock-Allen's wife), Tom Walls and a sex-bomb of the time, Christine Norden, were the stars.

Robert Hamer, who somehow got to hear about the deal, met Valerie Hobson and told her she would never get a usable script out of me. He had bad luck with his timing, because I delivered the script the next day and she liked it; but I must give him full credit for consistency, a consistency which was not reflected in his own later work, which rapidly degenerated into the second rate.

Interrupted Journey received a kindly press. The only shocking notice came from the critic of the *Daily Sketch*, who not only tore it to shreds, but also broke the unwritten laws of the game by giving away the fact that the story was a dream. My ability not to take bad reviews as a personal affront is illustrated here in that the critic was Jack Davies, with whom I was currently working. It did not affect our friendship in the least.

Jack and I collaborated on another film for Bobby Garrett. This was a screen adaptation of a stage play, *Curtain Up*.

The first task we were given was to seduce Robert Morley into playing the lead. He was another of those choosy actors who, we were told, had to be handled with great delicacy. We were to tell him the story and try to persuade him to play. We met him in his dressing-room after a matinée of the play *The Little Hut*. He was with his agent. He welcomed us with open arms, then promptly pushed us out, saying that he was discussing filthy lucre, a subject which he detested, but had to be dealt with. He would meet us at a nearby café in a few minutes. He joined us there, sat down, took out a pencil and said: 'Well, come along, tell me about your lovely, lovely story.'

I had detailed Jack to do the talking and he got off to a disastrous start.

'Bob,' he said, 'the first thing you should know is that yours is the *only* good part in the film.'

'In that case,' said Robert Morley, 'I don't want to do it. If the film falls flat on its face every time I'm not in a scene, I shall merely be picking up the pieces when I reappear, instead of making people laugh.'

Jack threw me a supplicating look, and I started to pick up our pieces. I told the story. Robert listened in silence, constantly doodling with his pencil on a napkin. At the end he said he liked it and would probably do it. He left us to return to the theatre.

I am a dedicated doodler myself so I picked up the napkin on which he had been doodling while I told the story. On it was written:

'£10,000 . . . . Ten Thousand . . . . Dix Mille . . . . Diez mil . . . . Dieci mille . . . . Zehn Tausend . . . .' etc.

Robert may have disliked discussing filthy lucre, but he had certainly been thinking about it while I told our tale. Anyway, he accepted the role, starring with Margaret Rutherford, and very funny he was, too.

I was still actively engaged on plays which still caused me a good deal of titubation.

Dick Rawlinson and I had re-written *Chain Male* for the fourth time. We deserved full marks for trying. John Counsell produced it at Windsor. It received a good press, several managements dickered with it, and Warner Brothers showed an interest in the film rights; but it all came to nothing.

I wrote two plays with Roland. The first, *Rough Shooting*, was also produced at Windsor. Hugh Latimer and Geraldine McKeown were in the cast. The play was a curious mixture of farce, comedy and thrills, concerning the downfall of a ruthless millionaire aboard his yacht. It sank without a trace.

The second play, *In the Bag*, was our first attempt at pure farce. It was tried out by the Folkestone Repertory Company, and provided us with another traumatic first night. The middle act contained the bones of the very complicated plot. There were two rather similar lines of dialogue in the act, both spoken by the same character. One line occurred ten minutes after the curtain rose; the other came three minutes before the curtain fell. On the opening night the actor concerned inadvertently spoke the second line first, and the actor to whom he was speaking followed on with his later speech. The result was that the curtain fell after an act of only twelve minutes instead of forty-five minutes. The entire plot, which would have made the third act comprehensible, had been cut out.

This was bad enough, but what we found even more depressing was that nobody noticed. As a result, we re-wrote the play, cutting out a good deal of the plot, which seemed a good idea, since no one had missed it the first time. The new version was tried out at Windsor by the ever faithful John Counsell, with Elspet Gray,* and William Franklyn (Sssch!) in the cast. The play is still available.

During these years John Counsell proved himself a most loyal and encouraging friend, and in no case could I blame either the direction or the acting performances for the failure of my plays to transfer. I only wish that some of my more recent efforts could have reached the West End *via* Windsor so that he could have reaped some little benefit from the faith he showed in me.

I was approached by Jack Waller to write the book of a muscial comedy. This was to be his return to the big time musical. He had originally presented the record breaking *No, No, Nanette!* His house was even called 'No, No, Nanette!' in memory of it.

The musical was an adaptation from the play *French, for Love*, by Margaret Steen and Derek Patmore. It was about the seduction of a young man by an older woman. After my experiences on the Paris—Biarritz train I seemed a good choice.

William Mollison, a brother of the actor Clifford Mollison, was the director. Geoffrey Wright wrote the music. He was the composer of *Transatlantic Lullaby*, which had been a big hit and is still heard today. The lyric writer was an unknown quantity. He was a quiet, withdrawn young man with a pale, worried face. Jack Waller forecast that he and I would team up to be the new Rogers and Hammerstein. He was wrong; but Sandy Wilson went on to write *The Boy Friend* and other successes.

---

*Brian Rix's wife.

The cast included Henry Kendal and Sally Ann Howes, Bobby Howes's daughter. It was her first musical. She had a lovely voice, but was inexperienced. The orchestra leader used to ring a little bell before each song to set her on the right course. Once locked in she was a delight to hear, and was a delightful girl, too.

The musical's title was *Caprice*—and it was a disaster.

Jack Waller fell ill and went away. During rehearsals it was apparent that William Mollison did not have a sure grip on the reins. He let the whole thing slide along, despite the fact that the show was obviously overlength.

We opened in Glasgow for a two-week run. The Glasgow *Evening News* said:

> 'Allowances must be made for the first night problems but the show will require drastic tightening and speeding up.'

This was putting it mildly. The show ran well over three hours and needed to be cut by at least three quarters of an hour. We waited for a rehearsal call, but William Mollison appeared satisfied, and made no comments at all.

After the second night Henry Kendal came to me in desperation, and said that if William Mollison was not going to call a rehearsal, then I should, so that some of the deadwood could be removed.

I called a rehearsal, and we cut half an hour, which improved things considerably. William Mollison watched the show that evening, asked why the cuts had been made and insisted that they all go back. That was the only firm action he took. The show then remained as it was. It moved on to Manchester where it quite deservedly expired.

My private life was not without its titubation but eased as my four-year-long engagement finally came to an end.

Periodically, Carolyn came to stay with me. Her visits were now becoming a joy instead of being painful for both of us. In the early days her appearance had been a reminder to me of a continuing unhappiness, while, to her, they had been strange and frightening. She was homesick, and although she did her infant best to put on a brave smile, it would crumple at the slightest provocation, such as the time when she refused to eat her supper because she found the London cold ham was not nearly as nice as the Penzance cold ham.

My mother and stepmother both died suddenly within weeks of each other.

My mother lived in a village in Sussex where she was much loved. There was a mountain of wreaths and flowers outside the cottage before the funeral.

Uncle Guy drove over to attend the funeral. I knew he had arrived when I heard his voice exclaiming: 'Good Heavens! *Flowers!*'

Uncle Guy was always surprised by things like that. At Christmas he would exclaim: 'Presents!' as if he had never heard of people giving presents. He had only sent one Christmas card in his life and that was when he received a card that someone had forgotten to sign.

During the foregathering of the mourners in the living-room I noticed Uncle Guy had disappeared. I looked into mother's garden and saw him picking a big bunch of flowers. I imagined he was making up for not bringing any himself, and proposed to put the flowers with the others outside the house. I was wrong. He stuck them in his car and took them home. I remember reflecting sadly that, of all the people present, my mother would have enjoyed this more than anyone.

Jon went to Australia on a variety tour for which he was paid a fortune. Coby and I gave him a nasty fright by stealing some Admiralty notepaper and recalling him to the Navy for a limited period of service to start one day before he was due to leave for Australia. We closed every possible avenue of escape by stating that this special call-up, which was confined to officers who had been previously discharged from the Navy on medical grounds, could not be avoided for reasons of health, or on any personal grounds whatsoever.

Jon's agent knew Emanuel Shinwell, who was then War Minister. He telephoned Mr Shinwell personally to intercede on Jon's behalf, and Mr Shinwell promised to do what he could. Since it was an entirely fictitious call-up I can only think that there may still be someone at the Admiralty trying to trace its source.

On another occasion I telephoned Jon and he did not recognise my voice. When he asked who it was, I said I was Inspector Welling of Scotland Yard, and that I expected he knew what I was calling him about. There was a very long pause, then Jon said: 'Yes.'

He has steadfastly refused to tell me what it was.

I sometimes went to parties given by Stephen Ward. These parties were not the kind which were to make him famous and infamous a few years later at the time of the Profumo affair. There were lots of pretty people and quite a lot of pretty famous people. He was liked as a host, admired as an artist and used extensively as an osteopath.

We met Danny Kaye at one party. Jon and I chatted to him for some time and, looking at them standing together, it was quite uncanny. They might have been twins.

131

Other people were to notice this and when Mel Frank and Norman Panama (Mel was later to become an important figure in my life) made their film *Knock on Wood,* Jon doubled for Danny Kaye in all the London location shots.

One of the signs of growing older is a tendency to dislike what is happening in the world around one. I am no exception to the rule. I feel positive tubation at the modern film producers' excessive preoccupation with tits. I can even growl at some aspects of the permissive society—but I still feel sorry for Stephen Ward. It would be wrong to paint him in any way as an admirable figure. He was, according to the rules of our society, an immoral man. He was a victim of his own vanity, weakness and, above all, stupidity in trying to take on a vindictive establishment; but to hound him, try him, and convict him of being a pimp, who lived off the immoral earnings of women was ridiculous. He did not have to. Stephen had many friends, most of whom were conspicuous by their absence when he needed them, but I do not believe there is one person who knew him, who would come forward today and label him as a professional pimp. He was, if you like, a social pimp. He was known as a man who knew a lot of pretty girls. He was a snob and a social climber and this was a good passport into the kind of circle he liked. I firmly believe that if he were brought to trial today he would not be convicted. Anyone bothering to read the details of his trial and the frail and dubious evidence against him must be given food for thought; but they found him guilty, and rather than face prison and a second trial on even frailer abortion charges, he killed himself.

Another great party-giver during the postwar years was Arthur Ferrier, the cartoonist, whose lovely ladies graced the *News of the World.*

Arthur Ferrier's New Year's Eve party was the most sought-after occasion in London. If you were not asked to Arthur's you were definitely not 'in'. Here, every year, gathered an array of stars who gave a cabaret which would have cost thousands of pounds. One after another they would get up and do their stuff, Peter Ustinov, Theodore Bikel, Frances Day and, of course, brother Jon among them.

One party was attended by a handsome young man, whom nobody knew. After a particularly stellar cabaret, the lady who had brought the stranger announced that he would like to perform. He rose, carrying a copy of *The Bedside Esquire.* He opened it and read aloud for about twenty minutes. He read well, but it was hardly guaranteed to entertain a hundred tipsy people. However, we listened politely, a little stunned. When he finally closed the book he received a nice round of applause, perhaps in recognition of his nerve. Then everybody began to ask who he was, which, I am sure, is exactly what he wanted. His name was Laurence Harvey.

I did not meet Larry personally until about twenty years later, at a party at the Trattoria Terrazza in Soho, given by Sammy Davis Jnr and Peter Lawford. As we stood chatting on the pavement outside the restaurant, fortified by a good deal of wine, I mentioned to Larry that I intended writing a piece about him in my autobiography. He asked what it was and I told him. He uttered a great shout of laughter, and gave me a smacking kiss, to the astonishment of quite a crowd of people. I have taken this as his permission to write the story.

I suppose, from the point of view of my ego, the most satisfying event of this period was my collaboration with W Somerset Maugham.

In 1949 was published *A Writer's Notebook*, a series of notes on characters and ideas, which Maugham had jotted down from 1894 to 1944. He signed the book for me and wrote:

'A book to dip into here and there and now and then.'

I dipped into it avidly as I did with everything he wrote.

I came across a story that someone had told him in 1938. Two tea planters, A and B, lived together in the hills. A used to receive a lot of letters by every mail. B never received any letters at all. After many months, B, who hankered to have a letter, just one letter, offered A five pounds to sell him one of his letters. A laughingly agreed, let him have his pick from the next batch of mail, and accepted five pounds in payment. Later, A casually asked B who the letter had been from, but B refused to tell him. It was now his private letter because he had paid for it. Nothing would shift him, and A nearly went mad trying to find out what the letter was.

That was all. The story ended there without disclosing what had happened. Of it Maugham wrote:

'I suppose if I belonged to the modern school of story writers I should write it just as it is and leave it. It goes against the grain with me. I want a story to have form, and I don't see how you can give it that unless you can bring it to a conclusion that leaves no legitimate room for questioning.'

I thought of an ending to the story. Somewhat nervously I wrote to Maugham, told him my suggested end, and asked if he would allow me to write a television play around it. He replied with a charming letter, congratulated me on a very good idea, and gave his permission to go ahead.

The result was an hour's BBC Television play called *Rainy Day* starring George Cole and Edward Evans as the planters. It was quite remarkably successful. The *Star* wrote:

> 'High marks to Somerset Maugham who started it, to Michael Pertwee who carried it on and finished it and to Eric Fawcett who produced it so admirably.'

The *Daily Herald* voted it the best TV play of the year.

Some time later, Alfred Hitchcock bought the rights and re-made it, directing it himself, for his hour long American series, *Suspicion*. In this version Robert Flemyng took over from Edward Evans.

This was not the end of the story. Following the American showing, I was sued for three million dollars damages, together with Hitchcock, the Ford Motor Company and CBS, by the widow of an American gentleman, who I think lived at Atlanta. She claimed that, jointly, we had stolen a story, written by her husband some twenty years before, which had been published in a local newspaper.

This was no frivolous suit. I have no doubt the lady felt she had a cast-iron case. On the face of it she had, when one considered the evidence, having read her late husband's story.

(a) The situation of the two tea planters and the sale of the letter was identical.

(b) The end twist (which I had invented) was also identical.

(c) The story had been submitted by her to the Hitchcock organisation some months previously, *and had been rejected and returned.*

On paper it looked a strong case indeed. On the other hand, there was no reason to doubt that Somerset Maugham had himself written down the situation some twenty years before. There was absolutely no doubt that I had never seen the American story and had thought up the ending myself.

There was, of course, a simple explanation. The story of the two planters was one of those tales which was being bandied about in the 'thirties. Maugham heard it, and so did the American.

As to the coincidence of the same ending, there were not very many dramatic endings which could be invented. Mine had been that planter A was driven mad by not knowing what his letter had contained. He flipped and killed B to get at the letter, only to find it was an advertisement for a raincoat.

It is not really surprising that two people came to the conclusion that a man, living in the jungle, might be driven to insanity and murder over such a trivial irritation.

There remained the unfortunate fact that the story had been submitted to Hitchcock and rejected. The answer to this was that he had not read it personally but someone in his scenario department had done so, and had not liked it.

I had to undergo a very rare legal proceeding. I appeared in a small court at the Old Bailey. There were only three people in court—myself, a judge, and Mr Sidney Silverman, MP, who had been retained by the plaintiffs to cross-examine me. I can honestly say that the four hours I spent being cross-examined by Mr Silverman are among the most unpleasant of my life. From the start he elected to act as if I was a thief and a brazen liar. He hissed, scoffed, ranted and occasionally shouted. His inferred contention was that Somerset Maugham and myself must have conspired together. It was all very well for Maugham to produce a book in 1949 and say that a story he put in it had been told to him in 1938. What if the story had been told to him in *1948*? How else could I possibly explain the unbelievable coincidence of the identical endings? He would not let me try to explain anything. I know he was only doing his job. He probably had nothing but the kindest feelings towards me, but he made me hate him. It was therefore with enormous satisfaction that I finally knocked the wind right out of his sails—through a piece of amazing good fortune.

At the time of the American showing of the play I had been living at 3 Justice Walk, Chelsea, SW3. One of Mr Silverman's main points against me was that I had been sent a letter by the plaintiff's lawyers which I had ignored. Had I received this letter? If so, then why hadn't I answered it? I honestly could not remember whether I had received the letter or not. It is possible that I had and, on reading that some crazy American was preparing to sue me for three million dollars, I had shoved it in the wastepaper basket. I said I could not remember if I had received it or not.

Mr Silverman then produced a copy of the letter and handed it to me. He asked me to read it, which I did. He then implored me to speak the truth 'for once' and say whether anyone in their right mind could forget receiving such a serious communication. I could only repeat I did not remember receiving it.

'Is that your name on the letter?'

'Yes.'

'Is that your address on the letter?'

I was about to reply that it was, when I noticed that the address was 3 Justice Walk, Chelsea, SW3. As it happened I had just moved to another address which, by a fortunate coincidence, was 3 *Paradise* Walk, Chelsea, SW3.

'No,' I said. 'This is addressed to 3 Justice Walk, SW3. My address is 3 Paradise Walk, SW3.'

Both Number 3; both Walks; both SW3; but I was no longer in Justice. Mr Silverman threw down his papers as if there was no justice in the world, and glared at me as if wishing to see me in hell for being in Paradise. He asked no more questions.

It was fortunate that he did not. I had answered his question literally, so had not committed any perjury; but I had only moved the week before, and would have been bound to say so had he phrased the question differently or cared to pursue the matter.

I was not bothered again, but heard afterwards that some small settlement was made out of court.

Jon, meanwhile, was going great guns on radio, the music-hall and, it seemed, in bed.

One day a formidable lady in a mink coat arrived at Roland's house, forced her way in and confronted Roland with the words: 'Your son, Jon, seduced my daughter and she has never seen him since.'

'Let's get this straight,' said Roland. 'Are you complaining that he seduced her, or that he hasn't continued to do so?'

I gained a reputation of another kind. Mario Zampi offered Jack Davies and me a long-term contract, so Jack quit the *Daily Sketch* and we set up as a writing team.

Mario gave this news to someone in Wardour Street, who said:

'Yes, they're queer as coots, you know. Michael made him give up the *Sketch* and they've set up house together.'*

He may have been surprised when, shortly afterwards, still grimly following in Roland's footsteps, I fell in love and married for the second time.

---

*It always puzzled me why, supposing we were queer, I should force Jack to leave the *Daily Sketch*. I assume that he was to stay at home to do the cooking and housework.

Part 13

★★★★★★★★★★★★★★★★★★★★★★★★★★★★★★★★★★★★★★

Wife Dropping (Two)

★★★★★★★★★★★★★★★★★★★★★★★★★★★★★★★★★★★★★★

VALERIE HARRISON WAS twenty-four, and an extremely efficient film production secretary. She had worked for Danny, who originally introduced us. She had dark hair, flecked with grey, a big, wide smile, cat-like eyes, a distracting figure, a quick mind and, on occasion, a biting tongue. She possessed a natural flair for interior decoration, and was a cook of Cordon Bleu class. We were married in the spring of 1952, and spent one very happy year together.

Robert Clark, who was then running Associated British Film Studios, under whose banner *Laughter in Paradise* had been made, asked Jack and me to write an original musical film for Gracie Fields. Before the war her films had been immensely popular. Robert felt she could still be a big draw, given the right subject. Mario Zampi would produce and direct. The major problem, it seemed, was going to be persuading Gracie to do it. She had more or less retired to Capri, where she owned a restaurant and a swimming pool. She had been married for many years to Monty Banks, the Italian film director, who had died suddenly. Had she remained a widow, the task of persuading her to return to the hustle and bustle of film making might have been easy, but she had recently startled the world by quietly marrying Boris Alperovici, a resident of Capri. It was said they had met when he came to her house to repair a radio set.

Gracie did not need to work and, as a newly-wed, might require considerable persuasion.

We thought up our story, then, with Robert Clark and Mario Zampi, set off for Capri to sell the idea to Gracie.

137

The short sea crossing from Naples to Capri was the roughest I have ever endured. When we docked at Capri I was barely able to stand, and Jack had to help me ashore.

We drove to Gracie's house on the other side of the island. Gracie opened the door herself, and said: 'Hullo!' I said: 'Lavatory! Quick!'

She looked a bit startled, and pointed to a door in the hall. Without another word I left them. They adjourned to the dining-room for a meal. No one came near me for half an hour. This was unfortunate because, although it was a very nice lavatory, there was no toilet paper and I was too shy to yell for paper. Eventually someone came to the door to find out if I was still alive, and I was able to explain my predicament.

Boris, Gracie's new husband, proved a lovable character. He is a born handyman and loves gadgetry. He and Gracie were ardent amateur ciné enthusiasts, and were convinced that we should enjoy seeing their films. Boris, believing in a captive audience, rigged up a curious device which enabled the films to be projected on to the ceiling. He ran them during mealtimes, so that we sat around the table with necks craned upwards, only looking down briefly to steer food safely into our mouths.

Boris gave another astonishing exhibition of do-it-yourself handywork. The weather was cold, so Gracie suggested a log fire. This proved difficult to light. Boris thereupon fetched the Hoover, and dismantled it before our eyes. His intention, he explained, was to make the Hoover blow rather than suck. Having made his adjustments, he levelled the instrument at the fire and switched on. The Hoover then blew a concentrated jet of air which I estimated came out at over 100 mph. The result was cataclysmic. Flames and smoke shot out in all directions, together with a cloud of blinding ash, which put the passive Mount Vesuvius to shame. Coughing and spluttering everyone fled from the room, except Boris, who stood at his post amid the smoke and ash, continuing to direct the blast into the now nearly empty grate.

'He's stubborn, you know,' said Gracie, fondly.

Gracie and Boris gave a big lunch party in the open air at their pool restaurant. Robert Clark, who is the most respectably married man I know, sat next to a French lady, who did not speak one single word of English. This resulted in a somewhat silent meal so far as Robert and the lady were concerned. Finally, toward the end of the meal, he leaned towards her confidentially and said, in his Scottish accent: 'I'm verra sorry that I haven't been able to talk to you, but I don't speak a word of French.'

138

The lady looked completely blank, not having understood a word of this either. Robert smiled, nodded and continued: 'Except,' he said, '*Voulez vous coucher avec moi?*'

He chuckled at his little joke. The lady let out a furious 'Augh!' and turned her back on him. Robert looked hurt and thereupon set about making it far worse, by saying: 'I didn't mean "*Voulez vous coucher avec moi?*" ye understand. I meant that "*Voulez vous coucher avec moi?*" is the only French I know.'

So far as the lady was concerned here was a man who would not take 'Augh!' for an answer, and just went on propositioning her in an inexusably brash and typically British manner.

Since the film was to take place in a Capri setting we were allowed to write the picture out there, and were joined by Dorothy and Valerie. Jack and I worked. Jack complained endlessly about the foreign cooking, and once sent back some sardines because they were fresh and not tinned. He travelled badly in those days. Dorothy lapped up the sun, and Valerie lapped up the torrid looks of a cloud of beach boys who settled round her like flies every time she went to the beach.

Gracie and Boris paid a visit to London and read the final script.

We were in Robert Clark's house in Hendon when the verdict came—an enthusiastic 'Yes'. Robert was so pleased that he dashed from the room and returned with a bottle of whisky in each hand. He presented Jack with one and me with the other.

A few days later there was a conference of all the ABC top brass at Elstree. High on the agenda was the Gracie Fields script. Mario, Jack and myself were invited to attend.

Jack and I sat like Cheshire cats. This was our moment. Robert Clark would rise and tell all those present how we had triumphed. He rose all right—but only to announce that the subject was no good and was to be shelved.

I wish I could have seen the expression on my face. However, I saw Jack's and it was a picture.

We never received an explanation for this *volte-face*. I can only guess that Warner Brothers, who had some say in ABC, may possibly have thought that Gracie was no longer a box office attraction. Certainly the decision was political, and not on account of the script. Jack and I had our whisky to prove that.

This was not the end of the Capri film. Mario sold it to the Americans, Mel Shavelson and Jack Rose, who made it under the title *It Started in Naples*.

Some years later, by sheer chance, I found myself in Capri on holiday at the same time as they were making the picture there. I introduced myself to the charming Jack Rose, who was very kind about our script, and almost apologetic for having made 'a few' alterations to it. Our story had Gracie as a Yorkshire spinster making her first trip abroad, who comes to Capri in search of an orphaned child, who was being looked after by tough Capri fisherman—an Anthony Quinn type.

Jack Rose introduced me to the actors who were now playing these two roles. The star playing the Gracie Fields part was also most complimentary about the role. I found myself slightly at a loss for words—for it turned out to be Clark Gable, who was not exactly type-cast for a Gracie Fields part. The same could be said about the casting for the rough, tough Capri fisherman. This role was played by a young actress called Sophia Loren. Vittorio de Sica was also in the cast, and a thoroughly enjoyable film emerged.

The second picture Jack and I wrote for Mario was *Top Secret*, starring George Cole, Oscar Homolka and Nadia Gray. It was a story of the little man in charge of the sanitary department of Harwell, who inadvertently goes to Moscow with the plans of Britain's atom bomb instead of, as he thinks, his design for a new lavatory complex. It was quite funny, but did nothing like the business that *Laughter in Paradise* had done. Oddly enough, it became a little classic in America under the title *Mr Potts goes to Moscow*.

To Mario any excuse to return to Italy was a good excuse and, on the assumption that he could keep our noses to the grindstone, he took us to Ischia to write it. Ischia, unlike Capri, was completely undeveloped at that time.

Ischia is a volcanic island, famous for its thermal mud baths. While we were there we met Tony Havelock-Allen, for whom I had written *Interrupted Journey*. We ran into Tony, a lithe and sprightly figure, walking in the town. He had come, he said, to take the thermal baths, not that there was anything wrong with him, but just for the experience. A couple of days later we met an old gentleman, walking very slowly with the aid of a stick. It was Tony Havelock-Allen. He had taken his thermal bath and, the following day had found himself almost paralysed, either with rheumatism or a slipped disc. It may have been sheer coincidence, but it caused me abruptly to change my plan to try a thermal bath.

I suppose 1953 can be marked as the year in which I became 'famous'. As a reasonably successful writer it was a little irritating to become a nationally known figure, with a large fan mail, entirely through my regular appearance on two BBC Television panel games.

These were *Down you Go!* which was a kind of visual crossword puzzle, and *Guess my Story*, in which the panel had to guess the identity of 'guests' who were connected with the previous week's headline news stories.

I do not know why I proved a reasonably popular TV personality. I rarely said anything clever or outrageous. My most sensational moment was being bitten to the bone by one of the 'guests', a monkey, which had fallen madly in love with James Robertson Justice's beard, but evidently disliked me on sight. James had recently returned from a South American film festival where the local paper had written:

> 'Among the British stars arrived today is the lovely English actress James Robertson Justice.'

Success on TV is an elusive thing. Many panelists, specially the women, are desperately keen, swotting up like sixth formers and hissing: 'Good luck everyone! *Good luck!*' just before transmission.

Others try too hard to be controversial. I think Ken Tynan, a man of enormous intelligence, did himself little credit by being the first person to say 'fuck' on TV. Anyone can do it, just as anyone who feels in the mood can write it on a wall. I think he should have left it to one of the many thousands of TV personalities, who have less intelligent things to say than he.

The secret of being successfully controversial is to appear not to try to be controversial. The outstanding example was Gilbert Harding. You either loved or hated Gilbert. His anger was often unreasonable. His bullying tactics against unfortunates whom he considered to be of inferior intelligence were unforgivable, but he was completely sincere. Gilbert's tragedy was that the more successful he became on television the more ashamed he was of it. He really resented becoming a national figure through shocking the public on *What's my Line?*

Gilbert was the original choice for Chairman of *Guess my Story* with a panel consisting of myself, Jack Train, Joy Adamson and Helen Cherry.* He clearly detested the whole thing and was replaced by Kim Peacock who, in turn, handed over to Peter West.

---

*Helen Cherry is married to Trevor Howard.

141

Helen Cherry and I survived into the main run of the show. Helen was, like me, one of those who did not take it too seriously. She looked gorgeous, was relaxed and came across as the charmer that she is. Marghanita Laski on *Down you Go!* approached the whole thing with a touch of the Gilbert Hardings about her and could be deliciously sour on occasions.

On the whole, professionally funny men, whether writers or actors, fail to come across on panel shows. Comedians without a script are often a disaster, while humorous writers need more time to think up their verbal gems than television allows. Frank Muir and Denis Norden are notable exceptions to this. Paul Jennings on *Down you Go!*, to my mind, never lived up to his proven capabilities as a humorist. He appeared to try too hard.

The television camera can also be cruelly deceptive. Wolf Mankowitz came on one week. He was very nervous, very anxious to do well, and completely open to advice from all the old hands. He came across as aggressive, over-confident and rather rude, which was absolutely false.

I suppose our most exciting night on *Guess my Story* was when Gerald Kersh, the novelist, was a guest panelist. There is at the BBC a room with drinks and refreshments called *Hospitality*, where the chairman, panel and producer have a quick drink before transmission. It was all too clear, while we were in *Hospitality*, that Gerald had received hospitality before he arrived. A conference was hastily convened at the end of a passage, attended by Peter West, Ronnie Waldman, Head of Light Entertainment, and our producer. The question was, should Gerald be allowed to appear or not? It was reminiscent of Eisenhower's agonising decision about invading Europe. There were only minutes in which they could come to a decision one way or the other. As they whispered together at the end of the passage, I came out on my way to the loo and, for a bit of fun, staggered towards them and fell flat on my face. This was not a popular joke.

Finally, they decided to risk it, and Gerald took his seat in the Studio. The ensuing half hour was clearly a torment for poor Peter West, who was fairly new to the game and did not give the impression of a man who could cope easily with a crisis.

Ninety-nine per cent of the programme passed miraculously without trouble. Every time the camera turned to Gerald Kersh he raised a finger and, very loudly, said: 'Beep!'

Before the final notes of his 'Beep' echoed away, the camera moved quickly on to the next panelist, and so it continued. A little colour returned to Peter West's cheeks as the half hour neared its end. As always, he thanked the team individually, ending with Gerald Kersh who, when the camera rested on him, now spoke clearly for the first time: 'I would have answered all these questions,' he said, 'if I had not been suffering from worms.'

It would be a lie to say that I did not enjoy the panel games, and my temporary fame, which, I suppose, lasted for about two years. One of my few remaining fantasies was to become an actor and this was the closest I had come to it. Everyone, or nearly everyone, enjoys being recognised and receiving fan mail. I still keep my favourite letter from J Beecher, aged 12, which simply said:

> 'Dear Sir,
> Please may I have a photo of your person?'

I consulted a legal friend about this and it was decided it would be safer just to send the normal photograph.

I went to Blackpool, with a number of other celebrities, for some enormous charity fête, where I had to auction a tie which had been presented by none other than Jon Pertwee. It received rather a poor reception and was bought in for 10/6d by Al Read, who was so popular up there that he nearly lost his own clothes every time he appeared in public. When we got back to the bus he found he had left his hat behind in the official tent. I offered to retrieve it for him to save him being mobbed again.

'Oh, no!' he said. 'I love it.'

He is one of the few celebrities I know who quite openly admits relishing the adulation.

Jon was a bit jealous of my new-found notoriety. He thought I was doing quite well enough as a writer without invading his market. He got a little of his own back when he asked me to write some material for his television show, and also to play straight man to him. I leapt at this as being another step in the direction of M Pertwee, actor. I carefully wrote the material and it sounded pretty good in rehearsal. However, when it came to transmission, Jon, who is an expert at ad libbing did not speak one of the lines I had written, or stick to the script in anything but the vaguest way. Since I was making my first appearance as a performer I was struck dumb. I don't know if he did it on purpose but I never risked it again.

The public's attitude to meeting a television celebrity is interesting. It is almost as if they think of him as two different people. I once went into a florist to send some flowers. The pretty girl serving me said: 'Aren't you Michael Pertwee?'

'Yes.'

'There!' she said. 'You know you *look* exactly like him!'

I had a curious experience walking through Berwick Market, Soho, one day. I heard a piercing whistle and turned to see a small, middle-aged cockney, in charge of a fruit barrow, who beckoned to me. I approached him and he said: 'Aren't you Michael Peewee?'

'Yes,' I said, pleased, as ever.

'Are you the brother of Jon Peewee?'

'Yes.'

'Then tell 'im he's a cunt,' he said.

I called Jon and gave him the message. He was very hurt and wanted to know why. I told him that I hadn't waited to ask for reasons.

About five years later Jon was walking through Berwick Market when he heard a whistle. He turned to see a man in charge of a fruit barrow beckoning to him. He went over.

'You're Jon Peewee, aren't you?'

'That's right.'

'Well, you're a cunt.'

The man must be given full marks for consistency.

By the time Independent Television arrived, my star was already on the wane. I did one commercial for Cadbury's Drinking Chocolate, and the two panel games on BBC finally expired.

The transient nature of television fame was well illustrated a couple of years later, when I was buying a ticket for the Motor Show at Earl's Court. The ticket seller looked at me closely and said: 'Aren't you whatsisname?'

'Yes,' I said.

'I thought you were,' she said.

I started another career in 1953, writing the story and balloons for a strip cartoon in the *Daily Herald*. It was called *Bruce Hunter*, who was a kind of poor man's Rip Kirby. It had been running for about seven years and was reputedly a firm favourite. Its artist was Maz, a very pleasant Dutchman, who could draw as sexy a girl as I have ever seen. It appeared he needed some assistance in stories. They paid me over £3000 a year for work which averaged about two hours a week. One day's dialogue would be three balloons saying: 'Hands Up;' 'Go to Hell;' 'Don't be a fool man, you're cornered!'

There seemed absolutely no reason why I should not continue to earn £3000 a year for at least another seven years. Unhappily, after only a few weeks, there was a big shake-up on the *Herald*, and a new Editor took over. To everyone's chagrin, one of his first actions was to kill Bruce Hunter. We were in the middle of a story in which bodies were lying all over Europe. It was going to take at least three months to tidy them all up. This did not suit the new Editor at all. I was told to dispose of them in ten days.

The Art Editor took Maz and me out to lunch and told us not to worry. He said that this was an extremely foolish action on the new Editor's part. Bruce Hunter was one of the paper's most popular features, had been running seven years and the public outcry would have him back in no time. He was wrong. I met him again some time later and asked, as a matter of interest, how big the outcry had actually been. He shook is head, looking very puzzled.

'Extraordinary!' he said. 'Seven years! Seven years! There was only *one* letter, and that said "Thank God!"'

Also in 1953 I wrote a six part television thriller serial for the BBC entitled *Strictly Personal* which achieved big ratings.

One of the fan letters I received was from J. Smedley (aged 13) which read:

> 'I am one of the admirers of the thrill-a-second *Strictly Personal*. In the last episode I was covered in sweat near the end.'

Its star was Ann Crawford, who was married to Wallace Douglas. She was a lovely girl and a talented actress. Unhappily, this was one of her last performances for she died soon afterwards.

I managed to get Valerie a tiny part in the serial. Wally and Ann were very kind to her and helped with after-hour rehearsals, which she badly needed in view of her comparative inexperience.

I cannot say that 1953 was the year which made Valerie famous, but it did make her bosom famous. We had somehow got on to the theatre first night list, which is my idea of a fate worse than death. We solemnly trooped along to every opening night, whether or not it was anything we wanted to see. For these occasions Valerie produced a series of plunging necklines, which sent the photographers wild, and must have infuriated numbers of other first nighters who aspired to get their pictures in the papers. We were no sooner in the lobby when, like hounds at the kill, the photographers leapt forward and dragged Valerie away. They stood on chairs, balconies and stairs to get high-angle shots. It was a sad breakfast indeed the following day if at least one paper did not carry her cleavage prominently displayed.

I had by this time become fairly resigned to the fact that what I had taken to be an ambition on her part to become an actress was, in fact, an absolute obsession, which took precedence over everything.

Looking back I am astonished at the amount of words I turned out in 1953.

I wrote two stage plays. The first, *Death and Brown Windsor*, based on the Haigh murders, has never done anything more than reps and amateurs. The second, *Tell the Marines!* was another collaboration with Roland, in which we decided we had found the key to a fortune.

At this time a young actor named Brian Rix, who had not been notably successful in provincial repertory, had suddenly burst into the West End and was packing them in at the Whitehall Theatre in an army farce by Colin Morris, *Reluctant Heroes*. Roland and I went to see it. When we came out, we decided it was all too easy. Harmless slapstick, discreet lavatory humour, no subtlety, a series of mechanically, although cleverly worked out 'routines', and yet the public lapped it up, and the author raked it in.

So we sat down and wrote a sequel. All went according to plan. Brian read it, liked it and optioned it. Too easy, as we had thought. He decided to send it out on tour to test its strength. Wally Patch starred as a bullying sergeant major. Brian directed the play himself. On its opening week it did better business than had *Reluctant Heroes*, at the same provincial theatre. We started to work out how we would spend our fortune. Then, as the tour progressed, business dropped and, with the drop in business, so Brian's enthusiasm waned. At the end of the tour he decided not to go ahead with it.

I learned a valuable lesson from this. It is *not* easy to write farce—successful farce. It is probably more difficult than any other type of play. It is absolutely fatal to approach farce writing in a cynical frame of mind which says: 'Anything for a laugh.' Farce has to combine the incredible with being credible. Nothing fails like excess. Laughter dies the moment audiences cease to believe what they are seeing. A man losing his trousers can only be funny if there is a good reason for him to lose them. If it is done for the sake of a cheap laugh, it will not raise a titter. You cannot afford to let up in a farce. A pleasant verbal love scene, which would be quite acceptable in a play by William Douglas-Home, would kill a farce stone dead. Thus the farce author has a constant, desperate search for action which moves from one high spot to the next, giving the audience the minimum of time to think and dissect. You cannot write anyone really unpleasant into a farce. Even the 'heavy' must be funny and reasonably sympathetic. You cannot be too near the knuckle, because the farce audience is a family audience. Thus a fine balance must be struck between good honest vulgarity and a deeper exploration of sexual problems. A study of the majority of farces will show that however evil the intentions of any character he very rarely makes it with a woman. Most of the fun of

David Niven laughs his head off at the script of *Happy Ever After*. Co-writer (*left*) Jack Davies and myself react suitably.

Dining after the premiere of *Happy Ever After*. (*l to r*): Me, Valerie French, (Sir) Charles Forte, Yvonne de Carlo, a guest, and Jack Davies.

With Julie Andrews on the set of *The Sound of Music* in Hollywood. They told me at the time they thought they were making 'a nice little picture'—it took more money than almost any other film in history.

farce is found in a *failure* to score. A farce is not so much written as constructed, piece by piece, to form a whole. I would advise nobody to try their hand at it who is not prepared for months of hard, and sometimes soul-destroying, work.

The debacle of *Tell the Marines* had one positive result in that it laid the foundations of an abiding friendship between myself, Brian and his wife, Elspet. However, this was not enough for me. I hate to be defeated, and I swore that I would one day write him a farce, which he would not only option, but also present in the West End. I had to wait sixteen years to achieve this.

In the summer I found time for a brief and happy holiday with Valerie in the south of France. From there she flew to Rome for a scheduled three days, to make a film test. She departed in floods of tears at the thought of three days separation, and stayed in Rome for nearly three months.

It was an unhappy situation after barely fifteen months of marriage and left me with little confidence in the future. I was partly assisted in coping with the situation by an involuntary feeling of sympathy for her childlike capacity for lapping up the tired old lines with which she had obviously been saturated in Rome, then the world's capital for fringe producers, who produced little else but tired old lines. Anyone as wide-eyed had to be due for fearful disillusionment.

I still recall the mixture of irritation and compassion which I felt when she turned on me one day and said:

'Have *you* ever bought anyone an entire flower stall?'

I said I hadn't, but only because I'd be worried what the girl would do with a bloody great barrow in her sitting-room.

My image as a romantic figure had become severely tarnished by the Roman holiday, and the result was a temporary separation followed by a more or less successful reconciliation.

Jack and I had written our third picture for Mario, an 'Oirish' comedy called *Happy Ever After*, which starred David Niven, Yvonne de Carlo and Barry Fitzgerald. Also in the cast was that great old actor A E Matthews, who played a master of hounds. In the film he died after being thrown by his horse over a six foot wall. Matty insisted on riding the horse on location, which alarmed everybody. There was a scene in which he had to approach camera on horseback, rein in the horse, then speak a couple of lines of dialogue. His memory for lines was not too good and he fluffed several times. Mario had to take the shot about fifteen times before it was safely in the can.

147

I travelled back to London in a car with Matty. He was very cross, frowned fiercely all the way and only growled when spoken to. Suddenly, as we neared town, his face cleared and he gave a broad smile.

'You know what was wrong with that shot?' he asked.

'No,' I said.

'The horse didn't like Mario,' he said. After that he was in the best of spirits.

During the run of one of William Douglas-Home's plays, in which Matty played a leading role, the call-boy knocked on his dressing-room door to give him the half-hour call. Not receiving any reply he opened the door to find Matty spreadeagled on the floor. He panicked, and rushed down the corridor shouting: 'Mr Matthews is dead! Mr Matthews is dead!'

By the time the first person arrived in Matty's dressing-room they found him sitting in a chair, looking perfectly well. He had indeed fainted, but this did not prevent him going on for the performance.

At the end of the show Matty summoned the call-boy and said: 'If, on some future occasion, you should enter and see me lying on the floor, you will *not* rush round shouting: "Mr Matthews is dead". You will rush round shouting: "I *think* Mr Matthews is dead"'.

I was one of the party which met Yvonne de Carlo at London Airport. She did not know many people in England and, in the absence of Valerie in Rome, I showed her round London.

Our first night out at the 21 Room was slightly embarrassing. A drunk weaved his way up to the table and stood swaying in front of us muttering: 'Famous face! Famous face!'

I started to tell him to buzz off, but Yvonne shook her head at me. She was obviously used to it. He then fumbled in his pocket and produced a piece of paper and a pen.

'May I have the honour of an autograph?'

Yvonne nodded graciously. The man then put the paper in front of me and said: 'Thank you very much, Mister Pertwee. Sign right there.'

I signed, and he walked off, quite oblivious of Yvonne de Carlo.

We went to see one of the few plays which I had not seen on the first night. We sat in a tiny box at the Ambassadors Theatre, where they were performing *The Mousetrap*. Richard Attenborough played the villain, and gave us a broad wink during one of his more sinister scenes. We both decided we were glad we did not have money in the show, which would surely fold when Dickie and his wife, Sheila Sim, went out of it. They were not paying Dickie very much. The poor chap was on a percentage of the profits. I believe he still is, after twenty-one years, and looks like being so for another twenty-one.

Yvonne had heard about London's famous fish restaurants, and wanted to visit one. So I took her to Bentley's where, thank God, they recognised her and not me. Everyone rushed round asking her what she would like.

'Fish,' she said.

'What kind of fish?'

'Any fish,' she said. 'With chips.'

Yvonne was the most coolly professional and well-organised actress I have ever met. She carried a little book and the moment she met anybody new, she would write down their name with brief details about them. As an inveterate forgetter of names I have often wished I had followed this example.

I seem to spend half my life agonizingly trying to put names to familiar faces in an effort not to offend people. My most classic case occurred in Dunhills, Piccadilly, where I was buying a lighter. Standing next to me was a most familiar face. I knew him well; but my mind went blank on the name. The moment panic set in I knew I was lost, so I fell back on the well tried: 'Hullo! How *are* you? It's been a long time. How are things?'

He was well and things were apparently all right. My purchase arrived and I made a quick escape, before being found out. As I reached the door I realised I had been talking to the Duke of Windsor.

Yvonne made me organise her birthday party. It was a small affair, with a few friends, and was not publicised at all. It was held at the Pheasantry Club in Chelsea, with the price firmly and unalterably fixed in advance. I gave her an antique silver something as a birthday present. Before leaving London, at the end of the picture, she gave me a pair of underpants on which was printed a picture of a Red Indian dancing in front of a camp fire, together with the inscription: 'Heap much smoke—no fire.'

I liked to think she had stocked up with these from The Farmers Market in Los Angeles before she came to Britain; otherwise the gift might have appeared to imply some criticism of my impeccable behaviour towards her.

I did not get to know David Niven well. He was always pleasant, uncomplicated and professional. The only thing worthy of note about his appearance in *Happy Every After* is that a number of 'boys in the know' from Wardour Street shook their heads gloomily and doubted whether he was worth the money he was getting (which was very little). He was a fine actor, nobody disputed that, but he'd had a long career and looked to be over the top as a major star. I doubt if even David himself could have dreamed that he was,

149

in fact, standing on the threshold of enormous success. The box office returns from *Happy Ever After* did little to prove the 'boys in the know' wrong —and it was not an unfunny picture. Yet, before long, he was to rocket back to stardom and award-winning in films and had huge success in television production with his Four Star company. He is certainly a much greater star today than ever he was in 1953.

I was elected to the Thursday Club, an exclusive mens' luncheon club, which met once a week in the top room of Wheeler's Restaurant in Old Compton Street, thanks to the generosity of Bernard Walsh, who owned Wheeler's.

I have never been much of a one for outings with the boys, but, in its heyday, the Thursday Club was tremendous fun. Members included Baron Nahum, the photographer, his twin brother, Jack, who was a barrister, Peter Ustinov, Larry Adler, Arthur Christiansen of the *Daily Express*, Gilbert Harding, James Robertson Justice, Patrick Campbell, Tibby Clarke, the screenwriter, Danny Danischewsky and Vasco Lazzolo, the artist.

You were entitled to bring one guest, but it was advisable to pick him carefully, since members were merciless with anyone who proved to be pompous, talked too much or resented being interrupted while trying to tell a funny story. Interrupting stories was an integral part of the proceedings.

The club had few hard and fast rules. Vasco was responsible for one of them. Like all artists he had his financial ups and downs and the rule for which he was responsible read:

'In future no member shall be the guest of his guest.'

There were a number of unwritten laws. Baron was never, at any cost, allowed to finish a story. Any member who achieved something notable such as fathering a baby, would become 'Champagne Charlie', and had to treat the entire gathering to champagne. This could prove expensive if it was a well-attended lunch. It was on one of these occasions that we witnessed Arthur Christiansen drinking a shoeful of champagne.

Every month the club solemnly elected a 'Cunt of the Month'. This award was not confined to members, but could be a politician, a police officer, a film star, or anyone who had made a complete idiot of himself during the previous month. At the end of the year one of the twelve was elected 'Cunt of the Year'.

I hold the dubious and unique honour of having been twice elected. The first time was for putting my own money into one of my plays and the second was for allowing my wife, Valerie, to go and work for Harry Kohn in Hollywood. Since no one had previously been elected twice, a resolution was passed that, if I won it a third time, Henry Moore would be commissioned to make me a small sculpture with an appropriate hole. Unfortunately, I did not qualify again.

Baron was a wonderfully egocentric character. One of his friends was the Siamese Prince, Bira. Baron never lived down something he said at one club lunch.

'I'm taking Prince Bira to Siam with me next week.'

Baron used to give a large party every year at his London studio. It was a glittering occasion with about two hundred guests, all of whom were asked to bring a bottle. Baron sent out his invitations at least three months ahead, so that he could be sure that those he wanted to attend would have no previous engagements.

One year Vasco received his invitation three months in advance and replied by return of post: 'So sorry I can't come but I'm going to the cinema that evening.'

On another occasion, in answer to the request to bring a bottle, Vasco arrived at the party with a bottle of Airwick.

I took Valerie to one of the parties—a fancy dress affair. I went as a big game hunter, complete with solar topee. Valerie, attached to me by a chain, was virtually undressed as an extremely *décolleté* tiger. Her costume caused a sensation both with her old friends the press photographers and most of the male guests. One of these, very drunk, staggered up and started to make a pass at her. I gently pushed him away, saying: 'Lay off. This is my tiger and I shot her.'

'Oh, yes?' he replied. 'And did you stuff her, too?'

On this occasion Gilbert Harding arrived in ordinary clothes and in one of his more belligerent moods. He entered, looked critically at the multi-coloured throng, and exclaimed. 'What a bloody awful party!'

He then left. Baron was hurt and this was the beginning of the end of a long friendship.

Baron had been a long time friend of the Duke of Edinburgh. Occasionally he would give a private dinner party for Prince Philip, who always came with Mike Parker, his Private Secretary. These were held in Baron's home in Kinnerton Street, where he had a large studio filled with canaries, pictures of himself and of the Royal Family. Baron provided the food and on one occasion Prince Philip produced the wine from the Buckingham Palace cellars. A few close friends made up the rest of the party.

151

I still have the menu from this dinner, signed by those present and including an 'Annigoni' sketch by Peter Ustinov. The liquids provided included Liebfraumilch '33, Dom du Chevalier '37, Chateau d'Yquem '21, Hine '14 and '22 and a J & B of 1896.

They were relaxed and, at the same time, stimulating evenings with a lot of good conversation. When you put Gilbert Harding and Peter Ustinov at the same table this was inevitable. It was difficult to decide who was the better raconteur. Both were brilliant. Gilbert's choice of words and phraseology could make even an old story sound fresh and new. Of the two, he appeared to be the more natural storyteller. Peter is more of a performer, a brilliant, multi-voiced cabaret act.

Odd recollections of the evenings come back.

We were discussing those circular blue plaques which are put outside houses where famous people have lived. Peter Ustinov had just bought a house in Chelesa, and said he was going to put up a blue plaque with: 'WATCH THIS SPACE!' on it.

There was Tony Wysard, an expert on wine, being asked by Prince Philip what he thought of the claret. I remember a feeling of shock as Tony shook his head dubiously and said: 'Needs to breathe and badly needs to be drunk. Another year and it'll be useless.'

I recall looking at Larry Adler and thinking what a mixed-up world it was. Here was an American virtuoso, barred from working in his own country because his leftish views were held to be dangerous to the state, seated happily next to the husband of Britain's Queen, who was prepared to listen to any views he expressed with perfect equanimity.

Prince Philip recounted an experience during his recent inspection of the Jewish Ex-Servicemens' Brigade. He had walked down the line stopping here and there for a word with some of the men. He paused by one and asked:

'What unit were you in?'

'RASC, Sir.'

'And what are you doing now?'

The man gave him a startled look. There was a pause then, finally, he replied: 'Well, I'm here, aren't I?'

Prince Philip moved on and whispered to Mike Parker: 'That'll teach me to ask stupid questions.'

Another story when the late King George VI had visited Montreal, where he was met by the Lord Mayor who, he noted, was not wearing any chain of office.

'Don't you wear chains of office?' asked the King.

'Oh, yes, Your Majesty, but only on special occasions.'

It was at one of these dinners that Gilbert Harding and Baron came to the parting of the ways. Television was being discussed and Baron jokingly accused Gilbert of pandering to the public by trading on his reputation for rudeness. Gilbert visibly froze.

'Rude?' he said. '*Rude?* I have never been rude in my life.'

Baron laughed, told him to come off it, and said he was famous for his rudeness. Gilbert rose, in a towering rage.

'I challenge you to give me one example—just one—when I have been rude to anybody.'

'Certainly,' said Baron. 'You were rude to me at my party, when you looked in, said: "What a bloody awful party!" then walked out.'

'That wasn't rude,' cried Gilbert. 'It *was* a bloody awful party.'

With that Gilbert bade everybody a dignified goodnight, told Baron he regretted this was the last occasion they would meet socially and stalked out.

Baron's brother, Jack, also became a close friend. He was a successful barrister, working mostly in the North of England. He had a very quick mind which was well illustrated in a somewhat sordid case when he defended a huge Scandinavian seaman, who was accused of having carnal relations with a duck. It was, if I may put it that way, a fairly open and shut case, with little hope of a successful defence; but Jack decided to have a go. Dramatically, he drew the attention of the court to the gigantic dimensions of the accused seaman, who stood almost seven feet tall, and was immensely broad. Jack assured the court that the rest of the man's body was in proportion to his enormous size, and then asked them to consider the proportions of a little duck. Could anyone, for one moment, imagine. . . . At this point the judge intervened. 'Have you ever noted the size of a duck's egg, Mr Nahum?'

'Yes, my lord,' said Jack. 'But I've never seen one put back.'

When Jack and Baron, twins, died within months of each other I lost two good friends, and London lost two very colourful characters. The Thursday Club was never quite the same after they had gone. The membership of the club was largely middle-aged, thus the mortality rate was alarmingly high. The club had one thing in common with the RAF squadrons during the war, in that no sombre mourning was allowed, however loved the member had been. Thus, when Baron died unexpectedly from an embolism after a comparatively minor operation, his epitaph, spoken by Vasco Lazzolo, was: 'If old Baron could have known how much publicity he'd get when he died, he'd have committed suicide years ago.'

In 1954 I devised and sold to the BBC the first British Television soap opera. It was entitled *The Grove Family* (Lime Grove—get it?). Having conceived this brilliant notion and had it accepted, I was appalled by the prospect which lay ahead, and ran to my Daddy, yelling for help. Roland seized eagerly on the idea, which was exactly the type of thing which he had been looking for, since he was now suffering badly from emphysema, which in no way affected his working capacity, but prevented him rushing about to film studios. We collaborated from the first episode. He proved a tower of strength and, in the long run, contributed a great deal more than I did. No one knew how the idea of a lower middle-class family's adventures, week by week, would work. It was something quite new to British TV, and could have been a dire failure.

Immediately prior to its opening I appeared on the panel game *Down you Go!*, then quickly changed studios, and talked for ten minutes, without a script, to introduce the family to the public. I had risen from a sick bed to make both appearances, and was also sick with nerves. Everyone afterwards congratulated me on my utter calm, but when I rose from the table I discovered I wasn't wearing any shoes. I had kicked them off and they were about ten feet away.

Jonah Barrington in the *Daily Sketch* wrote:

> 'Fascinating to compare Michael Pertwee's two personalities; one a rather jaded panel player with no more adult duty than to say: "I'll have an E", and the other an eager author bearing the heavy responsibility of launching a new TV family upon millions. . . He did it with modesty, sincerity and charm and made friends for *The Groves* in advance. I'll defer further criticism until tonight, except to say this: If the stories are as attractive and genuine as the family appeared in this brief trailer then viewers are in for a happy time. Good luck, Mr Pertwee.'

Within a few weeks, an estimated quarter of the entire population were tuning into *The Grove Family*, something over 11 million people a week. The show ran three years, was made into a film, and a strip cartoon. Roland wrote a novel about them, and, together, we wrote about fifteen one act plays for amateurs, which still produce a tiny annual income.

Mum and Dad were played by my old friends Ruth Dunning and Edward Evans. He had previously appeared in my Somerset Maugham play. A centenarian Grandma, who became a nationally famous figure, was played beautifully by Nancy Roberts. The elder son was played by Peter Bryant, who later deserted acting, and is now a literary agent. My daughter, Carolyn, made her first professional appearance in one of the episodes.

A spin-off from my television appearances and from writing *The Grove*

Family, was an offer from the magazine *Woman* to write a regular weekly article of about 1200 words. Since I was a well-known face it was evidently considered that anything I cared to write about sex, the aged, marriage, or children would be of immense value to *Woman*'s public. I was, in effect, being asked to do what Beverley Nichols and Godfrey Winn had done so well, so successfully—and so lucratively—for years. I was excited at the prospect. The work was a little more arduous than the balloons for Bruce Hunter, but the money was larger and this could last for twenty-five years. I was put on a probationary period of nine weeks. So I sat down and wrote under such headings as:

'SEX IS A DIFFICULT WORD.'

'Even in families where frankness is the rule, open mention of sex can embarrass.'

or:

'THOSE WERE THE DAYS.'

'Children never think of yesterday. And, in this respect, happiness keeps us all children. Only when the brightness fades do we look back—and dream. . . .'

I thoroughly enjoyed myself, but the lady editor, Mrs Jordan, wasn't so sure. She was unfailingly polite and encouraging, but kept on saying: 'Lovely, but can you make it just a *little* bit more from the woman's angle.'

At the end of nine weeks I was fired. I had been unable to project the woman's angle, and had evidently remained far too masculine-orientated. A few weeks later, just for fun, I asked a girl friend, who was a journalist, to write an article as if by me, in the style which she thought might appeal to readers of a woman's magazine. I gave her the subject material and left the rest to her. The result was a hideously embarrassing piece. Apparently, according to the article, we all of us remain children at heart and I had to admit I still took my old teddy bear, Mr Tiddy-Biddy, to bed with me when I was feeling particularly low, but that was a secret that I only told a *few* people, so not a word!

As a matter of interest, I sent the article to Mrs Jordan, who read it and wrote back that it was *exactly* the type of thing she had been looking for and why, oh why, hadn't I done it before?

At the end of three years writing *The Grove Family*, Roland and I realised that we were nearing the point of exhaustion, although the public seemed perfectly prepared to take more, despite the intervening arrival of Independent Television. I approached the BBC and suggested that, if they wanted the

155

show to survive, they should build up a team of different writers, thus allowing Roland and myself gradually to ease off. They expressed themselves as extremely grateful for my generous attitude. This was not reflected in the corporation's later actions.

I have always had the best of relations with the BBC, but I am bound to say that their actions over the survival of *The Grove Family* were both shoddy and stupid. Without realising it, I was well ahead of my time in suggesting to them a way to make a show run indefinitely—a formula later successfully adopted by ITV with such shows as *Emergency Ward Ten* and the never-ending *Coronation Street*.

The BBC's immediate response to my 'generous' approach was to offer us £5 per episode as a royalty payment for any scripts which we did not write. This was a derisory, if not insulting offer, and was treated with the contempt it deserved.

Secondly, they took up the idea of using other writers but inexplicably forbade Roland or myself permission to read their scripts and comment on them. It was the equivalent of taking a three-year-old child away from devoted parents, handing it to total strangers, and refusing to allow the parents even to give the benefit of their experience. Naturally, this proved disastrous, and the show collapsed within weeks.

The cast received a nice compliment shortly before the show closed when the Queen Mother expressed a desire to meet them at Lime Grove. She was evidently a fan. I say the cast received this compliment, because the authors were not invited to share in the occasion.

I refuse to be ashamed of *The Grove Family*. It had no message, no pretensions, but it gave enormous pleasure to millions of people, which is all it was designed to do. Although it bore little resemblance to real life, the public closely identified themselves with it. If Grandma had a birthday, Nancy Roberts was inundated with presents. In one episode I had the old lady appear as a guest on a TV panel game, and I played one of the team on the panel. I gave Grandma some dialogue in which she made rude remarks about me, saying that, in her opinion, I had a nasty, smarmy personality. The following day my lady cleaner, who daily used to watch me writing the scripts, came to the house and asked me if I had watched the previous night's episode. I said I had. She shook her head disapprovingly and said: 'The things that old Grandma said about you.'

During the run of *The Grove Family* I received a letter which read:

'I wondered if you would be interested in a char in your script? I really do go out three times a week charring and if you are not suited I would like the opportunity of a try.'

It was also remarkable how angry the series made people, who did not like it. Gilbert Harding used to attack me every time we met, ranting wrathfully against it. This did eventually give me the opportunity of getting the better of him verbally—which was a near impossible task with Gilbert. He seized me by the lapels at one Thursday Club lunch and started off again: 'How can you, an intelligent, reasonably gifted man descend to such depths. I watch it, appalled, every week. . . .'

'Say no more, Gilbert,' I said. 'The fact that you still watch it every week is all I want to know.'

Another friend who became almost obsessive about *The Groves* was novelist Nicholas Monsarrat, who took one cruel see, then switched off half-way through. Long after the public have forgotten it, Nick still remembers and shudders. He even found space to attack it in the second volume of his autobiography, published in 1971, though he coated the pill by giving me credit for a very funny line which I quite forget saying to him. More often than not Nick still addresses letters to me as 'Mr Grove'. He let up a few years ago when I wrote the book of the musical comedy *The Four Musketeers*. He then wrote me a letter addressed to Alexander Dumas Jnr, which our cleaning lady tried to return to the postman saying that no Mr Dumas lived there. Luckily, John the postman knew more about what goes on in show business than any showbiz columnist, and told her to give it to me just the same.

Having dealt immodestly with success I now come to a succession of disasters writing, financial, and family-wise.

I wrote a comedy play entitled *It's Different for Men*, collaborating with Danny Danischewsky and his wife Brenda.

It's Different for Men was independently backed by a consortium of backers. It was presented under the banner of EP Clift and Alec Rea. The leading man was Naunton Wayne and the leading lady was Yolande Donlan, the delicious American comedienne, who had made a big hit in *Born Yesterday* and who had remained in England to marry my old non-collaborator and friend from Gainsborough, Val Guest. Valerie got a little part in it, too.

We toured the provinces before a scheduled opening at The Duchess Theatre. We did reasonably good business. Naunton was a most polished performer, and Yo was splendid in a part which might have been written for her. Unfortunately, during the tour she decided that the play was not right. Shortly before we were due into town she announced her intention of quitting the show.

This was a hard blow and, if we had been sensible, we should have taken the count; but we didn't.

June Clyde popped up, announced she would like to play the role and said she could produce a backer, who would be prepared to pump a lot of money into the production, if she was in it. We settled for this.

I have previously said that authors can generally find good excuses for failure. I do not believe any author can produce a better one than I am about to unfold.

Our opening coincided with the first national newspaper strike in British history. From the day we opened there were no papers for five weeks. Nobody knew the play was on. In a desperate search for publicity Naunton Wayne even paraded up and down the Strand with a sandwich board. We tried to get an excerpt on the BBC (ITV had not opened yet) but they refused.

At the same time June Clyde's backer backed smartly out. I had, meanwhile, personally guaranteed the theatre for, I think, five weeks. I was thus legally responsible for all financial losses over and above what the original production figure could pay for.

The strike lasted five weeks and the play lasted five weeks. I do not know how many people actually saw it during that time, but it ran into dozens. It cost me every penny I had painfully saved over the years.

I will never again have as big a failure combined with as good an excuse for one.

Next, Jack Davies and I parted company as a team. This decision was entirely mine, and was an extremely difficult one to make, because I was almost part of his family. During my bachelor years theirs had been my second home. There was also no valid reason to make the break. Apart from being great personal friends we had no difficulties in collaboration. It was simply my same old problem of an in-built resistance to being tied. As part of a team I did not feel a free agent. It was, in effect, like having a second marriage; in some ways even more tying than a marriage. A member of a team cannot suddenly say: 'I'm off to the South of France for a month.'

In the long run neither of us has had cause to regret the move. We have both done better separately than we could have as a team, and our friendship has never suffered.

Jon deserted the ranks of bachelors and married actress Jean Marsh, having teetered nervously for about three years before taking the plunge.

The collapse of my marriage to Valerie was partly caused by a beautiful Italian girl called Marla Sportoletti-Baduel. As Marla Scarafia she was a model. As Marla Landi she was an actress, with a photogenic face and considerable talent. She is now Marla Frye, and is married to an old friend of mine, Jack Frye.

Should Marla, by chance, read this and decide to sue me for libel and defamation of character, I must quickly add that she is unaware of the part she played in the collapse.

A friend, Harold Rose, decided to try and help Marla with her film career. He invited Marla and her husband Pepino to dinner to meet Mike Frankovich and his wife Binnie Barnes. Mike was then the lively head of Columbia Pictures in Britain. Harold did not want the dinner to look like a set piece so he called me to ask if Valerie and I would mind coming to dinner, too, as window-dressing. There would be just six of us. With any luck, Mike would take one look at Marla and a nice fat contract might ensue.

Everything went exactly according to plan, except for a slight deviation in the direction of Mike Frankovich's eye. He took one look at Valerie, and precisely two weeks later she was in Hollywood, at the start of a seven-year film contract with Columbia Pictures Inc.

Sic transit Valerie.

When she left Britain we had been married 36 months and her vital statistics were 40-27-39. She returned nine months later, a svelte 37-21-36, in a blaze of publicity to appear at the première of her first Hollywood picture *Jubal*, a Western, starring Rod Steiger and Glenn Ford.

Columbia Pictures Publicity Department told me they hoped I would co-operate in playing down any cracks which might have appeared in the marriage, so that full coverage could be given to the picture rather than to our personal problems. They might have been better employed in suggesting this to Valerie, who had already been reported in a Sunday paper as saying that she did not find that absence made the heart grow fonder.

This was a time when British popular journalism had sunk to an all-time low, and Editors were allowing free rein to the gossip columnists—a bevy of dirt-probing men and women, sheltering under such umbrella names as Tanfield (*The Daily Mail*), Simon Ward (*The Daily Sketch*) *et al.* They were not quite as bad as their American counterparts in *Confidential* but they did their nasty best, bearing in mind British libel laws.

For months before the *Jubal* première my private life had been made a hell by them. Anyone reading the papers at that time might have been tempted to believe that only one important world problem remained to be solved—was my marriage on the rocks, or wasn't it?

I dutifully met Valerie at London Airport and kissed her several times for the benefit of the photographers. I accompanied her to the Savoy Hotel, where a suite had been reserved. Here I made my first big mistake by exclaiming how nice it was. I realised this when she shot me an angry look, then informed the Columbia entourage that the suite was unsatisfactory, and that she required another with a better view of the river. With somewhat strained faces those concerned conducted a quick negotiation with the hotel authorities, who produced another—and to me very similar—suite, which satisfied her.

A harassed Publicity man drew me aside, and asked me if I would attend the official press reception and begged me again to put up a smiling front of marital happiness. I said they could rely on me. Nothing would have suited me better. The subject was beginning to bore me almost as much as it must have been boring the public. Once again Columbia neglected to brief their star. As soon as we were left alone I said that the most sensible thing was for us to give exactly the same answers to any embarrassing questions at the reception, in view of the way the columnists twisted anything that was said. Valerie cut me short. She wished to make one thing clear. This was her première and her reception. She was there as Valerie French and not Valerie Pertwee. She did not want me standing beside her at the press reception, and was perfectly capable of handling any questions herself.

I promised her full co-operation on this, left the hotel, rang up the nearest blonde and disappeared.

The news that I would not be attending the reception reached Columbia, I assume *via* Valerie, and there started a panic search for me all over London, which got them nowhere. I heard later that I was considered to have behaved very badly.

My absence was duly noted by the columnists, as was the fact that Valerie was not wearing her wedding and engagement rings. She was questioned about this and, handling the answers in her own way, as promised, said that she did not wear them because the fact of people knowing she was married was bad for her career. This might have been a tolerable answer in British Honduras but in London it caused raucous laughter. I was, at the time, a great deal better known than she was, and the whole country had been saturated for months with headline stories about our marriage.

Having become bloody-minded at last, I had an enjoyable time with the gossip columnists. I managed to tell three representatives of the Simon Ward column to go and bugger themselves on three different occasions, once when they pretended not to be Simon at all. I mistakenly let a sour looking lady with sour breath into the house then merely said: 'No comment' for half an hour to anything she asked. ('No comment', said Mr Pertwee, nervously tapping the ash off his cigarette.)

After one totally untrue statement in the Simon Ward column, I wrote a letter to the Editor of the *Daily Sketch*, Bertie Gunn, whom I knew personally, protesting, not at the publicity, but at deliberately inaccurate and malicious reporting. He wrote an ungracious reply, saying that a public figure had to expect publicity. Such were the depths into which Fleet Street had sunk in 1955.

We attended the première together. As we drove up to the Odeon, Marble Arch, I felt one sudden uprush of warmth and sympathy when, looking out of the hired limousine, I saw that there was not one soul standing on the pavement outside. However the première went well. Valerie's performance was good and the critics were kind. There seemed no reason to doubt that she had a promising career ahead of her. That this failed to materialise was not through any fault of hers. No one could have tried harder or with more dedication. She was merely another example of the sad fact that from every hundred girls who go, starry-eyed, into show business, only about one ever makes the grade.

Valerie returned to Hollywood still starry-eyed. I set firmly and not unsuccessfully about the task of de-castrating myself.

We were not divorced until the end of 1959.

Part 14

Anchor Dropping

A SMALL HEADLINE in the London *Evening Standard* announced:
NO CRUMPET INCREASE.

It appeared that: 'When the crumpet season opens the cost will be the same as last year—two for $2\frac{1}{2}$d.'

This was not my experience at this time of my life. I found an enormous increase at a relatively high cost.

Having rediscovered my youth, aged about forty, I also took up gliding, at the instigation of Prince Philip's Private Secretary, Mike Parker, thus finally achieving my ambition to fly. I proved an apt pupil, flew solo after thirty brief flights, and soon owned my own glider, in partnership with a dentist friend, Paddy Pitt-Roche. I cannot begin to describe the joy of soaring above the English countryside in complete silence, or the sense of triumph in keeping a machine without an engine in the air for over five hours at a time. Sir Peter Scott*, the naturalist, learned at the same time and made me jealous by going on to win the National Gliding Championships within a very short time. This was not surprising in a man who knows as much about birds as he. I became no more than an average pilot, owing to my inability to read a compass and map reference. On one occasion I flew into cloud, without my artificial horizon working, lost control, spun out upside down, and found myself about nine hundred feet above a thick wood. I saw what I thought was my base, Lasham, and headed desperately towards it, with the trees growing alarmingly closer. When I reached the airfield I found

---

*Son of Robert Falcon Scott of the Antarctic.

it was Odiham RAF base, where they were holding a jet exercise. I had neither the time nor the height for niceties and since they did not fire a red light at me, I landed neatly in front of the main control tower, where a line of handlebar moustaches bristled angrily at me through a window. I was fined £2.10, and was towed safely away behind a tiger moth half an hour later.

I wrote a film on gliding for the Rank Organisation, who paid me a lot of money but never made the film.

Life was a paradise in Paradise Walk owing to a Portugese maid, 'Saum', who not only cooked like a dream but did all the laundry, suit pressing and washed my car twice a week. Her only failing was English, which still defeated her after thirteen years in this country. I never received a telephone message which was more informative than: 'One friend telephone you.'

Vasco and Leila Lazzolo had suffered in the same way. They insisted that their maid must leave them messages — or else. Having delivered this warning, they returned to their flat that night to find a sheet of paper prominently displayed in the hall. On it was written:

'Urgent!'

I invented a television panel game called *Yakity-Yak*. I went into partnership with a friend, Leslie Goldberg, who is a tremendous organiser. The idea was simple; a panel of four gorgeous girls who gave impromptu answers to such questions as:

'Does a kipper swim sideways or flat?', or 'Look at this globe of the earth. If a plane flies from England to Australia it must be upside down when it gets there. How does it right itself to land?', or 'What is circumlocution?' (This proved a dangerous one.)

The show was completely unrehearsed, and the answers the girls gave were the first thoughts that came into their pretty heads. The answers were often hilarious. The girls had to be beautiful, able to talk freely, and not appear to be trying to be cute or funny.

We interviewed literally hundreds before we got a panel together and produced a dry run of the show for Val Parnel, Lew Grade and others. They bought the show on the spot. It was not exactly praised by critics but it achieved enormous publicity. It so enraged Gilbert Harding that he never mentioned *The Grove Family* again.

We chopped and changed the panel, but, finally, the most successful girls were Therese Burton, a cute little thing with slightly prominent teeth, who was the only one who could think up a funny answer without seeming to do so, June Cunningham who was a pink blonde, Jean Clarke, a ravishing model, who looked like a young Marilyn Munroe, and lovely young red-head, Shirley Ann Field, who gave the most sensational answers of the lot.

Our chairman was MacDonald Hobley, who was occasionally replaced by myself or by show business journalist, Peter Noble, a charming man with a quite incredibly encyclopaedic mind who can instantly give you the names of the entire cast of any picture ever made.

I can claim to have discovered Shirley Ann Field. Some time before, when she was about sixteen, I had met her at a party, and sent her to an elocution teacher, as a first step towards becoming an actress. She finally did well and played in *Saturday Night Sunday Morning* and other films. Shirley's telling remarks were not only confined to the television screen. I once took her to a film première, after I had not seen her for some months. As we had dinner later, she said: 'It *is* nice to see you again. I've been out with nothing but intellectuals recently.'

I made a new friend, David Wynne-Morgan, a blue-eyed boy of Lord Beaverbrook, who was currently writing the William Hickey column. He left journalism to become a successful PRO. We met through half-sharing the same girl friend. In those days the only place to go to in London was Les Ambassadeurs and its night-club, The Milroy, upstairs. Even if you hadn't a date, it was worth while dropping in to Les A for a drink at the bar, where you were sure to meet someone you knew. David and I had a glaring relationship over a period of some months, since, on roughly alternate nights, we used to take out the same girl. One night I would glare at him with her, and the next he would glare at me with her. One evening we were both in the Les A bar, unaccompanied, at opposite ends of the bar, when through the door came Stirling Moss with *our* girl. This caused an instant bond and we had our first drink together.

David's complicated sex life has always been a source of joy to me. Like his motor cars it is accident prone. Things happen to him which never happen to the ordinary, run-of-the-mill Lothario. On one occasion he spent the night with a girl he had just met. The following morning he went into a well-known florists, who shall be nameless, and sent the girl some flowers with an appropriately grateful card enclosed. At the same time, stricken by conscience, he sent his regular girl friend a similar bouquet with an affectionate card enclosed. The well-known florists got the cards mixed, with disastrous results.

David was then in partnership with another good friend of mine, Frederick Mulally, now a thriving novelist who, when he heard about it, told David he should sue the florist. David said he would like to, but on what grounds could he possibly sue them?

'You can sue them,' said Freddy, 'for destroying your reputation for being the most successful double-dealing bastard in London.'

I had always wanted to look at a film festival. I conned Reg Willis, then editor of the London *Evening News*, into sending me to The Cannes Film Festival as their correspondent.

I watched a seemingly endless stream of films, some good, some appalling. One of them was *I'll Cry Tomorrow*, starring Susan Hayward, a turgid drama about an alcoholic. When it drew to its tragic end, the journalist next to me shook his head, wiped his brow and said: 'Well, that's cured me. I'll never go to the pictures again!'

Looking through my *Evening News* articles I see that I reported the arrival of Mario Zampi, who had come to promote his latest picture, *Now and Forever*, a simple love story about two teenage elopers, which starred Janette Scott and Vernon Gray. I wrote:

> 'I have seen this admirable film no less than eight times already. It is a story by R F Delderfield* and Michael Pertwee.'

I had also played a small part in the picture, but even this added attraction did not stop it being one of Mario's few flops.

At the Palais du Festival I went to check the names of the British stars attending. They included Mr J Arnal, Mrs Muriel Ponlow, Mr Gray Vernon, and a sinister sounding Swede, called Mr Swonson. These were, in fact, Julia Arnal, Muriel Pavlov, Vernon Gray and Maureen Swanson.

Diana Dors came for the launching for her film *Yield to the Night*, in which she played a serious role for the first time. She also represented the *Daily Sketch* at the Festival. I had known her since she was a dark, podgy fifteen and we interviewed each other for our respective papers. She came with her husband Dennis Hamilton. Her picture had been made by ABC, and Robert Clark was among those attending the Festival. Dennis objected to Diana's accommodation at the Carlton. His method of expressing disapproval was more violent than Valerie's at the Savoy. He stood, floodlit, on a balcony above the front door of the hotel and, as Robert Clark arrived, yelled unrepeatable insults and tossed down a handful of coins which, he claimed, would help to pay for a better room.

Diana had a serious rival for the glamour stakes at the festival in Belinda Lee, who was beautiful. Dennis was not going to have any of this. One night

*R F Delderfield wrote the long running farce *Worm's Eye View*.

he went round Cannes with a piece of chalk, drawing a moustache on all Belinda's photographs.

I wrote a picture for Diana a year or so later in Rome, after she had separated from Dennis. It was called *La Ragazza Del Palio*, and was made in English and Italian. The producers were in a great hurry for the script since they were only five weeks away from the start of shooting. I collaborated with four Italian writers and the director. Despite the rush, nobody met until four o'clock in the afternoon, and then worked exactly four hours until eight. This allowed me to sneak away to Rieti, where I spent many happy hours gliding over the Italian alps in some very rickety machines. The club had a nervous flying instructor who was ordered to test me out before I was allowed to fly solo. He clearly entertained deep suspicions about foreign pilots, and was determined not to be killed by one. After a couple of flights, I was convinced that his hands never left the controls of the dual trainer. As we came in to land after a flight I took my hands and feet off the controls. We made a perfect landing despite this.

'*Very* good,' he said. 'Now, you go solo.'

Coby came over to stay in Rome and was present when I broke my endurance record, and stayed up for seven and a half hours, which gave him a boring day.

I had an Italian girl friend, who looked like a miniature Gina Lollobrigida. We took Diana and her new boy friend out on the town for an evening which was not without its embarrassments. As we came out of the Excelsior Hotel, a crowd outside started to mob us. Diana looked delighted, but they made straight for my girl friend to demand her autograph, thinking she was La Lollo. Later, when we were visiting the floodlit ruins of the Forum, an American, who had been eyeing us, finally plucked up courage and approached Diana for an autograph. Diana complied. The man put the paper back in his pocket, shook her warmly by the hand, and said:

'Thank you, Jayne Mansfield.'

It was definitely not Diana's night.

I took my daughter Carolyn for her first trip abroad when I came out to write this picture. We drove down together. She stayed a couple of days in Rome, then flew back to England on her own. I think we both enjoyed every minute of it.

Time was flying and sex was rearing its head in her life. I had already received a letter from school, which included the following paragraph:

'A little girl called Sandra Wilson who is in the babies form wants a pash on me but I said "No". Firstly, I have three already and it should not be encouraged so early in the school.'

Remembering Roland's failure ever to discuss sex with me, I decided that Carolyn should not be neglected in this way. I took her out to dinner at The Caprice with the idea of combining a slap-up meal with a few down to earth facts of life. We found ourselves sitting next to a very famous actor. I pointed him out to Carolyn. She nodded and said: 'Yes, isn't it a pity he's queer?'

I abandoned the projected talk and never raised the subject again. She seems to have managed very well without it.

The day the Russians startled the world by lobbing up their first sputnik, I sat down and wrote a television play called *Man in a Moon*. In those days it seemed it might be years before the re-entry problem was solved. My play was based on the assumption that the British had developed the first rocket big enough to send a man into orbit. He could not be brought down alive, so the authorities approached a condemned murderer, due to be hanged, and offered him the chance of becoming a dead hero instead of a dead villain. He accepted but, at the last moment, changed his mind, which he was entitled to do. However, the scientists involved would have none of that, and sent him up just the same. Thus, man's first words to be heard from space were: "You bastards!" It was, though I say it, quite a good play. It was sold at once to ABC TV. Dennis Vance produced and Donald Pleasance starred. Halfway through rehearsals the ITA stepped in and threatened to ban the play unless it was completely re-written. Their reason was that no British government could be seen to act in so inhuman a fashion. This was such a ridiculous attitude that, for once, I threw a temperamental fit. I refused to have anything to do with the re-writing, and made them change my credit on the screen to 'Based on a Play by'. The row was widely reported, and it was unfortunate that the TV Times, which is printed well in advance, chose this week to write glowingly of the plays by Shaw, Michael Pertwee and Balzac, in that order.

With memories of the gossip columnists fresh in my mind I wrote an original film story, *The Naked Truth*, about the threatened publication in Britain of a magazine like *Confidential*, and the attempts by several of its victims to murder the blackmailing editor. Mario Zampi bought it, and the film starred Terry-Thomas, Dennis Price, Peggy Mount, and a comparative newcomer to films, Peter Sellers. It was Peter's first big role, and it made him a star overnight.

'Britain's master goon Peter Sellers, unchallenged king of inspired lunacy, is at once the star and joy of *The Naked Truth*. For twenty dazzling minutes at the beginning this Rank comedy launched 1958 in the cinema on a tidal wave of hilarity.'

'For Peter Sellers the film is a personal triumph and he emerges as a brilliant screen comedian.'

'*The Naked Truth* is always funny, and three quarters of it is brilliant. Peter Sellers establishes himself as the finest film comedian since Chaplin. His is the brand of lunatic genius that British films need.' (Philip Oakes).

I was paid five thousand pounds for the picture and so was Peter. I only wish my fees had risen as sensationally as his did thereafter.

Mario had an option for a second picture for Peter Sellers, which was my next assignment. I called it *Too Many Crooks*. It was another black comedy, and concerned a bungling gang of crooks, who intend to kidnap the lovely daughter of a millionaire and hold her for ransom. They kidnap the millionaire's wife by mistake. The millionaire hates his wife and answers the ransom note by saying he is delighted to be rid of her.

It was again intended for Terry-Thomas and Peter Sellers. At this time it was widely believed that Peter was considerably influenced in making decisions about his career by the late astrologer, Maurice Woodruff. Mario even went to the lengths of consulting Maurice Woodruff himself, and quietly plugging the film, but it was to no avail. Peter turned us down.

Mario had an eye for star material, as he had already shown with Audrey Hepburn and Peter. He now followed another hunch by announcing that he would like Tony Hancock to play the Peter Sellers role. Hancock, up to then, was mainly known as a funny man on radio. Mario invited Tony to lunch asking him to come to the office first to listen to me tell an outline of my story. Tony arrived with his agent, and listened glumly while I told the story. When I had finished, he shook his head and said he wasn't interested. When he made a picture he was going to be the star, the *only* star, and he had no intention of sharing the honours with Terry-Thomas or anybody else. Mario accepted this with his usual urbane good humour, and suggested we went out to the prearranged lunch. Tony shook his head again.

'No point in having lunch now, is there?' he said, and departed with a cursory farewell. The seeds of self-destruction were sadly evident here before he had even made the grade.

The film was finally made with Terry-Thomas, George Cole and Brenda de Banzie.

Mario had another idea, which was about twelve years ahead of its time.

Jimmy Edwards was starring in one of the most popular shows on TV, Muir and Norden's *Whacko!* in which he played the bullying, crooked headmaster. A film of the subject could not fail to do well. I sat down and wrote an original story outline called *Bottoms Up!* Frank, Denis and I wrote the script together. I am no judge of whether it was a bad picture or not. All I can claim is that it was no better and no worse than the TV show, which attracted millions of viewers every week. It proved to be our second box office disaster. No one, it seemed, wanted to see a film based on *Whacko!* Those ever present 'boys in the know' from Wardour Street nodded their heads and said they had told us so. It was madness to expect the public to pay to see something in the cinema, which they could see for nothing on TV. There was a certain logic in their argument, and they appeared to be right; but I wonder what they said later, in view of the fantastic success of *On the Buses, Dad's Army, Up Pompeii* and others which in the 1970s, have done exactly what we tried to do in 1960.

Bottoms Up! was also the last script I was to write for Mario, who died from a heart attack after making only one more picture.

I had, in a sense, become Mario's writer, but I also worked for a number of other producers. I wrote two pictures for George Brown (not the Labour politician), *Ladies who Do*, starring Robert Morley and Peggy Mount; and a Cliff Richard musical *Finders Keepers*, which also starred Peggy Mount and Robert Morley. I wrote three pictures for Hugh Stewart, *Make Mine Mink* with my old friend Terry-Thomas, which did well here and in America, *The Magnificent Two*, starring Morecambe and Wise who, in my view, are grossly neglected by film makers, and a comedy about a vet called *In the Doghouse* with Leslie Phillips.

A funny thing happened after the press show of *In the Doghouse*, which was not a good film. My cousin, Angela Huth, Harold's elder daughter, had married journalist Quentin Crewe, who had just become film critic of the *Daily Mail*. I was seeing a lot of them at the time, and when he heard I had a picture coming out, Quentin groaned and said he hated reviewing pictures written by friends. I told him not to worry. I was immune to criticism and did not expect him to enjoy it anyway. After this, I confidently expected him to dismiss it in a couple of lines. When I opened The *Daily Mail* on the day after the press show, I found that Quentin had not dismissed it at all. He had devoted a full column of vituperation such as I have rarely read in any review. I was actually reading it a second time when the telephone rang. It was Quentin on the line, speaking in a rather diffident voice, as well he might. He did not, as I had anticipated, refer to the review, but asked me if I could come to lunch that day. Someone had approached him about writing a film and, since he knew nothing about the art, he could think of no one better to advise him than me. I was so startled that I resisted the temptation to say that I would have thought I was the last person whose advice he would have sought, and accepted his invitation. We had lunch. He picked my brains. At no time was the review referred to. At the end of lunch, when conversation reached more general terms, he said he could not understand how certain pictures came to be made at all. He had seen a film that week which was bad beyond belief. I suddenly realised he was talking about *In the Doghouse*. I also realised, simultaneously, that he must have arrived at the press show too late to read the credits, and had no idea I had written it. I let him finish, whereupon he played straight into my hands by saying: 'I don't suppose you've seen it?'

'Several times,' I said: 'I wrote it.'

I have never seen a man so stricken. All he could do was gasp: 'And you still came here . . . You didn't say anything.'

I am sure he did not enjoy the lunch, but I did, and went away happily convinced that whatever he thought about my next picture, he would bend over backwards to give it a good notice. Unfortunately, he moved on to other things before the occasion arose.

I tried my hand at writing one of the *Carry Ons*. I sold an idea verbally to Peter Rogers, who fell for it at once, and paid me a nice sum of money to write a first draft. I dashed it off happily and submitted it, convinced that it was as good, if not better, than anything they had previously turned out. Perhaps I had fallen into the same trap as I had in my initial approach to the Rix farces. Some weeks went by without my draft being acknowledged. Finally, I called Peter Rogers and asked if he had received my *Carry On*.

'Yes,' he said. 'And I hated it so much I couldn't even bring myself to talk to you about it.'

This was quite a severe blow to my ego.

Shortly afterwards I took daughter Carolyn for her first trip to the South of France. My ego received a nice boost here, when a young couple we had met at Eden Roc asked Carolyn if she and her 'husband' would like to join them for lunch. After that I felt I could carry on.

I must now hark back to the autumn of 1956, to a day when friends of mine, Dick and Joan Wills, invited me to go to the theatre to see Arthur Miller's play *Over the Bridge*. Making up the fourth was actress Ursula Howells, once unhappily billed outside a theatre as 'Ursula Bowels'. At the last minute Ursula went down with glandular fever. Joan Wills asked me if I wanted to produce a bird, or would care to risk a blind date with a girl they knew, who was free. I said I had never been on a blind date, and was prepared to do anything once.

My first glance at the blind date gave me the impression that she was the most beautiful girl I had ever seen. My second glance confirmed it. She was tall and slim with smooth dark hair almost to her waist. She had enormous dark eyes and an olive skin. She wore a sari, which effectively hid the longest pair of legs in London. She was half-Indian and half-Scottish. Her father was a Bengali, Chief Engineer to the Government of India. She had only been in England for a few months. Her name was Maya Guha. She was twenty-one years of age and still a spinster. She was just starting on a modelling career, starving bravely in a permanent job at £8 a week.

We sat in a box at the Comedy Theatre, and I offered to buy her a box of chocolates. She said she would like that very much—and meant it, since she had not eaten lunch. For some reason, I forgot to buy the chocolates, an omission which took me a long time to live down.

Our appearance in the box caused a sensation. Dick Wills looked so like Arthur Miller that he could have been his twin brother. My face was widely known from TV. Within minutes, dozens of people were nudging each other and whispering that Michael Pertwee was in the box with the author of the play. When the actors took their curtain call they must have been surprised when large numbers of the audience directed their applause towards the box where we sat.

This blind date heralded the nervous beginning of a new life and marked the positive ending of the crumpet season. The change did not come easily. I had entirely recovered confidence in myself as a man, but after two marital failures the thought of a permanent relationship, which might lead to another marriage set my teeth chattering with fear.

Maya was not only beautiful; she possessed an innate intelligence and sensitivity, which was astounding in anyone so young and, I have to say it, so much in love. In the ensuing three years, during which we were constantly together, not once did she bring up the question of marriage. I was never able to issue any well rehearsed warnings, or give vent to my fears, because the subject never arose. At times, I must admit, I found this quite infuriating. How can you discuss the serious problems of a relationship, if one of the parties apparently refuses to admit there is a problem?

On 17th July 1959 I obtained a divorce on desertion grounds in a case lasting nine minutes. It made the front page of The *Daily Mirror*, complete with a picture of Valerie, taken by one of our photographers at some far off first night.

In December 1959 I flew from Los Angeles, at the end of a Hollywood assignment, to Hawaii, one of those dream places I had always longed to visit. My recollections of Honolulu are of enormous secondhand car lots; of crowds of middle-aged and overweight tourists; wearing leis and learning the hula-hula; of endless canned Hawaiian music, with that well-known Hawaiian, Andy Williams, singing *The Hawaiian Wedding Song*, and of the words of the hall porter at my hotel, who, in answer to my question as to what I should see during the few hours at my disposal, said: 'There is the world's biggest supermarket just down the street.'

From Hawaii, with a splendid view of a volcano in full eruption, I flew to Tokyo, one of those oriental cities I had always longed to visit.

My recollections of Tokyo are of rain, cold and fog, which reminded me irresistably of Manchester in November; of taxi drivers who were unquestionably ex-Kamakazi pilots, bent on killing themselves and anyone who got in their way; of shop window dummies who, inexplicably, had European eyes and blonde hair; of night-club reviews of quite excruciating badness; of a population wearing white gauze masks over their mouth and nose; of a huge store with a railway running straight through the second floor; of the longest hour I have ever spent, watching a Kabuki play, which apparently ran all day. During the hour I stayed the only action was a man, uttering shrill cries, crossing the stage and opening a door; of a visit to a tourist Geisha house where hideous Geisha girls, with blacked out front teeth, made the visitors play infantile games such as who would be the last to sit down when the music stopped; of an overwhelming desire to get the hell out of Japan at the earliest possible moment.

From Tokyo I flew to Hong Kong, another of those places I had always longed to visit—and I am glad I did. My recollections of Hong Kong are of astonishment at the immensity of the new building projects in view of the fact that it all has to be handed over to Red China in a fairly short time; of the elegance and beauty of the Chinese girls in their Cheong-sams and, finally, of the kindness and hospitality of an Indian tailor, Mr Dayaram, who not only made me four suits in three days, but who fed me curry every time I looked into the shop, who hired a car and took me round the island, who made me return everything I had bought from other shops and procured me the same items at a cheaper price, and who even offered to find me a woman to help while away my four nights. I accepted everything he offered except the woman, which I regretfully declined. I am sure she would have been first class, like everything else he provided. I explained I was on my way to Delhi to get married—to an Indian. He was delighted.

'You are marrying an Indian?'

'Yes, and a very beautiful one.'

He looked surprised:

'Oh! You've met the girl?'

I wanted to meet the girl again so badly that I abandoned my plan to visit Bangkok and flew straight to Delhi, where Maya was already staying with her parents, having flown from England a few days earlier.

I had forgotten that my future father-in-law was an important man in India. There was no question of them standing behind some barrier in the air-port building. Through a window of the cabin I saw Maya and her parents waiting to greet me near the foot of the steps.

I can only speculate on what was in her parents' minds. I know how I would feel if my daughter announced she was marrying a twice divorced man nearly twenty years older than she. Maya did not make things easier for them as they waited. I was among the last to leave the plane, but every time an unattractive, elderly man tottered down the steps she nudged her mother and whispered: 'There he is! That's him!'

Perhaps she was exhibiting her innate intelligence again, for when I did appear, comparatively upright and well tanned after weeks of Californian sunshine, their faces positively radiated relief.

Her father looked like an Indian Frederick March and her mother like a Scottish Marlene Dietrich. I have never been rude enough to enquire her age, but she certainly looks a lot younger than me. They have always been wonderfully kind and the only thing I hold against them is that they live much too far away.

They had a lovely house with a nice garden where five gardeners came twice a week to do work that one British gardener would finish in an hour.

My one complaint was that it was perishingly cold at night, also that no one thought to warn me that packs of howling jackals roam through the gardens of New Delhi after dark. On my first night there I thought someone in the house was being murdered—perhaps on account of me.

I was in Delhi at a time of crisis for the Republic of India, which was hovering on the brink of open war with Red China. Large scale fighting was actually in progress, and emergency debates were to take place in both Houses of Parliament. I was invited to attend the debates by an old friend of the family, who was an MP and a member of the Congress Party, Diwan Chaman Lall.

It was a fascinating experience. Except for a communist member, who spoke Tamil, which few present understood, the debate was carried out in English. It was immediately apparent that Pandit Nehru stood head and shoulders above the others. Most of the speeches were almost ludicrous. If they had taken place in Britain one would have gained the impression that they were designed to make headlines in the local press of the constituency for which the member had been elected.

'It is time to stop gabbing, stand up and give the Chinaman a black eye.'

Nehru was weary, irritable and logical. He treated them like a class of young children. It was all very well to talk of giving the Chinaman a black eye—but with what? Did they really wish him to plunge the country into a full scale war which they could not win?

While he was talking he turned suddenly on one of his senior ministers and hissed: 'Stop rustling those damned papers while I'm talking.'

The minister stopped rustling instantly.

I felt enormous sympathy for Nehru as the inconclusive debate ended and he gathered up his papers preparatory to going to the Upper House and starting it all over again.

At this point Chaman Lall said: 'Would you like to meet the Prime Minister?'

I would very much have liked to meet the Prime Minister, but could not imagine a less appropriate time for him to be asked to meet a complete stranger. He was obviously tired, harassed, and completely preoccupied with the crisis. Chaman brushed this aside. Nehru was an old friend of his. They had been at Oxford together, and imprisoned by the British together. He would be delighted to meet me.

Chaman waylaid Nehru in a corridor, as he was making his way to the Upper House. I was standing about four feet away when he said: 'Prime Minister, I'd very much like you to meet a friend of mine, a famous writer from England. . . .'

Nehru turned on him and shouted: 'I don't want to meet any damned writer. Do you think I have time to meet writers?'

I thoroughly agreed with him, and only wished there was some corner into which I could rush and hide.

To my astonishment Chaman did not move. He remained firmly standing

174

in front of Nehru, effectively blocking his way and, quite unabashed, said: 'No, really. I do think you should meet him. He's a very interesting fellow.'

I wished I was dead. Nehru stared at him; then said: 'Oh, very well.'

Chaman beckoned me forward. I approached with quaking knees. Nehru shook my hand and chatted pleasantly for about three minutes before politely excusing himself.

I can think of no other Prime Minister of any country, large or small, who, in these trying circumstances, would have shown such remarkable restraint and courtesy.

India, to a visitor with no preconceived ideas, is a country of paradoxes. What possible reason can there be for the undoubted popularity of the British of all people? Why should a Hindu happily accept his daughter marrying an Englishman, and yet fight to the last gasp to stop her marrying a Muslim Indian? Why does the average Indian have little time for communism, when, ten miles outside Delhi, people are living in the same primitive conditions which existed a thousand years ago? Why are Indians colour conscious? I sat in the New Delhi Club (where up to twelve years previously the colour conscious British had allowed no Indian to tread) and heard a member of the Congress party express the view that a pretty girl sitting nearby would never find a good husband because she was too black. Why would 'Settled Bachelor' advertise in the marriage columns: 'Wanted. Tall, beautiful, *fair*, educated virgin.'

The marriage columns in themselves are both funny and sad. 'No objection to aged virgin.' 'Brahmin girl, age 20, reading MA final. Corneal opacity in right eye but no outward ugliness.'

The visiting Britisher, after years of liberal brainwashing, finds it hard to accept the rigid class distinctions prevailing in what is proclaimed to be a socialist democracy.

We visited the residence of the present Maharajah of Jaipur, driven by one of my father-in-law's officers. He drove with Maya beside him. I sat in the back with his servant, who was only with us to open the car doors. When we left the residence, and got back into the car, Mr Kumar drove straight off, leaving his servant in the middle of the road. He was very old and started to trot hopelessly after the car. I tapped Mr Kumar on the shoulder and told him he had forgotten his servant. He did not reply, but drove straight on. We reached the first corner of the road, made the turning then he stopped the car and waited. A few minutes later the old servant tottered up, climbed in and we started off again. The only conceivable explanation was that Mr

175

Kumar did not want one of the Jaipurs to see me sitting in the back of his car beside a servant.

Other brief impressions; the utter beauty of the Taj Mahal, the only building I have ever seen which is far more beautiful than one imagines it will be; the horror of the huddled, white-clad figures lying in rows along the pavements of Calcutta at night, like corpses laid out after some plague— not corpses, but human beings with nowhere else to go; huge snakes gliding majestically in the Delhi equivalent of Hyde Park; the lovely spectacle of families of chattering monkeys playing among the rooftops in the middle of a teeming city; cows wandering and—as Shirley Ann would have said— excruciating all over the market, where delicious hot foods are served from open stalls; the unbelievably generous hospitality, with dinner served to any number of people at no notice at all; vultures at a busy cross roads eyeing the passing traffic with hungry eyes; the intense disappointment of every shopkeeper if you paid the price he asked and did not haggle; the realisation that although Indians naturally know how to make a good hot curry, they have not yet discovered the value of a nice hot plate; the strange sight, on the Republic Day Parade, of a pipe band of an Indian regiment, dressed in kilts.

The night before our wedding day I started to tremble violently and was found to have a temperature of a hundred and four. Whether this was some last psychosomatic symptom of subconscious resistance I shall never know, but it had disappeared by the morning.

We were married on New Year's Eve in the garden of the Guhas' house. Coby, who was with the World Health Organization in Manila, flew over to be Best Man. Maya wore a white sari. We both wore leis of golden marigolds round our necks, which prompted Danny, when he saw a photograph, to dub us as: 'The two best leis in Delhi.'

We honeymooned at the old palace of Jaipur, now a hotel, and at the Ashoka Hotel, New Delhi. On the first morning at the Ashoka I was standing on the balcony when a glider flew overhead and landed nearby. There was a gliding club five minutes away from the city.

I went there and presented my gliding certificate to their Chief Instructor, a handsome Sikh, who seemed overjoyed to meet a glider pilot from overseas. I expected to have at least one proving flight with an instructor. The Chief Instructor pointed to a two-seater which already had someone in the front seat, a pretty Indian girl. I vaguely remembered reading that Nehru had recently taken a gliding flight with an Indian girl instructor, so felt no qualms.

My own instructor had been Ann Welch, who had been great. I put on a parachute, and the Chief Instructor helped me into the rear seat. Just before lowering the canopy, he leaned forward confidentially and whispered: 'I'd be very grateful for your opinion on this girl. We can do nothing with her; keeps losing her head.'

Before I could shout for help, he closed the canopy and we were whisked into the air. I have rarely been so scared. I was comparatively inexperienced, flying in a German machine I had never seen, with controls in positions which hadn't even been pointed out to me, being piloted by a girl who, apparently could not fly. In addition, I had never soared with three hundred hawks before. They refused to obey the rules and most of them flew in the opposite direction, flashing over our heads with inches to spare. There was not much thermal activity, and we soon had to prepare for landing. Up to this moment my pupil had behaved in an exemplary fashion, circling tidily and keeping a nice constant speed. I discovered her weakness as we made the final approach— she was terrified of landing. Instead of increasing speed she decreased it. Up went the nose and down went one wingtip to signal an incipient spin. She threw up her hands and gave up. I scrambled into the emergency routine—stick forward and opposite rudder. We went into a steep dive, straightened out and landed at about sixty miles an hour. I did a lot of flying there, periodically waggling my wings at my father-in-law as he rested after lunch in the garden—but I refused to do any more instructing.

I left Maya in Delhi for a few weeks. I twice set off for Moscow (another of those cities I had always longed to see), twice flew over the Himalayas and twice returned to Delhi owing to bad weather in Tashkent. As I had to get back to work I gave up and decided to fly straight back to London. In the airport lounge I left Maya for a few minutes to buy some papers. An airport official came up to her, looking for me.

'Miss,' he said, 'where's Dad?'

Somewhat disloyally, I think, she did not correct him and said he was across the lounge, buying papers.

My own Dad had sent us a telegram for the wedding which read: 'Third time lucky.'

It was well intended but it had *not* been read out at the ceremony.

Readers who have persevered thus far, and who may now be looking forward to reading my fourth marriage, can stop right here. We are still married and blissfully happy after fourteen years. I have finally dropped anchor.

Part 15

Insularity Dropping

ANGUS MACPHAIL ONCE said that no British screenwriter could consider himself a success unless he had been asked to write a picture in Hollywood before he was thirty. If this somewhat arbitrary statement is true, I am a failure.

I did not visit America until 1957 when, aged forty-one, I paid for a trip to New York in an attempt to sell *Yakity-Yak* to US television. This was the first of my many visits.

One of our more popular postwar sports, even exceeding Pakistani-bashing, has been knocking America and the Americans. I am surprised that the Americans sometimes resent this. They should have learned by now that if you lend enough money to impecunious friends, who have no hope of paying it back, you are bound to be disliked. In addition, of course, all Americans are brash, loud-mouthed, ill-educated and politically backward. Their food looks good but tastes of nothing. You can visit America but you could not possibly live there.

I am going to be very courageous, and dissociate myself from these views. I will even go so far as to say that some of my best friends are Americans, and that I would allow my daughter to marry one.

I like their warmth and hospitable nature. I like their steaks, super highways, central heating and air-conditioning. I like the efficiency of their film and television studios, where they know exactly what they want—even if they want what is sometimes bad. I like their stores where, instead of getting pleasure out of telling you that something is unobtainable, they will send to the other end of the city to obtain what you want. I like eighty degrees of sun in

Los Angeles in February. I like the green lawns and crazy, mixed-up architecture of Beverly Hills. I like their clean, over-heated swimming pools. I do *not* like the Pacific which is never pacific.

I received a tremendous welcome when I arrived in New York. Even in my heyday as a British TV personality I have never been stopped by so many strangers, nor received so much adulation. This was because *My Fair Lady* had recently opened there and everybody took me for Rex Harrison, whom I do resemble slightly.

I wanted to see *My Fair Lady* but it was impossible to obtain tickets, even on the black market. I knew Rex Harrison vaguely but resisted calling him. He must have been inundated with requests from nodding acquaintances, who would otherwise never have dreamed of approaching him.

By one of those coincidences, which keep on proving what a small world it is, I found myself sitting right next to Rex Harrison in a bar, on my second night in New York. Despite this, I stuck to my decision. We chatted for some time. The last occasion we had met was in Brussels during the war, when he had shown a passing interest in the play *Chain Male*. By not mentioning *My Fair Lady* I brought off a brilliant psychological coup. After several minutes chatting, a slightly strained look came into his eye. A little later, he could contain himself no longer and asked if I had seen the show. I said I hadn't because tickets were unobtainable. He told me not to be stupid. He had two house seats available every night. Which night would I like to go? I gave him a night, the address of my hotel, and left the bar feeling extremely smug. The only sad footnote to this story is that Rex forgot to arrange the tickets.

I happened to be in New York on Saint Patrick's Day, which is celebrated there far more fervently than anywhere in Ireland. This was a particularly big year, because the Mayor of Dublin, who happened to be Jewish, was in New York at the time.

I watched the giant parade down Fifth Avenue. Some of the banners on display were a little puzzling since this was America, 'Go Home England' being one of them. One of the largest banners simply had 'SINN FEIN' printed on it. An American, standing on the sidewalk next to me, nudged his wife, pointed to the banner and said: 'Sinn Fein. That must be the name of the Jewish Mayor of Dublin.'

I spent a few days in Chicago with a lawyer friend, Bill Rivkin. Here I met Adlai Stevenson. Bill was one of his aides in his unsuccessful bid for the Presidency.

179

Bill was later an active aide in John Kennedy's successful campaign and, as a reward, was made US Ambassador to Luxembourg.

Maya and I went to stay at the Embassy in Luxembourg with Bill and his wife, Enid. They gave a banquet in our honour, to which all kinds of important people were invited. Here I encountered my first experience of protocol. Although the banquet was in our honour, we could not be seated above certain important guests. Bill and Enid spent nearly all day shifting named flags around on a wooden mock-up of the dining-table. They were still shifting them ten minutes before all the guests arrived *en masse* promptly at eight o'clock. (Protocol again; you wait outside even if you are only a minute early.)

It was a most enjoyable dinner but for one thing. Something had happened to the distribution of the flags and, as we sat down, we found all the men were seated on one side of the table, and all the women on the other.

I made my first trip to Hollywood in 1958. I was to write two of the Hitchcock TV half-hour thrillers. The money was small, but it would pay my trip, enable me to see the place and meet people. In addition, Hitchcock himself was going to direct one of the episodes, which meant working with him. I felt this was an opportunity not to be missed.

My agent was Hugh French, an Englishman, who had started as an actor, then worked with various big agencies and had now set up on his own. Among his clients were Michael Rennie and Richard Burton. Later, Elizabeth Taylor joined his stable. Hugh was, I think, the first agent to achieve a million dollar fee for a client. He has now more or less retired on his well-gotten gains.

Hugh did everything to make my first visit enjoyable and useful. He loaned me a car, secured me many introductions and gave me constant hospitality at his beach house in Malibu. Hugh held open house on Sundays, with a cold lunch provided for any friends who cared to turn up. A lot of well-known people would come and lounge in the tiny patch of sandy garden on the edge of the ocean; James Mason, Christopher Isherwood and Marlene Dietrich were among them. On one occasion I spent an enjoyable couple of hours talking to a wonderful English actress. The conversation got around to the two films about Oscar Wilde, which had been distributed almost simultaneously, one starring Robert Morley, and the other Peter Finch. I said that although I was one of Robert Morley's most devoted fans, I had preferred Peter Finch's interpretation of Wilde. She listened politely—very politely indeed, as it turned out. She was Gladys Cooper and I had quite forgotten she was Bob Morley's mother-in-law.

On my first visit I stayed in an apartment on Wilshire Boulevard. In the adjoining apartment Danny and Brenda Danischewsky were staying. He was writing a film. Across the courtyard I could see Nigel Balchin, tapping away at his first draft of Walter Wanger's mammoth *Cleopatra*, which was to have many vicissitudes before it finally reached the screen, and brought Richard Burton and Elizabeth Taylor together.

Nigel was another of Hugh's clients. I used to look at him, and compare the two thousand dollars I was earning with the vast sum he was getting for his script. He was very friendly, but I suppose it was the enormous difference in our class of employment which made me feel somewhat in awe of him at the time.

One of my introductions happened to be to Walter Wanger. A few hours after I had returned from meeting him, there was a tap on my door. It was Nigel Balchin. He had heard I had been to see Wanger. Anxiously he enquired whether, during my interview, Walter Wanger had passed any comments, good or bad, on what he had read of Nigel's script.

It just goes to show that earning vast sums of money does not necessarily give a writer a feeling of security.

The Danischewskys gave a party. Here I met a slim, petite, attractive woman who talked about Roland, whose work she admired and whom she had met many years before during one of his visits. She invited me to dinner, and said Danny would give me the address. Like all ill-mannered Englishmen I had failed to get her name on being introduced and had to do one of those: 'Don't look now, but who is that nice lady I was talking to?' She was Lee Gershwin, wife of Ira Gershwin, who wrote the brilliant lyrics to the music of his brother George, I have never understood why the Gershwins took me under their wing. Hollywood is full of visiting firemen, and the Gershwins, although they know everybody, are notoriously choosy about making friends; but this meeting was the beginning of a friendship which has now lasted fifteen years; one sided, in certain respects, since they are impossible people to entertain. The only times I have seen Ira in a bad temper are when I have invited him out to dinner and he has had to accept. Ira has lived by words and lives for words. You need only question the meaning or derivation of a word and he will disappear upstairs, to reappear hidden behind a mountain of tomes, in one of which will lie the answer.

There is something very special about hearing Gershwin words and music in the Gershwin home, whether it be an old disc made at some rehearsal, with George playing the piano and making comments, or listening to the silken voice of Ella Fitzgerald.

In 1959 Ira sent me his book *Lyrics on Several Occasions*, a selection of his stage and screen lyrics with, to quote him: 'Many Informative Annotations and Disquisitions on Their Why and Wherefore, Their Whom-For, Their How; and Matters Associative.' In one of the disquisitions he writes that, since most of the lyrics were arrived at by fitting words mosaically to music already composed, any resemblance to actual poetry, living or dead, is highly improbable. Perhaps true, but I would commend anyone who thinks there are many comparable lyricists around today to read the book.

It was not surprising to meet many people connected with music at the Gershwins. Oscar Levant was always looking in. He gave an enormous party while I was out there, and professed to hate the whole idea. Two questions were on everybody's lips prior to the occasion: 'Have you been invited to Oscar's party?' and, more often, 'Is Oscar going to his party?'

I met Judy Garland, sad and withdrawn. I often met Arthur Freed, a gruff, down-to-earth character with a sly wit who, in contrast to Burt Bacharach, did not look to have an ounce of music in him. He was probably the world's greatest producer of musical films—*Meet Me in St Louis, An American In Paris, Gigi*, and *Singing In The Rain* among them. His talents were not confined to producing. He was a lyric writer of renown and wrote the entire score for *Singing In The Rain*. I remember Arthur reminiscing about Cole Porter, who had been very much of a gourmet. He nearly always ate his meals in New York's plushest and most expensive restaurant, Le Pavilion.

'Cole,' said Arthur, 'is the only man I know who sent back a jug of water at the Pavilion.'

I met Joe Bushkin, the pianist, a lively and amusing man with a reputation for being a great one for taking pills. I understood how he gained this reputation, when he cheerfully refused all food at dinner and placed a handful of multi-coloured pills on his plate, which he slowly consumed while the rest of us ate our meal. I am still not sure whether he did it as a joke or not. I met Burt Bacharach. He married Angie Dickinson, the actress, who has no right to look so pretty and play such good poker. I met Rosemary Clooney. I even listened to her husband, José Ferrer give a little concert at the piano, and he is no musician.

When Connie, my mother-in-law, visited Mexico and America on a shoe-string, she travelled round the States by Greyhound bus. She visited Los Angeles, where she settled contentedly into the YWCA. She called Lee Gershwin to send our love. Lee asked where she was staying and, when she

An unholy trio—(*l to r*) me,
Brian Rix and stage producer
Wallace Douglas during
rehearsals for *Don't Just Lie
There—Say Something!*, a
London theatre success, now a
film *and* a TV series. It doesn't
happen that way too often!

With my wife Maya, at one of
the celebrated Arthur Ferrier
fancy dress parties.

'Old Once-Every-Twenty-One Years'——with wife, Maya;
son Timothy, and canine friend.

'The two best leis in Delhi' at wedding in New Delhi (*1959*). (*Left*): best man and stepbrother Michael Colbourne; (*centre*): mother-in-law Connie Guha; father-in-law Biren
Guha; brother-in-law Arun Guha.

heard, abruptly told Connie not to move and hung up. Fifteen minutes later she picked her up, took her home and made her stay with them.

My first Hitchcock half-hour was received well. I then wrote a draft of the second one, which Hitch was to direct. This meant working with him in his house, which looked over Bel Air golf course. I have never met anyone who has lived so long in America and yet has remained as determinedly British as he, even to afternoon tea with crumpets.

The brief time I worked with Hitch was instructive, interesting, and unsatisfactory for both of us. He did not like my first draft, and was almost certainly justified. It was a difficult story, which could be handled in a dozen different ways. The problem I encountered was that Hitch sees his scripts entirely as pictures on a screen, acting and reacting as he will direct them. He could visualise exactly what he wanted, but could not translate his images into words which clarified to me what he wanted. Thus my words and his images kept failing to meet. He was patient and encouraging and polite but, despite substantial re-writes, I could not give him what he wanted and eventually someone else re-wrote it.

I made several trips to California, made many good friends, and wrote a lot of television scripts; but I did not get the big film assignment I had hoped for. The motion picture business was already in a decline, and the whole structure of the major studios, with large scale self-financed production, was beginning to disappear.

I took Maya there in 1960 for three months. We stayed in New York on our way back. We attended a debate in the United Nations on the day after Khruschev had taken off his shoe and banged it on the table. During the course of his violent diatribe Khruschev had said some rude things about the Philippines. When we arrived the Philippino delegate was making a spirited defence of his country. His theme was that, although the Philippines were a small nation and Russia was a large one, this did not give Mr Khruschev the right to insult his country. This received a tremendous ovation from all 'freedom loving' countries. Only the Iron Curtain delegates grimly glowered at the floor. Then, in the midst of the applause, an extraordinary thing happened. Grinning all over his face, Khruschev rose to his feet, raised his arms above his head, and also began enthusiastically to applaud the Philippino. The faces of the delegates from the other Iron Curtain countries were a picture of surprise and dismay. They just did not know what to do. Khruschev's action caused gales of laughter, and the applause continued with

Khruschev leading it. One by one, the other Iron Curtain delegates followed suit and, finally, everyone in the hall was applauding. The only people who looked displeased were the Philippinos, for Khruschev had cleverly turned the whole affair into a great joke.

I wanted to get a closer look at this intriguing man, so rose and walked over to where he sat. No one in the Russian delegation around Khruschev seemed concerned as I stood three feet behind him for some minutes.

As I stood there, it occurred to me that, since entry cards for the UN are reasonably easy to obtain, and since no one had searched me on entering, nothing could have stopped me assassinating Mr Khruschev (or anyone else in the hall) had I smuggled in a weapon, and been prepared to sacrifice myself. I found this a most disturbing thought.

This was quite a day for politicians. We were in bed asleep in our hotel at 2 am when the telephone rang. Bill Rivkin was on the line.

'Hi!' he said. 'Would you like to meet Hubert Humphrey?'

Two o'clock in the morning seemed an odd time to ask this, but I did not argue about that.

'Yes,' I said. 'When?'

'*Now*. Come over to Lindy's right away.'

So we dressed and took a cab to Lindy's. There were only two people in the restaurant, other than staff. They were Bill Rivkin and Hubert Humphrey. If there can be an equivalent between British and American politicians, I suppose one could describe Hubert Humphrey as being the Opposition Shadow Foreign Secretary at that time. He had just returned from a highly publicised trip to the Soviet Union, where he held a series of private meetings with Khruschev, during which every problem between Russia and the US had been thrashed out in frank detail. Humphrey had reported at length to President Eisenhower. Now, at Lindy's at two o'clock in the morning, surrounded by a crowd of goggle-eyed waiters, he reported to Bill Rivkin, Maya and myself. It was, at once, one of the most fascinating and incredible experiences of my life and to this day, I can still hardly believe it happened.

I wrote a picture for an extremely nice American, Walter Shenson, who had settled in England. This was *Mouse on the Moon*, a sequel to his successful *Mouse that Roared* which had starred Peter Sellers. It was a kind of farcical science-fiction tale, and did pretty well. Among the stars were Margaret Rutherford, Bernard Cribbins and, it almost goes without saying, Terry-Thomas.

The picture was directed by Richard Lester. It was his first full feature film. He proved efficient, modest and most willing to listen to advice from any quarter.

During this picture something happened, which illustrates the very special quality inherent in the older British actors and actresses. At the time this picture was made Margaret Rutherford was about seventy. One day she drew Walter Shenson aside to ask his advice on a problem which was worrying her.

'Mr Shenson, Metro Goldwyn Mayer have offered me a long term film contract. Should I accept or would it be bad for my career?'

Another British-based American to employ me was Stanley Donen, who asked if I would care to write an original film comedy for Cary Grant. I was thrilled, and we started work immediately.

A week after signing with Donen, Walter Shenson called to ask if I was free to write a small picture for him. He could not offer much money, as it was a small budget affair, but he could offer a good percentage of any profits.

A trifle smugly I thanked him, but said I was writing a big picture for Cary Grant. He congratulated me, hired someone else, and then went on to make his picture which was called *A Hard Day's Night*, and starred four chaps called the Beatles. If I had written that picture I could have retired on the proceeds. I plugged on with my Cary Grant subject, which Stanley Donen disliked very much and which ultimately fell through at the halfway stage.

Such are the tricks of timing which make mine the fascinating and infuriating profession that it is.

My first picture to be made in Hollywood came from a collaboration with Melvin Frank writing the screenplay of *Strange Bedfellows*, a slick, glossy comedy.

Mel Frank, and his partner Norman Panama, had settled in England, and planned to make a number of pictures there. They had been partners for some twenty-five years, starting as gag writers for Bob Hope and going on to write, produce and direct a string of successful movies—Bob Hope's *Monsieur Beaucaire*, some of the Hope Crosby *Road* pictures, including the most recent *Road to Hong Kong*. They also made the delightful Bob Hope, Lucille Ball comedy *Facts of Life*.

After *Strange Bedfellows* I worked a lot with Mel and we have become close friends. Ten years later I still do not know how we work so well together, because no two men could be more diametrically opposed in their approach to writing. I am extremely fast and like to rush out a draft in order to have something to tear to pieces. Mel is exceedingly slow, and cannot bear to start writing until the subject has been discussed, noted, re-noted, and analysed a dozen times. Perhaps this difference is the secret. I have certainly learned a great deal from the association, not least that it rarely pays to be satisfied with first thoughts.

Both Mel and Norman are proudly proclaimed hypochondriacs. They once named a house in which they worked 'Hypochondria', and had the name put on a board outside.

One day I was playing golf with Norman in Spain. He swung the club, winced, and clutched his stomach.

'Jesus!' he cried. 'I have a terrible pain. I hope I've twisted something.'

The above may have to be read twice before the reader grasps his meaning.

In ten years I have never known Mel admit to feeling well. You ask how he is at your own peril, for he will tell you. Neither is it wise to tell him you are not feeling too good yourself for, before you are halfway through your symptoms, you find that he has the same trouble—only worse. Yet, in ten years, I have never known him spend a day in bed, nor met a man who can be writing three subjects simultaneously with a seemingly inexhaustible supply of energy and concentration.

Mel's amusing wife, Ann, can suffer, too. Her main problem is a deep suspicion of foreign food. We were once three months in Madrid together. They had a rented house, and imported their own cook from England. Thus the food was exactly the same as they ate anywhere else in the world. Yet, throughout the three months, Ann did not cease to complain of an upset, 'Spanish' tummy. As we prepared to return to England, I said I was going to write a book about her experiences entitled: *The Diarrhoea of Ann Frank*.

We finished the screenplay of *Strange Bedfellows* and the film was eventually made for Universal International in Hollywood, with Rock Hudson, Gina Lollobrigida, Gig Young and the ubiquitous Terry-Thomas. I just could not stop writing for him.

I flew to Los Angeles with Mel, when he went there to direct the picture, for we were already working on another subject together.

In the plane we sat near Cary Grant, whom I had never met. As Mel introduced us, I recalled that someone had just discovered that Cary Grant was the same age as the Archbishop of Canterbury, which was hard to believe. He looked incredibly young and handsome. The jet stopped at Montreal to refuel. Mel and I decided to stretch our legs in the airport. Cary Grant had written a quantity of postcards during the flight, and asked me if I would mind buying the stamps and mailing them for him. I did this, and on our return to the plane, he thanked me charmingly. He did not, however, offer to pay me for whatever it cost, perhaps on the assumption that I should like to tell my children how I once licked Cary Grant's stamps.

Americans sometimes accuse Britain of still being a class-conscious nation. Any American, no matter what his job, considers himself as good as the next man.

I noticed, when we arrived in Los Angeles, that Cary Grant was whisked off the plane first, shot through Immigration and Customs, and was well on his way home while the cold-eyed Customs Officers were still systematically searching every inch of our luggage. I do not disagree with the American view of Britain, but, nonetheless, I have never seen this happening at London Airport.

It would be easy to write a book about my American experiences, but I must content myself with a few random recollections.

Los Angeles is the biggest mix-up of a city I have ever known, architecturally, climatically (or is it climate-wise?) and legally. Where else in the world do you get headlines in July saying: 'Hottest Day Since February 1.?' Where else in the world do you risk arrest for taking an evening constitutional? No one walks. Tibby Clarke, who does not drive, was picked up twice by the police in one evening, for taking a stroll. I was once playing poker for peanuts with some of the richest and most influential people in Hollywood, when a Beverly Hills Cop entered on some business. I have rarely seen so many ashen faces as he glanced at the poker table. As my hostess started to stammer something, he waved an arm, winked, and said: 'It's okay Lady. I didn't see a thing.'

You risk arrest for playing poker for money in your own home in Beverly Hills, yet, ten miles down the road in another part of the city, every other building in the street is a licensed casino, where they play poker, smoking cigars and wearing stetsons.

I became friends with a Los Angeles detective. One night when I was there an armed gang, who had been raiding liquor stores, walked into a trap. Police were waiting in the store as they held up the proprietor. According to the papers, the gang refused to submit to arrest and, in the subsequent gun battle, they were shot down and killed. I asked my friend what kind of mentality men like these could have, who tried to fight it out, when they must surely know they were doomed. He shrugged and said: 'Well, it wasn't quite like that. It was a kind of execution really.'

The inference was that the police just shot them down without warning.

I said that the British police would have a hard job justifying an action like that, to which he replied: 'How many English cops have been shot dead during the last year? I've lost six men up to now.'

I was in a minor earthquake and did not know it. I thought it was a truck going by. I was amazed how many apparently sane and sensible people found reasons to leave Los Angeles for business elsewhere on the day that some astrologer had predicted that most of Los Angeles would disappear into the ocean, following an earthquake.

Astrologers flourish in Los Angeles. I spent a lot of pleasant days round Glenn Ford's swimming pool at a new house he had just built for himself. Glenn is a firm believer in astrology. He told me an odd story about his new house, which is built round two sides of the pool. It is a bungalow with one room below ground—his den, which houses a cinema (including cinemascope), and his own radio transmitting station, from which he did a weekly broadcast, thus saving him the trouble of going to the studios. When the house was being constructed, Glenn's current astrologer (whose name I forget, so I will call him H) visited the site, and said he did not like the position of the den *vis-à-vis* the swimming pool. He could 'see' water in the den quite clearly; a lot of water. Glenn was in a quandary. He had naturally hired the best architect and the best builders in the business. Could he go to his architect and say: 'My astrologer says the den is going to be flooded?'

So he compromised and, at the earliest opportunity, casually told his architect that an engineer friend had recently visited the site, and had expressed the view that the pool might burst and flood the den. The architect looked at him incredulously, and asked what kind of an engineer had made a ridiculous remark like that? He went on to prove without a shadow of doubt that such an eventuality was an absolute impossibility. Glenn told him to forget it.

The house was built. Glenn moved in and, within weeks, the den was flooded. The puzzled architect came to survey the damage, and asked Glenn the name of this prescient engineer. Glenn decided to tell him the truth. It had not been an engineer. It was H who had warned him.

'Why didn't you tell me?' said the architect. 'If I'd known that, I might have done something about it.'

I was so fascinated by the whole business that I went to consult one of Glenn's 'advisers', an old, foreign lady. She sat me down, looked at me with kindly eyes and said: 'Well, my dear, and what is your problem?'

I was silent. I am one of those lucky people who do not have problems. I

188

racked my brains, but could find absolutely nothing that was even vaguely troubling me. Her face visibly fell when I finally told her this. She cheered up a little on learning that I had a wife back in England, who was some twenty years younger then me. She proceeded to paint an erroneous picture of a rather dizzy creature, who was having a much better time than she should be in my absence. She also learned I had a young son aged two. Of him she said that she did not like the look of his right leg. I should watch this carefully. There was trouble there.

Three weeks after I had returned to England, Maya came to me and told me that Timothy, our son, could not walk. He had completely lost the use of his right leg. We stood him up several times, but he just fell down. We rushed him to the doctor, who gave him every conceivable test, without finding the cause. His leg was paralysed for two days; then, as suddenly, his leg recovered. We have never had any explanation of this, and I have never consulted another astrologer.

Las Vegas is a nice place to visit but you cannot gamble there. That is my experience. I have twice left this gamblers' paradise completely broke. Once I boarded the aircraft to return to Los Angeles and realised I had no money left to get my car out of the parking lot at Los Angeles airport.

If one can conquer the urge to gamble, which I now have, it is a wonderful place for a great weekend, with some of the finest entertainment in the world at reasonable prices. Occasionally you even get something for nothing. I watched a half-hour impromptu cabaret given by Sammy Davis and Debbie Reynolds to celebrate somebody's birthday, which was a joy. It concluded with Debbie kissing Sammy to huge applause. I was staying with him at the time, and that same evening he told me there were still casinos in the town where he could politely but firmly be refused entry.

You can visit Palm Springs but you could not live there, anyway if you were me. The air is fantastic. The climate is out of this world; but you can be bored to death if you don't know many people.

In Palm Springs I was one of a privileged few to have seen the only blue film ever to have been transmitted over a major US television network. I was lying in bed at my hotel. The channel I had been watching had closed down for the night, but I had not switched off the set. Then, silent, but graphically clear, came the blue film, showing every sexual deviation imaginable. Jack Nahum's Swedish seaman would have loved it. I could not believe my eyes. For one dreadful moment I thought six weeks monastic existence had affected my mind, so I woke up Mel Frank who was asleep in his house, and told him

189

to switch on. The yell of amazement which came over the phone at least put my mind at rest regarding my sanity.

It transpired that, after the day's transmissions were over, some of the staff at the local station ran blue films for their own amusement. On this occasion someone had forgotten to turn off a vital switch.

I spent some sad evenings in Hollywood with another old friend, actor Anthony Steel, who was in the process of seeing his marriage to Anita Ekberg go up in smoke. One evening he produced a little box, which contained nothing but a gold screw. It was, he said, her wedding present to him. He told me, with how much truth I do not know, that the card accompanying the gift had read: 'The most expensive screw you've ever had.'

I was responsible for a highly publicised marriage, although the couple may not be aware of it.

Peter Lawford threw a party for me, when I went out to stay with him at his house on the beach. The night before this party we had been together to another party, where I met an old poker-playing friend from England, actor David Hemmings. He had just arrived in Hollywood and was miserable. He did not know anybody and felt lost. I whispered to Peter that I thought it would be kind if he invited David to his party, so he did.

Peter told me that he had invited a very pretty girl for me to make up the numbers. She was very pretty indeed. I did get introduced to her—but so did David Hemmings. Her name was Gayle Hunnicutt, and that was the last I saw of David (or Gayle Hunnicutt) on that trip. They married not long after.

I first met Peter Lawford in London with his manager, Milt Ebbins. They asked if I would be interested in writing an original screenplay to star Peter and Sammy Davis Junior. I extemporised a story on the spot and they liked the sound of it.

Three weeks later I flew to America with a story outline to meet Sammy Davis.

Sammy was then appearing in a strange motel near Syracuse. It lay beside a main road, with no other building in sight for miles. It had an enormous dining-room, which could house well over a thousand people. It was full every night. I do not know where all the people came from. I asked Sammy what he did all day in a God-forsaken spot like that, and he said:

'I stand by the road and wave at the trucks as they go by.'

I was taken straight to Sammy's dressing-room to meet him, shortly before the evening performance. He was wearing nothing but underpants, and was playing cards with members of his entourage. He was a little reserved and, I thought, looked at me warily. Although I get on very well with Americans, I am, I have to admit, very British and probably, on first acquaintance, appear square and stand-offish. This is something Sammy will not tolerate.

We had a stilted chat, then I left him to get ready for the show. I was taken to the first floor to unpack. Here I nearly lost my life. There was a large verandah, which ran the length of the hotel. You could walk from one room to the other along it.

Milt, Peter and I stood on the verandah talking. I leaned back against the rail, which promptly broke. I started to fall to my death. They pulled me back when I was three parts gone. Very shaken, I accompanied them to the dining-room for the show.

My first surprise was to discover Peter Lawford's enormous popularity. In England no one takes much notice of stars when they come into a restaurant, no matter who they are. As Peter entered he was mobbed. It took about twenty minutes to reach our table. Thereafter four frightening-looking men stood guard over the table to keep people at bay.

Sammy's act was scheduled to run forty-five minutes; but on this occasion he performed exactly one and a half hours of singing, dancing and clowning of quite breathtaking brilliance. I am not ashamed of feeling some pride in the knowledge that this was done entirely for my benefit. He did not know I needed no convincing of his brilliance, but he was going to make damned sure that I was convinced. After it was over I felt almost as exhausted as he must have done; and the evening was only just beginning. Sammy's day only starts when the evening performance is over.

First, there was a dinner. I sat opposite Sammy who started a gentle probing of my ability to take it, by talking to me in his British aristocratic voice, which he does a great deal better than most Americans. An enormous amount of alcohol was consumed—though not by Sammy, who was on Coke following an attack of hepatitis. Later, a smaller number of us gathered together elsewhere in a thoroughly relaxed state. I say a smaller number, because being alone with Sammy nearly always means he has at least five other people with him. He asked me about myself, found out Maya's name and our telephone number, and then telephoned her in London to say that we had met, that he did not like me, but liked the sound of her, and would she care to sit with his wife, Mai Britt, at the forthcoming Royal Command

Performance at the London Palladium? Since he had woken her from a deep slumber she was slightly dazed by the whole business and, in the morning, was not sure it had really happened.

I got to bed at seven o'clock, slightly dazed myself because I had not closed my eyes since leaving England.

Next day I told my story and learned the valuable lesson that one must never tell Sammy a story without having a tape recorder handy. If anything appeals to him he gets up and starts to act out the scene. He ad libs brilliant dialogue. He is also extremely inventive, but the ideas pour out so fast that one needs a recorder to get them all down. He certainly has one of the quickest brains I have ever encountered. His power of instant repartee is, I think, unequalled.

Our excellent relationship, both personally and in working together, was cemented by one exchange, which took place in Las Vegas a little later. He was proving unnecessarily stubborn on one minor story point. I suddenly said: 'Sammy, now you're being niggardly.'

Without hesitation, he flashed back: 'Don't bring race into this, you English prick.'

After that, I was even able to get him addicted to White Port, when he eventually came to England to make the picture.

From Syracuse we went to New York now joined by Dick Donner, who was to direct the picture.

Here I had an odd experience, when I purchased a walky-talky radio set from a large Fifth Avenue store. I bought it because the store proprietor told me (he was lying in his teeth) that it was a very special piece of equipment, in that you could call up the party you wished to talk to, just as if it was a telephone.

After I had made the purchase I met Dick Donner, who was sure I had been swindled. He took me into another store, where they confirmed his fears. Dick told me not to worry. His uncle was in a big legal position in New York— something like High Sheriff. He said we had only to return to the store and ask for the money back, dropping the name of his Uncle. We returned to the store. I asked for my money back and the man laughed in my face. Dick then produced his High Sheriff like some piece of heavy artillery, and the man laughed even louder. We threatened to call the police and he nearly ruptured himself. We left the store defeated. I returned to the hotel and went to Sammy's suite. Sammy had a good laugh, too, and called me the same name as Happy had done during the war. Then a member of Sammy's entourage rose. He was one of the biggest black men I have ever seen. He stood about six foot six, with enormous arms and shoulders. I will call him Ben. Ungratefully, I have forgotten his name.

'Come with me,' he said.

I asked where? He said back to the store. I told him it was useless. We had threatened everything and the man had just laughed.

'He won't laugh again,' said Ben. 'Come with me.'

We returned to the store and walked in. Ben asked which of the men had done the laughing. I pointed him out. Ben then walked across, reached out with one arm and literally picked the shopkeeper up by the lapels of his suit, holding him about a foot off the ground. It is the first time I have seen this done outside of a film and I did not think it was possible. He then talked very quietly.

'Christmas is coming,' he said, which seemed an odd start. 'If you don't give this man his money back, I tell you what is going to happen to you. Tomorrow morning there's going to be six niggers (his word) just as big as me, who are going to be picketing this store, and no one's going to get in or out until the end of January. Now, what do you say?'

The man said nothing, but thirty seconds later I walked out of the store with my money back.

This is something else which could *not* happen in dear old Bond Street, and I cannot decide whether that is a good thing or not.

I started my return trip to London by taking to the air backwards, slowly, from the top of a tall building in the centre of New York in a helicopter— an experience which is both exciting and frightening.

Back in London I wrote the script, then returned to Los Angeles to stay with Peter at his house on the beach, while everyone read my story and made their comments. The house was one of the real, old-fashioned stars' homes, but complete, of course, with pool and sauna. Peter lived there alone, having recently separated from his wife, the former Pat Kennedy; but was still surrounded by mementoes of the Kennedy family. It was a curious feeling to find myself seated in one of the late President's rocking chairs from Camp David.

Peter and his manager, Milt, were extraordinarily hospitable. Milt is one of the most generous men I have met. He is also the most devoted manager that any star could want. It was said that when Peter had been ill in hospital Milt took a bed there, too, to be close at hand.

Milt is a born butt for practical jokes, which he suffers with remarkable good humour. In the days of the so-called Rat-Pack, his life must have been hellish, for none of them ever let up on him. Milt has a thing about wrist watches and electric razors. He never stops buying them. I possess two of his 'old' electric razors neither of which had been used. He once bought a new wrist watch, of which he was inordinately proud. Frank Sinatra asked to see it. Milt took it off his wrist and gave it to Sinatra, who looked at it, then threw it out of the window, which was some twenty storeys high. He let Milt suffer for a day, then gave him another, twice as good, to take its place.

Peter gave the party for me. Apart from bringing Gayle Hunnicutt and David Hemmings together, the party was also notable for the appearance of Martha Raye, who had returned that very day from entertaining the troops in Viet Nam. She was given a heroine's welcome when she arrived. The only thing which puzzled me was why she was still wearing full uniform and army boots. Perhaps she came straight off the plane.

I went to Las Vegas to talk with Sammy. His hours of work would have suited Nick Monsarrat better than me. Nick works all night and stays in bed until lunchtime. Sammy rarely surfaces before two in the afternoon, and I have never stayed up long enough to see him go to bed. I know he does, because I have seen him there at two o'clock in the afternoon.

The picture was made in England. It was called *Salt and Pepper*. It made little impression in Britain, but did so well in America that I was asked to write a sequel.

This entailed further visits to the States for talks. I flew to Reno where Sammy was appearing. Reno is a kind of poor man's Las Vegas. I was astonished at the number of pretty prostitutes, who stood openly in doorways, beckoning as one approached. I found they were not prostitutes at all, but representatives of the instant marriage parlours. Reno can be a dangerous place. You can walk down a street with a bird, say: 'Let's get married!' and you do.

I went to see Sammy perform at a casino. I was dressed in a silk shirt and tie, and wore a smart and expensive black evening cardigan. As I started to move into the restaurant I was grabbed by a tough looking man and told I could not enter. I was improperly dressed. It appeared I had to wear a jacket, and a black evening cardigan did not count. This was so ridiculous that I threw my weight about and said I was Sammy's guest. He clearly did not believe me. I only got in by abandoning my cardigan and borrowing a bright green check sports coat which reached to my knees. They then considered me properly dressed and allowed me to enter.

Sammy chose to open his show by talking about me and the two films. He said he was going to do some special bits and pieces for me, then made me stand up and take a bow, lit by a brilliant spotlight. The check sports coat must have looked quite dreadful, but the tough man at the door had completely changed his manner as I left at the end of the performance. He apologised for about five minutes.

Sammy and Mai Britt had just separated, and he was living alone in a huge house in Beverly Hills, where he looked a lonely and sad figure. After a meeting there one day, he asked me if I had ever played pool. I said I hadn't, which was true. He said he would teach me. I beat him in two consecutive games and, to this day, he is not quite sure whether I was hustling him or not.

For the second picture they abandoned Dick Donner as director and chose, instead, actor Jerry Lewis. Milt Ebbins was to produce.

Initially, I was very impressed by Jerry Lewis, if somewhat scared by his office, which looked like a high class junk shop in the Portobello Road. It contained everything from genuine antiques to the number-plates of motor cars. There was a mass of electronic equipment, and Jerry appeared to tape all conversations.

I have little doubt that Jerry Lewis theoretically knows more about the art of comedy than any man alive. He talks quite brilliantly on the subject. He can visualise a comedy situation, and instantly see ten ways of making it funnier. There is not a comedy film that has been made which he does not know backwards. Chaplin is his God.

Having said that, I must add that I wish he would put on the screen one tenth of the good things which pass through his mind before he starts directing.

This second picture was also made in England. Before many days shooting were complete Milt Ebbins disgraced himself by trying to insist that the script, as approved by Sammy, Peter, himself, Jerry Lewis and United Artists, should be shot as it had been written. The general consensus of opinion seemed to be that he deserved to be shot for daring to suggest any such thing. After he had been effectively gagged, everybody on the set had a wildly enjoyable time, with nobody to crack a whip or raise a warning voice.

Normally, visitors are discouraged from visiting a set when a picture is being shot. Jerry Lewis would have none of this. A large notice was posted outside the studio welcoming anyone to step right in and watch the fun.

Small roles were enlarged, a large role was completely eliminated. It was all such fun that, when the first rough cut was assembled, the film ran about forty minutes longer than it should have done. The story was a thriller with a complicated plot; but, at this length, something had to go, and by the time the film had been ruthlessly cut to bring it down to a viable length, such plot as remained was incomprehensible even to me, who had invented the story.

Some of the new 'comedy touches' were so excruciating that they caused me real physical pain. One of my favourite scenes in the original script had been a little gem of pure comedy. I can say this because it was entirely Sammy Davis's, extemporised by him at a meeting, and taped by me as he ad-libbed the lines. This was eliminated in its entirety, and in its place Sammy was shown walking through a field, saying he felt it was his unlucky day. As he said this, a very small shower of water descended on his head from above, hitting him and no one else. Get it? Subtle! Sammy's unlucky day; so unlucky that a tiny shower of rain six inches in diameter hits only him. A perfect example of incredible farce, guaranteed to make an audience disbelieve anything they saw thereafter.

I sat through the picture —— just —— then asked for my name to be removed from the credit titles. The first such request I had made in thirty years of writing films.

Milt got the picture back, and managed to cut a little sense into it. I believe he also cut out the shower of rain. He pleaded with me to put my name back and this I did. I need not have worried much either way, because few people ever went to see it.

All the same, it was sad. The second script was better than the first, and, with a little luck, Peter and Sammy might have become a team, and I might still have been writing films for them.

My son still proudly displays a signed photograph of Jerry Lewis in his bedroom. I have not asked to him to remove it, but I am gradually edging it closer and closer to the dart-board.

My second picture with Mel Frank was an adaptation of the stage musical comedy *A Funny Thing happened on the way to the Forum*, by Burt Shevelove and Larry Gelbart with music by Stephen Sondheim. This had been a big success both in New York, with Zero Mostel, and in London with Frankie Howard. Brother Jon played the Whoremaster in London.

Everybody who read our script was extremely complimentary, including Larry Gelbart. I valued Larry's opinion since, in my opinion, he should have written the screenplay rather than me. For a start, it was partly his child;

secondly, he was American, and the subject was pure American burlesque. Burlesque is the American way of describing farce. The musical was, in fact, based broadly on some of the old farces of the Roman writer Plautus (*circa* 200 BC). We did not try to tamper with its style, but treated it with the reverence it deserved as a proven success wherever it had played. We merely broadened the canvas cinematically.

The film was made in Madrid with Zero Mostel, Phil Silvers and Buster Keaton. Mel Frank was producer. Dick Lester was the director. I was one of those who enthusiastically endorsed his choice.

Dick Lester had greatly changed from the diffident man I had met on *Mouse on the Moon*, with the fantastic success of the Beatles' pictures and *The Knack* behind him. To say that he and Mel Frank collided would be putting it mildly. Once they had collided and extricated themselves from the collision, their minds were never to meet again. After this, Dick, with the full support of United Artists, went his own way.

Mel and I had seen the subject one way. Dick directed it in another. I have met people who loved the picture and people who hated it. My opinion is bound to be biased. I shall content myself with putting down the following:

> 'Lester hasn't so much directed it as dictated it; his own distinctive style (the cliché is "inimitable", I believe, and couldn't be further from the truth) is here gratuitously imposed on the material without justification, reference or reverence. Thus the picture is a living anachronism, a bastard child whose collision of styles does serious damage to the overall film. . . . Illusions are built only to be shattered, characters developed to be dissipated. . . .
> The sequences that come off best and give a tantalising glimpse of just what the film might have been, are those in which Lester is prepared to let music and lyrics speak for themselves without gimmicky camera embellishments.'

This was one critic's view, and there were others who felt otherwise, but it reflects my own opinion exactly. It gives me no pleasure to add that the paying public evidently felt the same way.

Part 16

★★★★★★★★★★★★★★★★★★★★★★★★★★★★★★★★★★★★★

Trouser Dropping (Two)

★★★★★★★★★★★★★★★★★★★★★★★★★★★★★★★★★★★★★

ON 19TH OCTOBER 1962, Carolyn celebrated her twenty-first birthday. Betty, her husband, Frank, and I gave her a joint party. Half way through the meal I received a telephone call from Queen Charlotte's hospital to tell me that Maya was about to deliver a baby. I left the party and arrived at the hospital in time to see my son, Timothy, having his first wash and brush up.

Thus my second child was born twenty-one years to the day after my first. As a result, I was known by some of my more ribald friends as: 'Old Once Every Twenty-one Years.'

I returned to Carolyn's party in time for the speeches and liqueurs.

In 1965 Timothy was joined by Tara, who was slightly premature, consequently not very beautiful, but has since made up for it by being the image of her mother.

Carolyn made a little name for herself, while on an Old Vic tour of the world, when she took over the second lead opposite Vivien Leigh in *Duel of Angels*, in Melbourne at a few hours' notice. The actress playing the part had gone down with mumps. She received a lot of publicity, some very good notices and immense help and encouragement from Vivien Leigh, who was absolutely sweet to her and continued regularly to see her long after the tour had ended.

During the tour Carolyn also found herself a fiancé, Coeks Gordon, Technical Stage Director to the Old Vic. They married in 1963, and, after a decent interval of six years, made me the grandfather of a bouncing girl, Danielle.

Jon's marriage to Jean Marsh had collapsed soon after my second marriage. In 1960 he married again. She was Ingeborg Rhoesa, a beautiful German girl he met while ski-ing in Austria. They have made me the uncle of two lovely flaxen-haired children, Dariel and Sean. At the age of seven, Sean deeply shocked our whole family by saying he did *not* want to play a leading role which he was offered in a projected film. Such a thing had never happened in our family before, and we are all waiting for him to improve.

Roland died in 1963. He continued writing up to the week of his death. I still sadly miss his quick wit and penetrating criticism.

The same year I was chosen as the screenwriter to be presented at the Royal Command Film Performance at the Odeon, Leicester Square. The film was Mick Balcon's *Sammy Going South*, which starred Edward G Robinson. It occurred on the day I came out of hospital following a badly slipped disc. I was tightly corseted, and could hardly walk.

The royal party consisted of The Queen Mother, Princess Margaret, The Earl of Snowden, Princess Alexandra and the Hon Angus Ogilvy.

Apart from my back, it was an awkward occasion, because I had not written the picture, and knew nothing about it. This made conversation difficult during the presentation, and I think the royal party were puzzled as to why I was there. That made six of us. In addition, I forgot about my back, bowed to the Queen Mother and barked loudly in her face.

Prince Philip, who is an Honorary Member of the Writers' Guild, agreed to come to the Annual Awards dinner as guest of honour. As Vice-Chairman of the Guild I was one of the party of three who went to Buckingham Palace to the office of one of his aides to discuss the details. He was a friendly man, who sat us down and asked if we would like a cup of tea. We said we would. An impressive manservant was given the order for tea. About five minutes later the manservant returned to utter a classic line, when one considers where we were.

'I am extremely sorry, Sir; but the kettle is being repaired.'

One of my briefest jobs was when a producer, having heard I was a very fast worker, asked me to dash off a draft screenplay for Bob Hope. It was based on a four page outline invented by the producer himself. The picture was to be entitled *Call Me Bwana*! The producer was going to Paris for the weekend and said he would like to see at least twenty-five pages of script by the time he returned on the Monday. He left two firm instructions. First, I must see to it that Bob Hope appeared in practically every scene. Secondly, I need not worry overmuch about Bob Hope dialogue, since Hope's own army of writers would be seeing to that.

He returned on the Monday and I gave him thirty pages. He read them, then became very angry, saying that I had gone against his instructions and written Bob Hope dialogue. I told him it was a little difficult to produce thirty pages of screenplay with Bob Hope appearing in every scene without writing *some* Bob Hope dialogue. The only other alternative would have been to present thirty blank sheets of paper; but he did not seem to get my message, any more than I had got his, so we parted amicably. This was a pity, because he was Harry Saltzman who went on to become the world's most successful film producer, and I would dearly love to be working for him now.

I firmly believe that to succeed in writing, acting, or playing poker one needs a measure of good luck. I have been very lucky. Unlike many much more talented writers than I am, I have never had to slog my way through a mountain of rejected works before getting somewhere. I have always had the encouragement of selling my first attempt at anything. Starting at sixteen by selling my first short story I went on to sell my first play, first film script and first TV play.

By the 1960s I had written over thirty feature films. There was not a year since the war during which I had not written at least one.

Midway through the 1960s the British and American film industries went into the rapid decline from which they have not yet recovered. This has resulted in much hardship for many experienced writers, to say nothing of the younger ones hoping for a break.

Here, I was lucky again in choosing the right moment to switch my attention back to the theatre.

There was no lack of television work, but television is a tremendous drain on the brain, and must be severely rationed. Apart from contributing episodes to most of the series such as *Danger Man* and *The Saint*, I wrote three series myself.

I brought the smiling gap of Terry-Thomas back to the BBC screen after a fifteen-year gap in *The Old Campaigner*. Also for the BBC, I wrote a series for Bernard Braden and Barbara Kelly, *B & B*, which proved a bit of a b. I thoroughly enjoyed writing *Never a Cross Word*, for Paul Daneman and Barbara Murray, for London Weekend Television.

In 1967 I was approached by Peter Coe who had directed *Oliver!*, to write the book of a musical comedy entitled *The Four Musketeers!* Herbert Kretzmer, theatre critic of the *Daily Express*, was the lyricist, and Laurie Johnson was the composer. The idea was to write a light-hearted send-up of Dumas' work, in which the Musketeers were to be shown in a far from heroic light. It will come as no surprise that Terry-Thomas was likely to play D'Artagnan.

The four of us formed an association, working together so that book, lyrics and music were firmly wedded from the start. It was broad, almost farcical, but, following the excellent example set by Larry Gelbart and Burt Shevelove in *Forum*, I resisted the temptation to put in anachronistic jokes.

Harry Secombe agreed to play D'Artagnan. Here we had both a big name and a great voice. Bernard Delfont was the impresario. The Palace Theatre was to be our home. This was an ideal theatre in size, location, and for the type of family show we had written.

Then, out of the blue, The Theatre Royal, Drury Lane became available. It would be the first British musical to be presented at Drury Lane for twenty-one years. Its capacity was, or course, enormous. Mouth-watering figures were bandied about. It is easy to see how this proved to be an irresistible temptation.

It is also easy to be wise after the event, but I am sure that this was the first big mistake to be made with the production. The show, although it was lavish and expensive—much too expensive, was essentially a British family-type musical, which seemed out of place at Drury Lane. The fact that it was the first British musical there for twenty-one years may well have led both audience and critics to expect something more sophisticated, and to feel a sense of disappointment which they would not have felt at the Palace Theatre.

From first to last the production was plagued with troubles. I so love the theatre that, in a strange masochistic kind of way, I enjoyed every terrifying moment of it.

Peter Coe must have been frightened by a writer once. This is not to say he in any way underestimates the importance of the writer. He became a great friend, and still is. He worked closely with me during the writing of the book, and contributed a lot himself; but, once in the director's seat during rehearsals, he wants to be alone. For the first week of rehearsals Herbie, Laurie and myself were asked to keep away from the theatre. I did not argue about this, but I did not agree with it. The book was at least forty-five minutes too long, which we all knew, and I felt that the major cuts should be made after the first read-through. Peter felt otherwise. He would make the cuts, he said, as the show progressed.

This had an unfortunate consequence for me. Bernard Delfont is the quietest and most polite of men. I had never heard his voice raised in anger until the day he came to see a run through of the show, halfway through the rehearsals. It was like Jekyl and Hyde. His face went red. For one moment I thought he was going to put his hands round my throat and strangle me. The show was miles too long. There was nothing but words, bloody words. This was a musical not a play. The damned thing had to be cut, cut, cut.

I felt like a naughty schoolboy being castigated by the Headmaster and, like a schoolboy, my inclination was to sneak and cry: 'It's not my fault! I wanted to! Blame Peter!'

But I merely nodded and said I agreed. The look he gave me seemed to suggest that if I agreed, why hadn't I already cut the thing?

Cuts were made as the show progressed but I still defend my method, because the cuts showed.

Three weeks before we were due to open, Sidney Tafler, who was playing Captain of Musketeers, a role which I had specially written for him, fell ill, and had to leave the show. Bill Owen took over as Captain with supreme confidence, gave a totally different interpretation of the character, and threw in some jokes about Green Stamps for good measure. He was severely reprimanded, but, since he could only see the part his way, he resigned his commission after one week. The part, cut to ribbons, was played by another member of the cast.

The role of the Queen was filled by a young American girl with a large bosom and the smallest voice in Europe. To disguise her American accent she adopted an unidentifiable foreign accent, which rendered her inaudible except to one or two fortunate members of the orchestra. As Queens sometimes do, she abdicated. Sheena Marsh then ascended the throne and ruled splendidly.

Harry Secombe was thrown heavily from his horse, but mercifully escaped serious injury.

The sets were by Sean Kenny, who had also designed the much admired sets for Lionel Bart's *Oliver!* Here again, I think a mistake was made. The public who would be drawn to the show would have liked a nice, old-fashioned set with recognisable castles, palaces and battlements. Sean's sets, at first glance, looked like concrete gun emplacements. They left everything to the imagination. They were a brilliant piece of mechanical design, and moved hither and thither, up and down by means of powerful electric motors. They were so silent that on one occasion a huge piece of moving battlement swept Harry Secombe off his feet while he was singing a song, unaware that Peter was using the song to cover a change of scene.

Our leading lady was Joyce Blackham, who had come from Sadler's Wells, and was better known as an opera singer than as a musical comedy performer. Peter had personally chosen her, but, as the rehearsals proceeded, it became clear that they were not seeing eye to eye. Miss Blackham was having trouble with her vocal chords, which greatly restricted the amount of singing and speaking she felt able to provide. This did not make things easier, for it is difficult to judge a singer's performance, if it is only mouthed, unless you happen to be a lip reader with a highly developed imagination.

With four days to go before the opening Miss Blackham announced that she would be unable to perform before a large preview audience that night. She was sent home to bed, and her understudy was put on, virtually without rehearsal. She managed the first act nobly. In the second act she made an entrance a couple of seconds too early, and was knocked out cold by a male dancer as he flung his arms wide. She recovered sufficiently to carry on with a mouth full of blood and four loose teeth.

On the same night, Harry, who had to make one perilous entrance on a kirby wire, was misdirected by the wire and fell heavily. Once again he escaped injury.

There were so many changes being made to the show that I was not unduly surprised when, in the middle of a scene during one rehearsal, a male member of the cast rushed across the stage with his face streaming with blood, pursued by a beautiful Jamaican girl from the chorus, who was armed with a knife. I began to wonder a bit, when they leapt across the orchestra pit and continued the chase up one of the aisles. I knew that it was unrehearsed when the man tripped at my feet and the girl flung herself on him, raised the knife and brought it heavily down on his back. With others I helped to separate them. He received two stitches in one cheek, and she was bound over for a year at Bow Street, after pleading guilty to assault and possessing an offensive weapon—a fruit knife normally used by the cast to peel apples. The knife was badly bent and the Magistrate remarked that she appeared to have done more damage to the knife than she had to her victim.

With two nights to go before the opening, Miss Blackham's voice failed once more, and the understudy again had to appear in her place, before a preview audience.

During this performance Harry again fell off the kirby wire and cut himself. During a change of scene one of the chorus girls got her dress caught in a piece of moving scenery. She was taken to hospital, suffering from shock but mercifully only minor injuries.

With three days to go, the grave decision was made to cut Miss Blackham's big operatic number in the first act. Miss Blackham instantly requested to be released from the show. The request was granted, and she left. Despite the fact that we were only two nights away from the opening, the news of her departure was received with admirable fortitude by the entire cast.

Her place was taken by Elizabeth Larner. I had to sit up all night writing an entirely new scene to suit Liz Larner. This also entailed a new dance routine.

Two nights later Liz opened in the show and went through the entire performance without faltering on one line or one note.

Throughout the whole of these nerve-wracking weeks Harry Secombe was a tower of strength. I had not really known him well before. I had known he was loved in the profession and now I knew why. He is a shining example of the good trooper, never ill-tempered, never selfish, always encouraging. I honestly believe that, but for his unfailing good humour, the show, with its many vicissitudes, might have collapsed before it ever opened.

I have only one quarrel with Harry and this is his predilection for the ad lib, topical and anachronistic gag. I knew that we would not be able to muffle him for long, but I did beg him to go easy on the first night. Even so, he could not resist a few of them, and I saw critical pencils flying as he threw in a quick one about Hush Puppies. I, of course, was blamed for them.

The critics were remarkably divided between those who hated the show and those who loved it.

'What with all the rumours of disaster ("They've had to cut over an hour"). . . . it seemed as if the scheming Richelieu and wicked Milady had defeated *The Four Musketeers* before the curtain went up. Happily rumour is proved a jade. The show, which crammed every nook and cranny of the huge Drury Lane stage last night, may be accounted a triumph.'

Felix Barker. *The Evening News.*

'At Drury Lane *The Four Musketeers* tries inexplicably to do for Dumas what *Twang** did for Robin Hood. I can only say, with brutal candour, that it succeeds.'

Ronald Bryden. *The Observer.*

The musical was not a failure. Neither can it be counted as a success. It ran for fourteen months, which is a respectable run; but it did not make money. It could not, because it was too expensive. If the papers are to be

Twang was a musical by Lionel Bart.

believed the show cost £150,000. In my humble view, if it had been budgeted at half the price, and been presented as a jolly, family romp at the Palace Theatre, it would have run twice as long and made money.

After sixteen years I wrote another play for Brian Rix. I took an idea from an old Vernon Sylvaine-Guy Bolton farce and wrote a new play around it.

I have already said that farce writing is no easy task. To tailor a farce for Brian Rix is doubly difficult. He has had over twenty years of uninterrupted success in the West End—a unique record, which will never be surpassed. You cannot tell Brian anything about any aspect of farce that he does not know better than you. He can forecast almost to the penny how much the takings will go down on Cup Final Day, Guy Fawkes Day and St Patrick's Day. On television he has performed every farce ever written—and remembers them all with a depressing accuracy, making it almost impossible to write him a scene which he has not already played in one form or another. He knows every pitfall, every situation which has been overworked.

He knows precisely how many laughs a play must have before it can be adjudged acceptable. His first action, on receipt of a draft script, is to go through it, page by page, marking: 'Belly Laughs', 'Laughs' and 'Titters.' This can result in an unequivocal demand for fifty more laughs. He will then study the distribution of those laughs, which is an important factor. The tendency must always be for the laughter to grow as the piece progresses. If there are five pages in which there are only three laughs the author may be required to go away and think up an entirely new situation, which must somehow be welded into the play without seeming to have been arbitrarily added on.

He carefully analyses how many laughs are his and how many go to other characters. He is only selfish to the extent that, as the star, he demands a certain fixed quota. Once he is satisfied on this point he will work tirelessly to help make the other roles as funny as possible. One of the refreshing things about working for the Rix organisation—and it is an organisation—is the way the whole company works to give other actors a laugh. There is no jealousy or upstaging. Some of the best bits of business arise from suggestions by actors for other actors.

As an author, I could never alibi a failure in writing for Brian Rix by blaming someone else, for I am consulted on the set design, the casting and before any change in dialogue. There is no question of being allowed to attend rehearsals. I have to find a very good excuse for missing even one.

In fact, Brian and I work closely together before any play goes into a first draft. We have both built little castles in the south of Spain, some forty miles apart. We meet on neutral ground at a deserted beach halfway between the two houses, consume enormous quantities of rough Spanish wine, bore our ever patient wives and devise outrageous scenes and lines, ninety per cent of which are subsequently discarded in the more sober air of London.

Admittedly, many writers would find the work intolerable. There is little that is inspirational about it. The basic idea may be inspired, but the actual execution is a carefully planned, mechanical operation—a delicate construction job, resting on perilously flimsy foundations.

More often than not Brian tries out his new plays somewhere out of London. This has advantages and disadvantages. The advantages are that any obvious weaknesses are revealed, and can be rectified. The great disadvantage is that, since the leading role bas been written specially for Brian Rix, the actor who plays the role knows that he is not going to move into London. Consequently, it is difficult to find a first class actor to take the part—and good farce actors are a rarity.

Brian elected to try out my play at Richmond, the scene of my triumphant first night thirty years before.

I felt this was a lucky omen—but I was wrong. If anyone had shouted: 'Author!' on the first night of this try-out I should have run a mile, because it would have been by someone who wanted to shoot me. I wanted to shoot myself. Beyond a brilliant performance by Derek Royle, as a dotty doctor, the laughs were scattered, and the play revealed itself to be full of holes. There was clearly no hope of a transfer to London unless I carried out a substantial re-write.

I girded my loins, sat down and re-wrote the play. I showed it to Brian, who demanded I re-write it again. I re-wrote it again.

The play was then given a second try-out at Palmers Green. In retrospect, it is difficult to see how the play could have been worse than it has been at Richmond, but somehow I had managed it. It was dreadful.

I began to think that while stubbornness can be a virtue, it can also be a sign of stupidity. Perhaps I was just not cut out to be a farce writer. Some people know how to make the dropping of trousers funny and some people don't.

I nursed my wounds for some weeks, then told Brian I was prepared to have one more shot at re-writing it. So I re-wrote it again from start to finish. I gave it to Brian and to Wallace Douglas, who would direct it in London, if it ever got that far.

We met in Brian's dressing-room at the Garrick Theatre for the verdict. Brian was silent. Wally Douglas entered, threw the script on a table and said: 'It's terrible!'

This was a crucial moment in my career. All my instincts, both logical and emotional, told me to rise with dignity, apologise for my failure, and depart from the scene, leaving trouser-dropping to someone else. Wally just stared at me. Brian stared at the carpet. I think he was a little embarrassed by the brutality of the verdict.

Then something inside me stirred. I remained seated, and told Wally to sit down and tell me in more detail what was wrong.

It was an important moment in more ways than one. Although neither of them said anything I think they were both impressed by the fact that I did not fly off the deep end. This has laid the foundation of a relationship between the three of us which allows us to say anything at any time with complete frankness, and without the fear of causing an emotional outburst.

The result was that I went away and I re-wrote the play for the fifth time. I handed it to Brian without much hope. I did not even feel much exultation when he and Wally accepted it. I think, deep inside me, I had lost faith in it.

We opened in Birmingham with Brian Rix, Leo Franklyn, a sprightly seventy-two, Anthony Sharp, Simon Merrick and Derek Royle. The girls included Anna Dawson, Hazel Douglas and a well-stacked newcomer, Margaret Nolan. It was an instant success.

When the company played Liverpool on the last week of the tour I returned to London, having completed any necessary re-writes. The telephone rang on the Thursday. Brian was on the line.

'Take the first train to Liverpool,' he said. 'You're on tomorrow night.'

'On what?'

'On the stage. Simon Merrick has an abcess on his throat, and you'll have to take over.'

The last of my Walter Mitty dreams had come true. I was going to step into the breach in the second leading role at three days notice, and open in London, never having appeared on the stage in my life. I could see the headlines. I felt no nerves; only a feeling of intense exhileration. I ran through the lines with Maya, who had gone as pale as any half-Indian girl can go pale. I acted so realistically that, when I gave a gasp and slumped into my chair, she thought I had suffered a heart attack, threw the script into the air and rushed to my side. When she realised I was only playing the part, she hit me hard.

I travelled to Liverpool, and went straight into rehearsal with the cast. I got through almost word perfect. Everybody was most complimentary. It was flattering to realise they all thought I had done a lot of acting before. I had to keep changing the subject when they asked which was the last play I had been in. Only Wally Douglas kept silent, and stared at me broodingly. He had done his homework, and he knew. It was all very well for me to canter through a rehearsal, but what would happen when I came before an audience? He would not let me go on that night, but let the young understudy continue to play.

The next day Simon Merrick's doctors announced that his abcess was responding to treatment, and that an operation would not be necessary. He recovered fast, and was well enough to open on the first night in London.

I am glad for his sake that he made it; but I would be a liar if I did not admit to wishing he had taken a little longer to get well. I think this is my one Mitty dream which will now never be realised.

She's Done It Again was, in many ways, an old-fashioned farce, showing traces of its early Sylvaine-Bolton origins. I was surprised by the excellent reception on the first night; but I still confidently expected a very lukewarm press.

Brian and I went down to Fleet Street to pick up the first editions of the papers. The result was simply staggering. The notices in the daily papers, and subsequently in the Sunday papers, were, without exception, the best I have ever received. They were the kind of reviews one dreams about.

> '. . . shows an immense development in comic skills compared to the lumbering old days in The Whitehall. It is easily the funniest show I have seen this year.'
>
> Irving Wardle. *The Times.*

> 'Compulsively enjoyable.'
>
> B A Young. *Financial Times.*

Harold Hobson in the *Sunday Times* wrote:

> 'I have no doubt at all about what has been the principal theatrical event this week. The Master is back again and London can once more be gay. Michael Pertwee's farce is the funniest in which the great Brian Rix has ever appeared. There are difficulties in the way of communicating a proper sense of its delicious and delirious qualities. But what looks feeble and hackneyed on the page glows with a glorious life in the Garrick Theatre. . . . Several times during the evening I was on the point of rising from my seat and demanding: "Where's your Georgie Feydeau now?"'

With notices like these, and others just as good, it is disappointing to have to record that the play closed after a modest run of ten months, which, by Rix standards, is short. The trouble in this case was not so much a lack of business as the fact that rising costs now demand a much greater volume of business if a play is to pay its way. A play which, five years before, could break even on a weekly take of £2,000 would now not break even under £3,500. Brian's public is largely a native one. British farce does not appeal greatly to the foreign visitor. His testing time is therefore the summer months, when theatregoers who enjoy his type of play prefer to remain in their gardens. The play could have continued, and would have run eighteen months or more had everyone been prepared to take cuts for about eight weeks. On these occasions a secret ballot is held and cuts are taken if there is a unanimous vote in favour. We held the ballot, and two people voted against the cuts, so the play was withdrawn and went on a sixteen week provincial tour, during which it broke several box office records.

Having broken the Rix barrier, and having thoroughly enjoyed the experience of working with him and with Wally, I set about writing Brian's next production at the Garrick Theatre.

I decided on a face-lift. I would abolish mothers-in-law. I would eliminate drag scenes of men dressing up as women. I would have nothing but pretty girls in the female roles. I would be a little less worried about offending 'the family audience', and try to attract another audience and add to Brian's faithful following. I would also write a good strong part for another major star.

This time the preparation, writing and re-writing went as smoothly as the previous play had gone roughly. Considerable changes were made, but without pain. To my immense relief, sufficient faith was expressed by all concerned to avoid the necessity of a try-out.

The play had a political background in that the two leading men were politicians, but the basic plot was pure bedroom farce.

Alfred Marks starred opposite Brian. Oddly enough it was his first venture into farce. I hope it is not his last, for he is a brilliant and inventive farceur.

Its title was *Don't Just Lie There, Say Something!* We opened in Birmingham once again, in the late summer of 1971. Leo Franklyn, Peter Bland and four lovely girls, Joanna Lumley, Deborah Grant, Donna Reading and Nina Thomas made up the cast.

It was clear, after the first night, that we had a hit. We beat the business of the previous play by a comfortable margin. We played to near capacity in Brighton, and broke the all-time box office record in Southsea.

Jilly Cooper of the *Sunday Times* covered the play from its first read-through to its opening at Birmingham, as copy for one of her pieces. She nearly cried for me when attending the inquest after the opening night, and listened to Wally and Brian's frank comments on what was wrong. Little did she realise that these were minor as compared with most such plays. She wrote a very nice article about us, for which we were more than grateful later.

We approached the opening night in London with complete confidence, for we had not played to an audience which had not enjoyed the show enormously.

One is never too old to learn, and I shall never again approach a first night in London with anything but trepidation.

The impossible happened. The audience sat in grim silence while the actors gallantly ploughed on, but with rapidly flagging spirits, as scene after scene died the death. The applause at the end was barely polite.

For the first time I did not bother to wait up for the newspapers. I knew I should not enjoy reading them. I was right.

I will repeat Ian Christie's words in the *Daily Express*:

> 'I find it absurd that anyone bothered to write it, that people agreed to perform in it and that customers managed to sit through it to the end.'

I have already said that no writer is immune from criticism, and I am no exception. I confess I was temporarily shattered, if only because I knew, with absolute certainty, that given the right conditions, the public loved the play; but how were enough of them going to come after notices like these?

I have no answer to that question, and it still puzzles me; but they came on the second night and poured in on the third night. Shortly afterwards we broke the all-time box office record at the Garrick Theatre on two consecutive weeks. The play grossed over £60,000 in its first twelve weeks and a quarter of a million pounds by the time it reached its anniversary. It has made a lot of people very happy—including myself and the actors who were on a percentage. To celebrate its year at The Garrick Brian threw a champagne party and we both threw flowers around. Alfred Marks, having completed his year's contract, departed from the show, presenting Brian with a quarter bottle of whisky to mark the event.

The show finally closed after over 600 performances, having broken The Garrick Theatre record seven times. It broke the theatre record in six out of eight provincial theatres while out on tour. It sold to eight foreign countries.

As to persuading people to perform in it, we started, as I have said, with Alfred Marks, an actor of great standing, playing the senior government minister. Terry-Thomas later played the same role in Australia. Leslie Phillips took the role in the film version and Warren Mitchell subsequently played the role in a television series, which used the characters from the play. Not a bad line-up of names.

It is the first West End play to have spawned a television series. It was made by Harlech Television and was entitled: 'Men of Affairs.'

The idea of starring Warren Mitchell with Brian Rix was inspired. Warren, seizing the chance of playing something entirely different to Alf Garnett, threw himself voraciously into the role of a lecherous, pseudo-suave Cabinet Minister.

Brian and Warren had never worked together and hardly knew each other. Brian invited Warren to come and see my play at The Garrick, so that he could get an idea of the character he was to play. Warren came. He went round to Brian's dressing-room after the show and they chatted of this and that. Warren expressed no views about my play. Finally, Brian asked him how he had liked it.

'Fucking awful,' said Warren. 'Horrible. I only laughed once.'

Brian was stunned and trembling with rage, which he could hardly contain. After twenty-one years in the West End he accepted that not everybody completely enjoyed his plays but, generally, even the doubters managed to say: 'That really was *something!*' or 'The audience certainly lapped it up, didn't they?' But for anyone to say it was fucking awful to his face was almost more than he could bear, and all the more unbearable in view of the fact that he and the person expressing that view were expected to work together.

The reader will now be in no doubt that this was the beginning of a quite horrific relationship. The reader is wrong. Warren sparked Brian and Brian sparked Warren. They worked amicably, enthusiastically and unselfishly together in one of the happiest series it has ever been my pleasure to write. Warren, like Sammy Davis, is not only a brilliant actor. He is an inventive one. I can almost say infuriatingly inventive because, given half a chance, he will go on inventing until the last second before transmission. Brian, himself, has never been better or happier.

The series was an ambitious project for Patrick Dromgoole of Harlech Television but his faith in it paid off. After we had completed six of the thirteen episodes it was sold for peak-hour viewing to the whole British network, one of the few occasions this has been achieved by one of the smaller companies.

Part 17

★ ★

Curtain Dropping (Two)

★ ★

ALMOST EXACTLY seven years before I was born, to be precise, on 17th March 1909, was founded the Dramatists' Club, the membership of which was confined to established British playwrights. Among those attending the first luncheon were Arthur Pinero, Alfred Sutro and W Somerset Maugham. Another founder member was J M Barrie.

The club still exists today, and meets four times a year for dinner at the Garrick Club. Among the members are Robert Bolt (President), Harold Pinter, W A Darlington, John Osborne, Alun Owen, Sir Michael Redgrave, R C Sherriff, Johnny Speight, Ben Travers, Ted Willis, Ray Cooney, Robert Morley, John Chapman and myself; a mixed bag of every different type of playwright, who enjoy gathering together and shamelessly discussing shop.

In 1972, I was made Honorary Secretary. This was not conveyed as an honour. I happened to be sitting next to the retiring Honorary Secretary, Robert Morley, who fixed me with a steely eye and told me I was elected.

I inherited the safe keeping of three beautifully bound leather volumes, which give details of every meeting of the club and the names of those attending. On looking through the volume dealing with the 30s I discovered that Roland had been a regular member; so I still follow in his footsteps. We are the only father and son to have been members.

I have dropped my last few names in a cluster, and now drop the curtain in order to get down to some less self-indulgent writing.

It has been a long road. The future still looks unnaturally rosy for one of my advancing years and in a profession which, at the best of times, is a perilous one. I have two plays awaiting production in the West End. One of

212

them, inevitably, is for Brian Rix. Here I broke my own record, established with the first play thirty-six years ago, by writing it in five and a half days. It is, perhaps, rash to mention this before I have seen whether it runs more than five and a half nights, but, with one exception, everybody who has read it thinks it is my best farce. The exception is Warren Mitchell who read it and said it was fucking awful, and that he'd only laughed twice. Since this was double the laughs he got out of the last play, I know Warren will not take it amiss if I look on this as a good omen.

I am not much given to self-analysis and therefore find it hard to sum myself up. I deserve little credit for being the hardest worker I know, since I enjoy writing as much now as when I was sixteen and am frankly bored doing anything else. I would view the prospect of six weeks lazing in the sun on some tropical beach with grim foreboding.

I think most of the people for whom and with whom I work are reasonably satisfied because I work fast, have a professional approach and do not burst into tears of rage when my favourite line is cut—which it always is.

I do not suffer from the sense of insecurity which plagues many writers far more talented and successful than I, perhaps because I have never really considered myself to be a success. I believe that a writer who feels he has achieved success runs the risk of having nowhere to go but down. A writer who feels that real success still eludes him is able optimistically to go on trying to climb the ladder with the top as his target. He will probably fall off on the way, but, at least, he has something to aim at.

Mercifully, I have few frustrated ambitions. My 'good' novel is all ready to be written and will probably turn out to be bad. I know my many limitations and accept them philosophically. I do not envy anybody's ox or ass and only occasionally wish to God I was Neil Simon. I have all the worldly goods I need to stay alive. I have five typewriters, three unusually nice and attractive children, and one lovely and understanding wife.

I have no desire ever to retire. This is lucky because I recently estimated that, should I so decide, I could afford to live in comfort for just ten days.

And so to work.